MAINE
BICENTENNIAL
COMMUNITY
COOKBOOK

200 RECIPES

Celebrating Maine's Culinary
Past, Present & Future

Foreword by Governor Janet Mills

Introduction by Don Lindgren

Compiled and Edited by Margaret Hathaway & Karl Schatz

Islandport Press, Inc.
P.O. Box 10
Yarmouth, Maine 04096
www.islandportpress.com

For more recipes, stories, and photos visit maine200cookbook.com

First Edition, June 2020
Corrected, June 2021

Cover and interior design by Ashley Halsey

ISBN: 978-1-944762-89-6
Library of Congress Catalog Number: 2020932259

ISLANDPORT PRESS

Maine Bicentennial Community Cookbook is distributed to the
trade by Islandport Press, Inc. and its partners, please contact 207-846-3344 or
email info@islandportpress.com for more information.

For you, and your family.

We invite you to personalize this community cookbook with your own family recipe, so that every family in Maine can be included in this bicentennial celebration of Maine cooking.

RECIPE _____

From the Kitchen of: _____

Our Family Story: _____

_____

_____

INGREDIENTS:

_____   _____

_____   _____

_____   _____

_____   _____

DIRECTIONS:

_____

_____

_____

_____

_____

_____

_____

_____

Maine Bicentennial Community Cookbook Map

16 Counties
118 Towns & Cities
200+ Recipes

CONTENTS

200 Years of Cultivating. The people of Maine have worked the land, reaped the rewards and savored every moment. Come get a taste of everything that has made Maine uniquely Maine for over two centuries.

Maine
BICENTENNIAL
VISITMAINE.COM

A Recipe for Public Policy

Governor Janet Mills • Augusta, Kennebec County

Choose ingredients with care.

Combine 186 fresh and seasoned lawmakers from farms, gardens and markets across the state.*
Wash with civility. Wait. Add herbs and spices to taste. Mix well. Marinate overnight. Wait.

Grease large pan with gentle compromise. Wait.
Heat slowly and let simmer. Stir slowly.
Do not burn. Wait.

Place in warm oven. Wait.
Brush with faith and empathy. Listen for bubbling or crackling of crust. Wait.
Bake until golden brown.

Let cool ninety days.

Serve with a side of County Yukon golds, backyard tomatoes, and organic greens
with Democracy dressing.

Pair with a hearty craft brew, Moxie, or homemade blueberry wine.

Serves 1.3 million.

*Those steeped for at least 21 years in experience, work, and service are best for this mix. Pick those with open eyes, open minds, and open hearts of different ages, races, genders, occupations, and orientations for robust flavor. Dirt under the nails will not impair taste.

About This Project

By Margaret Hathaway & Karl Schatz

This is a book about people. It is also a collection of recipes—both contemporary and historic—and a celebration of the bounty of the state of Maine. But mostly, at its core, this book tells a story of the families and individuals who make this state great.

When we conceived of this cookbook, a little more than a year ago, we aimed to take a snapshot of Maine's culinary traditions at the bicentennial of statehood. We hoped, through our collaboration with Don Lindgren of Rabelais Books, to share what Maine home cooking looked like in the early years of statehood, and to track its evolution to the foodie mecca it currently is. Having written several books about Maine's food in the past decade, we felt there was a story to tell. It's embarrassing to admit how narrow our gaze was at the beginning of this project!

For the past six months, since we put out a call for recipes and opened the digital floodgates, inviting people to submit their recipes, food stories, and photographs online, each day has begun in wonder. Every morning, we open our computers, check our email, and are met with new friends. Hundreds of families have trusted us with the most intimate details of their lives. We've received wedding portraits and baby pictures, unfinished memoirs and publication-ready essays, paintings, poems, and prayers. We've been invited into peoples' homes—both figuratively and literally—learning about their traditions, peeking into their family cookbooks, and, in a few cases, chatting for hours over tea and cake. We have shed more than a few tears.

As we worked our way through the submitted recipes, a number of things stood out to us:

- We knew it already, but it bears repeating: Maine has an abundance of resources. We are blessed to be situated in proximity to deep forests, fertile fields, and a sea teeming with life. Foragers, farmers, and fisherfolk make this state one of the best places to eat in the world.

- The food we cook at home forges connections across time, space, and communities. When we open a cookbook and consult a recipe, we are invited into the world of whoever happened to write down these instructions. We're in the kitchen with early-twentieth-century Lebanese immigrants to Waterville; Greek "Yia-Yias" preparing for a church supper in Biddeford; island boarding-house owners stretching their salt cod as far as it will go; and trained chefs creating elegant desserts at the Blaine House. With each recipe, we taste the world through new flavors and see it through new eyes.

- Our family food traditions often originate from community recipes. Many of the dishes that people submitted were originally found in local newspapers or previously collected community cookbooks and were adapted over the years. Spattered pages and yellowed clippings, annotated with slight (or substantial) changes, illustrate each family's preferences: spices are adjusted, techniques spelled out, family traditions created. Everyone's tastes are different, and they are all worth celebrating.

In creating this book, we used the model of community cookbooks described by Don in his short history. This book is by and for the people of Maine, and a portion of the proceeds from each book sold will go to fight hunger in the state. The words "crowdsourced" and "crowdfunded" have gained new currency lately, but they have a long tradition in community cookbooks, and it's one that we followed. In keeping with this model, we did things the old-fashioned way, albeit with the benefit of modern technology.

In early November 2019, we set up a website to allow recipe submissions online. We were overwhelmed by the response! Over the past few months, we've gathered more than 360 recipes from people all over the state, in each of the sixteen counties (and a few from people who've left, but maintain deep roots). When we've included a recipe submitted by someone who now lives "away," we've attributed the recipe to the town of its origin. Our goal was to include as many voices as possible, and we've been humbled by how many have contributed.

That said, we are sure that there are people who missed our pleas for recipes on social media, television, public radio, at libraries, and in the newspapers. We tried to solicit recipes through all the channels that we could think of, but we know that there are families full of wonderful cooks who may have missed our call. We want to make clear that this is not a comprehensive history of cooking in Maine—for that, turn to contributor Sandy Oliver's definitive history of New England food, *Saltwater Foodways*. Nor is it meant as a comprehensive collection of contemporary Maine cooking. This is just a sampling of the heartfelt home cooking Maine has to offer. What the *Maine Bicentennial Community Cookbook* aims to be is a celebration of the women and men (mostly, in these pages, women) whose cooking brings together their families and communities.

To fund the project, we've accepted paid ads, paid recipe and photograph sponsorship, and presale of books through a Kickstarter campaign. An arrangement with Islandport Press has given the book national distribution, with a publisher right here in Cumberland County.

Selecting the recipes for inclusion has been a challenge—in truth, we want to include them all. As it is, we prioritized including all 16 counties, as many individuals as we could, and as much variety as possible. There were many foods for which we received multiple recipes—molasses cookies could have had its own section, and we decided to devote an entire chapter to beans. In some cases, when we had dishes that were similar, we included the family stories, but not the actual recipes (these are differentiated by red titles). We solicited some recipes from notable Mainers, and some came in unsolicited from folks we were planning to approach. To help us winnow down the submissions, we enlisted the help of a team of food writers, who joined us for a memorable afternoon at Rabelais. Finally, in the interest of transparency and full disclosure, we have a confession: There are more than 200 recipes in this book.

Formatting the recipes has also been a challenge, as many are written in colloquial terms ("butter the size of a walnut"), with ingredients integrated into the instructions, and with an expectation, particularly in the older recipes, that a cook has committed most culinary techniques to memory. We've tried to edit the recipes as little as possible, and only for the sake of clarity. In most cases, the recipes have a distinct ingredient list, standardized measurements, and enough instructions to guide the most novice of cooks. In a few cases, recipes were so charmingly written that we abandoned our general formatting. The recipes from historic community cookbooks were left completely as they were found.

In contrast to many cookbooks, this book is illustrated entirely without pictures of food. We have received wonderful photographs, artifacts, and ephemera, which we've included, but we deliberately chose to leave the finished dishes to the reader's imagination. Home cooking is about comfort. In this age of perfectionist, Instagrammable meals, we hope this frees you up to plate them however you'd like. It's not important what the food looks like—it's how it tastes, and who you share it with.

Whenever possible, the notes at the top of each recipe are in the words of the person who submitted it. We are honored to begin the book with a benevolent recipe by Governor Janet Mills. We've also included five essays, written by scholars and activists in Maine, to help provide context for the state's food history and contemporary challenges. Professor Darren J. Ranco, of the University of Maine, writes about the Wabanaki Confederacy, who lived on this land for thousands of years before the arrival of Europeans. Author Nancy Harmon Jenkins writes of Martha Ballard, an early European settler, whose extensive diaries are filled with cooking and food, but don't include a single recipe. Scholar and historian Sandy Oliver contributes an essay on Marjorie Standish and Mildred "Brownie" Schrumpf, two newspaperwomen and beloved chroniclers of Maine food, whose columns shaped cooking in this state for decades. Abusana "Micky" Bondo, co-founder of the non-profit In Her Presence, shares her experiences as a "new Mainer" and her passionate belief that cooking together unites us. Finally, Jim Hanna, Executive Director of the Cumberland County Food Security Council, reminds us of the food insecurity that plagues many Mainers and helps strategize action steps for a better future. We are greatly indebted to these generous writers for making the cookbook that much richer.

One last note on the recipes: We did not test any of them, but instead trusted that the people who submitted them were sharing their best. Each recipe may not be to everyone's taste, but we took the maxim of Father Robert Farrar Capon to heart: "Man's real work is to look at the things of the world and to love them for what they are."

Our hope is that you will take the recipes in this book and make them your own. Adapt them to your tastes, make notes in the margins, and, above all, share them with people you love. May the foods in these pages connect you to those around you, start new food traditions in your home, and become the treasured family recipes of tomorrow.

DORCAS DISHES

A LITTLE BOOK OF COUNTRY COOKING

INTRODUCTION BY
KATE DOUGLAS WIGGIN

THE
HOUSEKEEPERS
FRIEND

A MERRY CHRISTMAS AND HAPPY NEW YEAR
Published By
JOHN GARNER,
DEALER IN
Choice Teas, Coffees, Spices, Fancy Groceries, Flour,
Butter, Cheese, Meats of all kinds, &c.
PASSENGER & EXCHANGE AGENT,   LEWISTON, ME.
Copyrighted   PRICE 25 CENTS   1879

The
rono
ook
ook

A Collection of
Practical Recipes

Furnished By

The Ladies of

Norway Grange

NO. 45

Patrons of Husbandry

"All labor of man is for his mouth,
yet his appetite is not filled."—Solomon.

"Eat, Drink and be Merry."

Machias
Cookery

1909

olwich Grange Cook Book
P. of H.
No. 68

REBEKAH

COOK

BOOK

Fish, flesh and fowl
FOWL, FLESH AND FISH
Each served up
IN A SEPARATE DISH.

The Community Cookbook in Maine

By Don Lindgren

Fish, Flesh and Fowl: A Book of Recipes for Cooking (Portland, 1877) is the earliest known cookbook to have been compiled and published in Maine. A small, brown cloth book with a gilt-lettered title, it contains 250 recipes, including Blueberry Cake, Rusks, Squash Fritters, Apple Dumplings, Indian Meal Pudding, Tapioca Cream Pudding, Citron Cake, Currant Cake, Hickory Nut Cake, Hermits, Peppermints, Mead, Pickled Lemons, and Pickled Eggs. The book is not the work of a single author but rather, "Compiled by Ladies of State Street Parish." The Ladies had formed a group to do good works for their church, in this case likely celebrating the twenty-fifth anniversary of their State Street Congregation. They gathered around kitchen tables, in church basements, and in meeting halls to collect and organize recipes. The recipes were themselves gathered from the favorites of friends and family, perhaps from a decades-old handwritten collection, or from one of the new and very popular contemporary homemaking magazines. The Ladies were doing the work of making cookbooks.

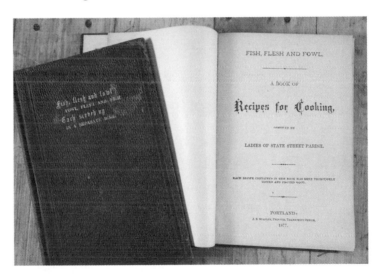

Fish, Flesh and Fowl was a community cookbook, a somewhat new genre of cookbook that was sweeping the nation at that time. Through the early and mid-1870s the nation was living in the aftermath of the Civil War, a conflict that created a tremendous amount of need, need responded to, in part, by the fundraising efforts of women's groups. At the same time, the nation was looking forward to its own centennial, and optimism about the future and aspirations of success were prevalent. It was into this environment that the community cookbook emerged.

Generally speaking, three characteristics define community cookbooks: first, the books were produced by members of a recognizable community (a church auxiliary, fishermen's wives, grange hall members); second, the recipes were compiled from sources within that community; and third, the cookbooks were sold to raise funds for a charitable or benevolent purpose. The earliest-known community cookbook was issued in 1870, seven years before Maine's *Fish, Flesh and Fowl*. A tiny book of just twenty-four pages, *Nantucket Receipts* was published in Boston for the benefit of the New England Hospital for Women and Children. By the end of the centennial decade, more than 250 community cookbooks have been published nationwide, perhaps fifteen hundred by the century's close. The books quickly spread across the nation; between 1870 and the turn of the twentieth century, community cookbooks had been published in forty-three states and the District of Columbia. Some call them charitable cookbooks, fundraising cookbooks, compiled cookbooks, local cookbooks, church cookbooks, and even "those spiral-bound books," but whatever you call them, community cookbooks became very popular, very quickly.

Within Maine, the community cookbooks also spread rapidly. Just a year after *Fish, Flesh and Fowl*, two Bangor women, "K. L. D. and E. K. H.," produced *Cuisine: A Collection of Family Receipts Contributed by the Ladies of Bangor*. No copy of the original 1878 book is known to have survived (perhaps one will emerge with this project), but thankfully the second edition of 1882 exists. The Woman's Christian Temperance Unions of Lewiston and Auburn issued the *Temperance Cook Book* in 1886, crediting the compilation to Mrs. E. M. Blanchard and Mrs. L. A. Robbins. In 1889, *The Teakettle: Recipes for Cooking*, was created by "the Ladies of Fairfield, Me. and Printed for the Benefit of the Fairfield Hall Association." And in 1891, "Ladies of the Independent Society," a Unitarian church group in Aroostook County's Presque Isle, produced *Choice Receipts From Many Homes*. These are but a very few early examples of the community cookbooks produced in every Maine city, town, and village, from Kittery to Houlton, Round Pond to Biddeford, Orono to Fryeberg. To date, some six hundred community cookbooks have been published in Maine.

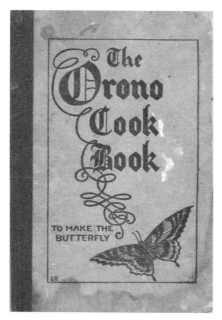

In Maine as elsewhere in the country, most community cookbooks were produced by groups affiliated with churches, but the books were popular with other organizations as well. Grange Halls, Fishermen's Associations, Hospital Auxiliaries, Civic Boosters, Temperance Crusaders, and all stripes of reformers employed the books to support their causes. Local Maine affiliates of national service organizations like the Rebekahs and the Dorcas produced books in multiple Maine towns. Over time, needs shifted: in the modern era we see books supporting Veterans of Foreign Wars (circa 1952), the Hurricane Island Outward Bound School (1967), the Waldo County Cooperative Extension Service (1974), The Maine Organic Farmers and Gardeners Association (1990), and Gay Rights Legislation (1995).

Maine community cookbooks, however, don't represent every group in the state. To date I've failed to locate community cookbooks by the native peoples of Maine – members of the Passamaquoddy, Penobscot, Maliseet, and Micmac nations. And I have yet to see books produced by recent arrivals from Africa and Asia, but that may just be a matter of time. Maine's earliest known Jewish cookbook was produced in Waterville circa 1951. The Levine Chapter of B'nai Brith, working together with the Waterville Chapter of Hadassah, produced *100 Selected Recipes*. Newer arrivals to Maine are represented in the genre, including the Franco-American community, represented by books such as Emma Marie Tourangeau's *Aunt Emma's Island Cookbook, with Old French Canadian Recipes* (circa 1960). Greek, Italian, Lebanese, and Armenian communities also produced the cookbooks. The compilations from Maine's immigrant communities often reflect a balance of dishes, with some recipes representing the origins of the group, while others their more recently adopted home.

You can expect the unexpected, like the *Camden Yacht Club Cook Book: Casseroles and Cruising Tips* (1972), or *Favorite Recipes of Maine Bikers* (Dixfield, 2015-16). But wherever and whatever the Maine organization, the members accomplished a great deal with these little books. Many of Maine's downtowns are specked with buildings, including churches, synagogues, grange halls, town halls, and libraries that were built, furnished, repaired, or restored in part by using funds collected through the sale of community cookbooks. Whether the cause was humble or grand, the impact on Maine's social and built environment was real.

Beyond meeting fundraising goals, the publication of community cookbooks had other results. They helped build a record of what people were eating in households throughout the state. Usually compiled by a committee (and it needs to be said, most often a committee of women), the recipe submissions were shaped, pondered, shared, and remade into a collection—"tried, tested, and proved" as many book titles say. Recipes are usually organized into sections. 1877's *Fish, Flesh and Fowl* had sections for Bread, Meats, Pie & Puddings, Cakes, "Fancy" (a catch-all phrase for sweet things; here it

includes creams, jellies, candies, and cake frostings), Salads & Pickles (really a section of preserves, but also including Cream Soda and a Currant Shrub), and Miscellaneous (medical or household recipes, such as Cleansing Glass Jars or A Remedy for Bad Breath). Until the last few decades, the recipes in community cookbooks favored those that required precision in cooking. Attention to detail was necessary to successfully create preserves, make candy, and bake, and those recipes were more numerous than those for which it was not, such as baking a fish, or grilling a piece of meat. Dishes that require a type of formula are also dishes one might see in an annual fair competition. They were also dishes one might be inclined to share with neighbors and friends. My own pantry contains a shelf full of delicious preserves given to me as gifts.

The recipes, more often than not, were accompanied by the name of the contributor. Sometimes a contributor is represented by initials alone or, alas, not at all. When present, attribution makes community cookbooks useful sources of information for local historians and genealogists. We read that Miss Lizzie U. Yates supplied the recipe for Angel Cake in *Tested Cooking Receipts* (Round Pond, 1887), or that Florence Kezar's Apple Muffins are included in the *Sunshine Sewing Circle Cook Book* (North Berwick, 1935). The compilation of locally sourced recipes—a centuries-old tradition for all types of cookbooks—meant there was no cost for the content that would become the book.

Compiled recipes in hand, the ladies (and sometimes gentlemen) often financed the expense of up-front printing and binding through a creative work-around. Advertisements were solicited from local businesses, including the printers and binders. Local advertisements could range from the expected, such as "Pyrex Baking Dishes" available at the Rockland Hardware Store (in *A Collection of Recipes of the Congregational Church* (Rockland, 1925)), to the exotic, "A Lover of the Beautiful Should Visit the Taxidermists Rooms of Mr. & Mrs. W.A. Herrick, over T.B. Seekins' Store" (in *Treasures: a Collection of Tested Recipes* (Dexter, 1885). Advertisements for businesses within the community helped finance the costs of book production, leaving the proceeds from sales of the books to be applied in full to the charitable cause. In today's terms, we might say that to get the books published women employed crowd sourcing (gathering the recipes from community members) and crowd funding (pre-financing of production through advertising).

Published outside of the traditional publishing industry, creative work-arounds were the norm for the makers of community cookbooks. When local printing and binding was less accessible (which, due to consolidation in the printing industry in the first half of the twentieth-century, was widely the case), new methods were employed. Maine's community cookbooks embraced new and cheap printing technologies such as spirits duplication, mimeo, and ditto, which may have been available at the school or church office, and home- or office-based binding methods like ribbon binding, saddle stapling, ring binders, machine sewing, brads, and wire and comb bindings (widely known as "spiral"). The materials used to make Maine community cookbooks were just as inventive and included wallpaper, linoleum, cardboard, decorated oil cloth, and in at least one case, woven asbestos. Cast off or repurposed materials found in the home or in local businesses became the covers of books. It was a "do-it-yourself" or "make-do" culture of cookbook creation.

Maine women (and later Maine women and men) came together in groups, informal and formal, to get things done. They creatively navigated the production and marketing of cookbooks, and they used the sale of the books to do good in their communities. But beyond the books themselves, beyond raising funds for the physical buildings that became the heart of downtown Maine, and beyond providing kindling for a range of Maine's social, cultural, and political movements, organizations in Maine used the cookbooks to build the very communities the books reflected. Each element of the process made connections and strengthened networks: compiled recipes were gathered from community members; small-town business advertisement supported the project while introducing the businesses into the kitchens of local families; local printing and binding (either professional or homemade) produced an object that in both process and material physically reflects the community. Each charitable contribution was accompanied by a parallel contribution to the social bond of Maine's communities. These dual achievements—solving a practical problem by organizing around the sale of community cookbooks, while building networks of social bonds within the community—are documented in the pages of each and every Maine community cookbook.

Despite our state's wealth of natural resources, Maine ranks 12th in the nation for food insecurity. According to the USDA's September 2019 Economic Research Service report, 13.6% of Maine's households are considered food insecure, and 1 in 5 Maine children are unsure of their next meal. $2 from every copy sold of the *Maine Bicentennial Community Cookbook* will go to organizations fighting hunger in Maine.

Land and Food Acknowledgment

The people of the Wabanaki Confederacy have been stewards of the land we now call Maine for thousands of years. They fished, foraged, hunted, and farmed these lands, woods, and shores long before the arrival of European colonists and the 200 years of Maine's statehood. Indigenous communities here in Maine and across the Americas continually demonstrate resilience and resistance in the face of efforts to separate them from land, culture, community, and food traditions. They continue to be on the front lines of environmental, racial, and food justice. We honor the pasts, presents, and futures of the Maliseet, Micmac, Passamaquoddy, and Penobscot peoples and support work ongoing to ensure Native land and food sovereignty for the Wabanaki Confederacy and all indigenous people.

Wabanaki Foodways and the State of Maine

By Darren J. Ranco, PhD

Like other indigenous people around the world, Wabanaki (Maliseet, Micmac, Passamaquoddy, and Penobscot) Tribal Nations and people have engaged, managed, gathered, planted, hunted, and fished the vast and diverse resources that form the core of Maine's food traditions for thousands of years. With the arrival of Maine's bicentennial, it is a good time to reflect on these food traditions and how they have been impacted by the creation of the State of Maine and, more generally, those who came "from away" during the last 200 years.

Wabanaki people continue to know and engage the precise location of every natural feature of their homeland, which stretches from the Connecticut River valley in the west all the way to the shores of Nova Scotia in the east. Before the arrival of Europeans and the creation of the United States and Canada and their colonial policies of control and assimilation, Wabanaki people knew where each resource was plentiful when they were wanted and roughly in what quantities. Major inland resources included white-tailed deer, moose, caribou, beaver, black bear, other fur-bearers (fox, lynx, bobcat, fisher, marten, otters, skunks), muskrat, porcupine, rabbit, fowl, berries, seeds, roots, tubers, nut trees, resident and anadromous fish, wild grasses, bark, maple sap, and plants for medicinal purposes. Upland game birds were plentiful—turkey, pigeon, and grouse (partridge)—along with raptors and birds of prey. The coast was abundant with lobsters, clams, oysters, and sea mammals such as seals, porpoises, and whales. Multitudes of waterfowl such as loons, ducks, cormorants, herons, and geese were seasonal inhabitants. Wabanaki people and others continue to hunt and fish these resources today, but it is important to note that the historical Wabanaki diet engaged a complex system of management, knowledge, and responsibility that included a great diversity of foods beyond the sources of protein we associate with hunting and fishing. From Wabanaki oral traditions, first-hand accounts, and anthropological reports, hundreds of plant species native to Maine have been documented for food, medicine, and sources of material culture.

Of course, beginning in the early seventeenth century, the arrival of Europeans started to change the ways in which Wabanaki people engaged and managed food and other natural resources. But change was not new, as Wabanaki people have been responding to ecological and climatic changes for thousands of years. The seasonal round, an adaptive management and resource extraction practice used by Wabanaki people, has for most of recent history focused on summer coastal and winter inland food resources for the last several hundred years. This was most likely an adaptation to changing ecologies and climate, and before this seasonal round was established there is evidence that it was just the opposite in deeper historical periods. Neither system is possible without a deep knowledge of ecology, seasonality, and locations of plants, fish, animals, and their lifeways.

At the time of Maine's founding in 1820, the majority of what is now the State of Maine was still Wabanaki space. Many inland areas, in particular, had a majority of Wabanaki inhabitants, most of whom used traditional Wabanaki food strategies to feed themselves. As the nineteenth century progressed, however, things started to change, often in dramatic ways. While the new state of Maine continued Massachusetts' policies to exclude Wabanaki people from some coastal resources, the increased settlement of inland areas created new pressures for accessing food in traditional places and traditional ways. Maine's colonial and economic policies worked to transform the state that made it almost impossible for Wabanaki people to harvest food and support themselves in traditional ways. The economic policies that encouraged and made possible the clearing of Maine's forest for the lumber industry transformed the ecology of inland Maine over the course of a couple decades, causing a major disruption in food gathering systems for Wabanaki people. Colonial policies, enforced by the state through Indian Agents, restricted Wabanaki movement across the state for food access. Furthermore, the state, like other states, passed hunting and fishing laws that hugely impacted Native and other people who were relying on the commons for sources of protein. Violating these laws could often have catastrophic effects for individual Wabanaki people—oral histories of infractions for violating these laws (which often ignored treaty-reserved hunting and fishing rights), could lead to serious injury or even death by the "authorities" enforcing these laws. The overall intent and impact of these colonial policies was to separate Wabanaki people from our traditional resources and diets, but luckily this was not fully achieved.

As the twentieth century progressed, Wabanaki people have inserted ourselves in powerful ways into the debates about resource management and food sovereignty. With recognition by the Federal courts and government in the 1970s that Wabanaki lands had been illegally seized by the states of Maine and Massachusetts, Wabanaki Tribal Nations were able to re-acquire about 300,000 acres of land in the 1980s in the aftermath of the Maine Indian Claims Settlement Act of 1980. Tribal management of these lands is almost entirely based on the hunting and fishing preferences of Wabanaki citizens, and habitats have returned to support these lifeways under Wabanaki management. At the dawn of the twenty-first century and beyond, we see each of the Wabanaki Tribal Nations in Maine—the Penobscot Nation, the Passamaquoddy Tribe-Indian Township, the Passamaquoddy Tribe-Pleasant Point, the Aroostook Band of Micmacs, and the Houlton Band of Maliseet Indians—charting a path for their citizens and Mainers in general for food sovereignty and local foodways. For example, the Penobscot Nation has been instrumental in removing dams on the Penobscot River, and the Passamaquoddy Tribe has provided critical leadership on along the St. Croix watershed—both of which have led to the return of important fish resources. The Aroostook Band of Micmacs is feeding a lot of people in Aroostook County through their Micmac Farms and trout fishery, and the Houlton Band of Maliseet Indians has been working for over 20 years to return a vibrant fish resource to the Meduxnekeag River by leading watershed management locally and internationally with Canadian partners. Taken together, these actions by Wabanaki Nations and people are helping support the food systems for all Mainers for the *next* 200 years.

Darren J. Ranco is the Chair of Native American Programs, Associate Professor of Anthropology, and Coordinator of Native American Research at the University of Maine. A member of the Penobscot Indian Nation, he is particularly interested in how better research relationships can be made between universities, Native and non-Native researchers, and indigenous communities

Photo: Charlotte Schatz baking in her family's kitchen in Gray.
Charlotte's great-great-grandmother's recipe for Meat Knishes is on page 62.

Sister Marie's Whole Wheat Bread

United Society of Shakers • New Gloucester, Cumberland County

Sister Marie Burgess (1920-2001) was born in Rumford, Maine. She joined the Shakers at age 19 and became an assistant cook a short time later, a role that she held for the rest of her life. She was a candy maker and an excellent baker of breads, pies, cookies, and desserts—and an avid Red Sox fan! She learned this bread recipe as a young baker and made thousands of loaves over the course of her lifetime.

1 cup milk
2 tablespoons sugar
2 teaspoons salt
¼ cup butter or margarine
½ cup molasses
2 packages dry active yeast

1½ cups warm water (temperature of 105°-115°)
2½ cups sifted all-purpose flour
5 cups *unsifted* whole wheat flour
2 tablespoons melted butter or margarine

Heat milk slowly until bubbles form around the pan, then remove from heat. Add sugar, salt, butter, and molasses. Stir until butter melts. In a large bowl sprinkle the yeast over water and stir until dissolved. Stir in the milk mixture. Add all-purpose flour and 2½ cups of whole wheat flour. Beat with wooden spoon until smooth, about 4 minutes. Gradually add remaining whole wheat flour, mixing in the last of it with your hand, until the dough leaves the sides of the bowl.

Turn dough out onto a lightly floured board and allow to rest for 10 minutes. Knead until smooth, about 10 to 12 minutes. Kneading is very important in making good bread so do not neglect it. Place dough in a greased bowl and turn the dough so as to bring the greased side up. Cover with a light towel and let rise in a warm place away from drafts until dough doubles in bulk, about 75 minutes. A good test is to poke two fingers into the dough and if the indentation remains, the dough is ready. Punch dough down with hands (this is a good way to let off steam about something troublesome). Turn dough onto lightly floured board, divide in half and shape each half into a smooth ball. Let rest for 10 minutes. Shape each portion into a loaf and place in lightly greased 9 x 5-inch loaf pans. Cover with a towel and let rise in warm place until double in bulk or until the dough reaches the tops of the pans. This takes approximately 1½ hours.

Preheat oven to 400°. Bake loaves 40 to 45 minutes. The tops should be browned and sound hollow when rapped with knuckles. Remove bread from pans immediately, brush with melted butter or magarine, and let it cool.

Bannock

1877 • *Fish, Flesh and Fowl: A Book of Recipes for Cooking*
Ladies of State Street Parish • Portland, Cumberland County

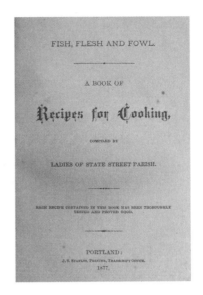

Bannock appears as the very first recipe listed in the first cookbook compiled and published in Maine. A simple flatbread, often eaten in times of scarcity, bannock is a dish with roots in both Native American culture and the cooking of the British Isles. Indian meal was the common name for corn meal at the time. —DL

One pint Indian meal scalded with one quart milk, six or eight eggs, a little sugar and salt. Stir in eggs when cool, and bake in high oven.

Steamed Brown Bread

Lois Widmer • Brunswick, Cumberland County

"This is my mother's recipe. She served it every Saturday night to accompany the traditional baked beans. During the 1970s and '80s, First Parish Church in Brunswick had monthly public baked bean suppers. We were known for our home-made brown bread, using this recipe. A team of members would make this, often tripling the recipe and storing the breads in our freezers until needed. One of our regular attendees, a lobsterman from Harpswell, offered to swap lobsters for a copy of the recipe. My mother's brown bread lives on in Harpswell."

1 cup Original All-Bran cereal
1 cup soured milk or buttermilk
    (not fat free)
¼ cup molasses
½ cup sugar

1 cup flour
1 teaspoon baking soda
¼ teaspoon salt
½ cup raisins

Mix all-bran, soured milk, and molasses in a large bowl. Let this sit while you grease or oil a 1-pound tin coffee can. Add enough water to a large, deep pot to come halfway up the sides of the can. Cover the pot and start water to boil for the steaming process.

Add sugar, flour, baking soda, salt, and raisins to the all-bran mixture. Mix well. Pour batter into coffee can and cover tightly with tin foil.

Place can in the boiling water, making sure the water doesn't boil over the tops of the can, and steam for 3 hours. When the brown bread has finished steaming, loosen with a knife around the edges and tap onto a rack to cool.

New England Brown Bread

Krista Marvel • York, York County

"I am the Department Chair of Culinary Arts and Hospitality Management at York County Community College in Wells. This simple bread represents the heart and history of Mainers. By using an old English cooking method of steaming baked goods, early New England cooks were able to create an easy, bread-like item on their open hearths without needing an oven. The ingredients often used to make brown bread, such as cornmeal and rye flour, were inexpensive pantry items that were readily available to these early settlers.

This bread is easily adaptable for gluten-free or dairy-free diets and is equally delicious with or without dried fruits and nuts. It can be served warm or at room temperature, like a muffin, and is also delicious sliced into 1-inch-thick rounds and pan fried in butter."

½ cup raisins or dried cranberries

½ cup walnuts (chopped and toasted), optional

½ cup whole wheat flour (or ½ cup gluten-free flour mix)

½ cup rye flour (or ½ cup buckwheat flour)

½ cup cornmeal

1 teaspoon baking soda

½ teaspoon salt

½ teaspoon cinnamon

⅓ cup dark molasses

1 cup milk (or coconut, hemp, almond or soy milk)

Preheat oven to 350 degrees. Using kitchen spray, lightly grease a 1-quart metal measuring cup, an old 1-pound coffee tin, or a tall, round pan. Lay a piece of kitchen twine across bottom and up sides inside the pan, leaving at least 1 inch of twine hanging over each side. Repeat with a second piece of twine, so twine creates an X on the bottom of the pan. (The twine will help you remove the finished bread from the pan.) Cut a long strip of parchment paper, the height of the pan. Paper the sides of the can, and spray again. Set prepared pan aside.

Place the raisins or dried cranberries in a small pan and cover them with water. Heat over high heat until water comes to a boil. Turn off and let sit for 5 minutes. Drain well and set aside to cool. If using nuts, lightly toast in preheated 350 degree oven for best flavor. Set aside to cool.

Combine the flours, cornmeal, baking soda, salt, and cinnamon in a mixing bowl. Stir in the molasses and milk. Fold in the raisins or cranberries and nuts if using.

Fill the pan or metal measuring cup with all the batter. It should come up about two-thirds of the way. Cover the top with a square of foil and tie securely with a string to make it airtight. Place in a deep baking pan and fill the pan with enough water to come halfway up the side of the mold to create a water bath. The steam will help it bake properly.

Bake at 350 for 2 hours, checking the water level after 1 hour. Add more hot water if needed.

Check by sticking a skewer into the bread; it will come out clean when done. Remove string and foil and allow to cool before unmolding.

Radnor Farm Place Cards

Cynthia Palmer Sherman • Damariscotta, Lincoln County

"These are place cards from my family farm, Radnor Farm, in Cumberland. Radnor Farm was a working farm from the 1920s through the mid-1950s, owned by the Smith family. Two of my great-aunts lived together in the big old farmhouse, feeding the farm animals, collecting the eggs, and picking blueberries in the summer. The farm was sold when the youngest sister passed away in 1956. The place cards were made for family members gathering at the huge mahogany dining room table for a family dinner in 1927. My dad is the little chick, he was 4 years old in 1927."

24-Hour Yeasted Peanut Butter Waffles (Gluten Free!)

Maya Flores • Kennebunk, York County

"I am 14 years old, and I have always lived in Maine. My recipe is not an old family recipe—it is a new twist on a family favorite. For many years, my family's favorite waffle recipe was an overnight yeasted batter that made traditional, fluffy waffles. We also love peanut butter pancakes. I combined the two! I used almond flour so my parents and other people who are gluten free can enjoy them."

2 cups whole milk
4 tablespoons unsalted butter, cut into 8 pieces
2 cups of all-natural peanut butter (just peanuts and salt)

2 large eggs
1½ cups almond flour
2 tablespoons sugar
1 teaspoon salt
1½ teaspoons instant yeast

Note: Batter must be made about 24 hours in advance!

Warm milk and butter in a small saucepan over low heat until butter is melted. Let mixture cool until just warm to the touch. Add peanut butter and eggs, and whisk until smooth. In a large bowl, whisk to combine the almond flour, sugar, salt, and instant yeast. Add the warm milk/eggs/peanut butter mixture gradually, whisking until the batter is smooth. Cover the bowl with plastic wrap and refrigerate approximately 24 hours.

For the fluffiest waffles, take the batter out of the refrigerator 1 hour prior to cooking and let it sit at room temperature. Stir the batter gently to recombine it and help it deflate slightly.

Heat waffle iron and spoon the batter onto the iron. It will likely plop onto the waffle iron rather than pour on like more traditional waffle batters. For best results, do not overcook so the peanut butter flavor can come through. Also, use a Belgian waffle iron instead of the smaller round kind to maximize the nooks and crannies to help create a crispy exterior and fluffy interior.

Serve with sliced bananas and Maine maple syrup. Enjoy!

Aroostook County Biscuits

Maureen Pease • Windham, Cumberland County

"Growing up, we visited the family farm in Hope nearly every weekend. My grandmother, Ruth, was very involved in the Knox County 4-H and Cooperative Extension, and was known for her many kitchen creations made with the cast-iron wood stove. These are more rolls than biscuits, but the name was my grandmother's, so the name stays. You can still find the farm, Barrett Homestead Farm, on Barnestown Road in Hope, humming along, as it has been for nearly 230 years."

⅓ cup butter, unsalted
⅓ cup shortening, vegetable
1¼ cups whole milk
⅔ cup water
3 tablespoons sugar, white granulated
4½ teaspoons yeast, active dry

6 cups flour, all purpose
¾ cup potato flakes
2 teaspoons salt, Diamond kosher
2 large eggs, slightly beaten
2 to 3 tablespoons butter, unsalted, melted
   for brushing

Melt the butter and shortening. Add milk, water, and sugar and heat to about 110 degrees. Whisk in yeast and let sit until bubbly and foamy.

While yeast is sitting, in a large bowl whisk together flour, potato flakes, and salt. Once yeast has proofed, add eggs and yeast mixture to flour and mix until dough comes together.

Turn dough out onto lightly floured board and knead dough until smooth and satiny, 5 to 10 minutes. Place dough in a greased bowl, cover with plastic wrap, and let rise until double, roughly 90 minutes.

Butter a 13 x 9-inch baking pan. Turn the dough out and punch down. Knead until smooth (should be fairly quick), and pat into a rectangle, roughly 10 x 12 inches. Using a bench knife, cut 48 rolls (8 cuts on one side, 6 on the shorter side). Arrange in baking dish. Brush rolls with melted butter, cover with plastic wrap and let rise for 1-1½ hours until almost doubled.

Preheat oven to 375 degrees. Bake rolls for 30 minutes, turning the pan once halfway through baking to ensure even browning.

Aunt Geri's New England Brown Bread

Barton Seaver • Freeport, Cumberland County

"Not long ago, my wife's father found a half sister whom he hadn't seen in many decades. A Mrs. Geraldine Varney of Newport, Maine. With this reconnection came a delightful troop of new aunts, uncles, and cousins. At the family reunion, Aunt Geri brought out her time-tested recipe for this New England tradition, a deliciously moist bread made the old-fashioned way, steamed for hours in a coffee tin, which rings the bread with ridges, like a can of jellied cranberry sauce. There is something so very fun about connecting to your history, both on the plate and around the table."

1 cup bread crumbs
1 cup cold water
½ cup cornmeal
½ cup flour

½ cup molasses, plus more for serving
1 rounded teaspoon baking soda
2 tablespoons butter, divided

Combine the bread crumbs and water in a bowl and let soak until completely absorbed, about 15 minutes. Add the cornmeal, flour, molasses, and baking soda, whisking until smooth.

Press the batter into a large coffee can, tamping down on it to remove any air bubbles. Place two layers of aluminum foil over the open end and secure it with rubber bands or kitchen twine. Place the can in a large deep pot and add enough water to come halfway up the can. Cover the pot and bring to a boil.

Reduce the heat to medium to maintain a consistent simmer and cook for 2½ hours, checking the water level periodically and adding more boiling water if it gets low. Test for doneness by sticking a skewer into the middle of the bread. If it comes out clean, the bread is ready. If still doughy, cook another 20 minutes and test again. Remove from the pot and let cool.

When it is cool, remove the foil and puncture the bottom of the can to allow air in. Gently shake the bread from the can and slice into 1-inch-thick rounds. Melt 1 tablespoon of the butter in a sauté pan over high heat. Working in batches, add the sliced bread and cook until crisped, about 4 minutes. Transfer to a low oven to keep warm. Repeat with the remaining butter and bread.

Serve the crisped bread with molasses or more butter, if you like.

Bernice's Refrigerator Rolls

Martha McSweeney Brower • Camden, Knox County

"My aunt Bernice had this recipe published in a women's magazine in the 1940s. My family loves these rolls for every holiday and my three sons always request little blobs of raw dough before they go into the oven."

2 yeast cakes
¼ cup lukewarm water
¾ cup butter
½ cup sugar

1 cup hot mashed potatoes (or ¾ cup
    instant potatoes and ¾ cup hot water)
1 cup warm water
6 to 6½ cups flour
1½ teaspoons salt

In large bowl, dissolve yeast in ¼ cup water. Add butter, sugar, hot potatoes, and water. (Mixture will be thin.) Add flour and salt, and mix. When dough is stiff, but not dry, grease top, cover tightly with plastic wrap, and place in refrigerator. Dough will keep in refrigerator for several days.

When ready to bake, knead for 10 minutes. Roll out dough to 13 x 20 inches. Cut in half lengthwise, then cut 8 triangles from each half.

Bake at 375 degrees for 10 minutes or until golden.

Lynn Reese's Pear Bread

Robert Bernheim • China, Kennebec County

"Some recipes are family favorites, cherished at special occasions like birthdays and holidays. Others are staples of daily or weekly life. Lynn Reese's Pear Bread is one of those staples; week in and week out, it anchors the rotation of meals as a steadfast and dependable choice for sandwiches, toast, or even the foundation for meatballs or meatloaf. Part of Lynn's repertoire for more than five decades, she has passed this Pear Bread recipe on to her nephew, nieces, and their families as a welcome, trusted, and indispensable part of the Bernheim and Campbell cuisines."

2¾ cups pureed pears (loosen with water if too thick, or substitute applesauce)

1 tablespoon yeast

¼ cup water (or warm apple cider)

1 teaspoon ground ginger (more if you like ginger)

2 tablespoons honey (more if you like it sweeter)

1 teaspoon salt (more if you like it saltier)

2 large eggs

7 to 8 cups white flour (can substitute 2 cups white wheat flour)

Puree pears in blender; add enough water to make 2¾ cups.

Dissolve yeast in warm water (or cider); proof for 10 minutes. Add fruit puree, ginger, honey, salt, and eggs to a large bowl and beat thoroughly by hand or with a mixer. Add 2 cups of flour and beat again. Mix in remaining flour and empty onto a board when it becomes thick enough to handle.

Knead in remaining flour and add more if necessary until bread feels right. (It should be soft but not sticky; almost like a clean baby's bottom—smooth with no tackiness.)

Turn into greased bowl. Cover and let rise until double, about 1½ hours.

Divide dough in half and knead; shape into loaves and place in greased bread pans. Let rise covered about an hour.

Bake at 350 degrees for about 40 to 50 minutes. Cool on rack before slicing.

Johnny Cake

Rachel Tremblay • Moscow, Somerset County

"My mother grew up on a farm in Bowdoin and although she and my grandmother were good cooks, their specialty was baking. My Grandmother Adams used to say, 'There's more in the baking than there is in the making.' Growing up, we always enjoyed homemade breads and pies and the cookie jar was never empty. This is my mother's recipe and we always had it with chili or pea soup."

1½ cups cornmeal	¼ teaspoon baking powder
½ cup sugar	½ teaspoon salt
1 cup flour	2 eggs
½ cup whole wheat flour	1½ cups of buttermilk or sour milk
¾ teaspoon baking soda	¼ cup vegetable oil

Sift or whisk together dry ingredients. In a separate bowl, whisk together eggs, buttermilk, and oil. Add to dry ingredients and mix until just blended. Batter will be lumpy. Pour into a greased 13 x 9 pan. Bake at 375 degrees for 20 to 30 minutes. Recipe may be halved and baked in an 8 x 8 pan for 15 to 20 minutes.

Grandmother Maggie's Molasses Blueberry Muffins

Allison Salisbury • Bar Harbor, Hancock County

"Back in the '30s when I was a child, we lived through the Depression, but we always had three good meals. Hens, a hog, and a cow provided us with everything Mother needed. I'm 91 now—please forgive me if I mess recipes up."

The handwritten notes in the margins of this Depression-era recipe read "NO eggs," and "heavy and delicious."

½ cup molasses	⅔ cup sour milk
¼ cup shortening (any cooking oil is also fine)	2 cups flour
	½ teaspoon salt
½ cup sugar	2 cups wild Maine blueberries, fresh or
1 teaspoon baking soda	Wyman's frozen, dredged in flour

Mix together all ingredients and pour into greased muffin tins. Bake at 400 degrees until toothpick comes out clean, 15 to 18 minutes.

United States Senate
WASHINGTON, D. C.

BLUEBERRY MUFFINS

+++++++++++++++++++++++++

Wash 1 1/2 cups fresh blueberries, drain
thoroughly. Mix and sift 1 1/2 cups flour with 1/2 teaspoon
salt, 3 tablespoons sugar, 3 teaspoons baking powder. Beat
1 egg and mix with 3/4 cup fresh milk. Stir the egg and milk
into the flour mixture, then add the berries and 3 tablespoons
melted shortening. Mix well and pour into greased muffin
pans, filling each one 3/4 full. Bake in a hot oven--400 degrees--
for 20 minutes. Makes nine to twelve muffins, depending on
size.

Pat Collins' Maine Blueberry Muffins

Senator Susan Collins • Bangor, Penobscot County

"I started making muffins for my husband almost every Sunday night a few years ago. It made me feel that I was doing something special for him to compensate for the many times that one or both of us had evening events that precluded our having dinner together. In addition, I knew that the muffins he was buying from the bakery near his office were loaded with fat, salt, and sugar. These were healthier and tastier alternatives.

My mother, Pat Collins, of Caribou, is the best cook I know, and it was natural that I would first turn to a cookbook that she published for family and friends called 'Fifty Years of Cooking: 1948 to 1998' for the first muffin recipes I made. These muffins are still my favorites."

1½ cups flour
½ cup sugar
2 teaspoons baking powder
½ teaspoon salt
¼ cup shortening
1 egg

½ cup low-fat milk
1 to 1½ cups wild Maine blueberries
Mixture of granulated white sugar and
   cinnamon to sprinkle on the tops of
   the muffins

Pick over and rinse blueberries, and let drain well on a paper towel.

Mix dry ingredients together. Cut shortening into the dry ingredients.

Beat egg slightly and combine with milk. Pour liquid mixture all at once into the dry ingredients/shortening mixture. Stir with a fork until flour is just mixed in. Fold in berries.

Fill greased muffin tins and sprinkle tops lightly with sugar-cinnamon mixture. Bake in a pre-heated 400-degree oven for 20 to 25 minutes.

Perfect Popovers

Nancy Wanderer • Falmouth, Cumberland County

"When I was growing up, my mother tried for years to make popovers. She tried every recipe and every kind of pan she could find. Time after time, the popovers flopped and tears were shed. In 1968, I married a man whose mother was an excellent cook. Most importantly, she knew how to make popovers that never flopped. I got the recipe and shared it with my mom, who was ecstatic to finally know how to make popovers successfully. The marriage didn't last, but the popover recipe did. Using this recipe, I have made hundreds—maybe even thousands—of perfect popovers over the past 52 years, and my son makes popovers every Sunday for his two sons in Uganda. That makes four generations of popover-lovers in this family!"

3 large eggs
1 cup of milk
3 tablespoons oil

1 cup flour
½ teaspoon salt

Whisk eggs, milk, and oil together. Stir in flour and salt. Let stand for awhile, if possible, to bring ingredients closer to room temperature. You can even stir the mixture up the night before and bring it out of the refrigerator to warm up a bit in the morning.

Pour batter into 5 or 6 greased crockery custard cups. Each custard cup should be about two-thirds full. Preheat oven to 400 degrees. Place custard cups on the lowest rack and bake until they have risen and gotten crusty and brown on top—about 30 minutes. Serve immediately with butter, honey, or your favorite jam.

One-Rise Cinnamon Rolls

Ginger Patterson • Mexico, Oxford County

"My parents owned Naples Packing Co. a wholesale meat and grocery business that my brother Jimmy runs today. During summer vacations, I would help make most of the meals, so my mother could do the books for the family business. I have made these cinnamon buns every Christmas morning for at least 35 years."

Topping:
1 cup heavy cream
1 cup brown sugar

Filling:
½ cup sugar
2 teaspoons cinnamon
½ cup butter, softened

Rolls:
3 cups flour, divided
1 package yeast
¼ cup sugar
1 teaspoon salt
1 cup hot tap water
2 tablespoons butter, softened
1 egg

Mix cream and brown sugar in an ungreased 9 x 13-inch pan.

In a medium bowl, mix sugar, cinnamon, and softened butter to make filling.

In a large bowl, blend 1½ cups flour and remaining ingredients, reserving 1½ cups flour. Beat 3 minutes at medium speed. Stir in remaining 1½ cups flour. Knead on floured surface for 1 minute, adding more flour if necessary.

Roll dough into a 15 x 7-inch rectangle. Spread filling over dough. Starting at the long side, roll tightly, sealing edges. Slice into 16-20 rolls. Place rolls cut-side down onto cream mixture. Cover and let rise 30 to 45 minutes.

Bake rolls in preheated oven at 400 degrees for 20 to 25 minutes.

Cool 10 to 15 minutes before turning out onto a serving dish. Also serves well right out of the pan.

Ployes

Norma Dionne • Van Buren, Aroostook County

"Ployes used to be served with most Acadian meals here in the St. John Valley in place of bread. They are very good accompaniments to any type of stew and baked beans as well as many other meals."

½ cup buckwheat flour
½ cup white flour

Dash salt
1 ½ teaspoons baking powder

Mix dry ingredients with cold water to form a very thick batter. Then add boiling water gradually, stirring after each addition until the consistency of crepe batter is achieved. Drop batter by large spoonful (about ¼ cup) on very hot griddle. Cook until bubbles have burst and top looks cooked. Flip and cook a few minutes more. Serve with butter, or butter and brown sugar, or molasses, or syrup, or creton, a French-Canadian pork pâté. Makes a small stack to serve about 2 people.

Gay Island Lobster Scramble

circa 1935 • *Just a Few Maine Sea Food Recipes*

Sea & Shore Fisheries Department "Old Fashioned Maine Housewives" • Cushing, Knox County

Feeding a family on a small island was difficult work for lighthouse keepers and their families. Provisions were brought by "tender" (supply boat), and might include corn meal, beans, salt pork, and some vegetables that put up well. But bad weather could mean weeks with no supply boat and no additional provisions. Joe Johansen, an assistant keeper at Ram Island Ledge from 1949 to 1950, recounted, "One time I was on there for 45 days. Couldn't get off. .. all we had was powdered milk and oatmeal for one whole week...."

So lighthouse families made do by foraging for berries, sea moss and shellfish. They kept chickens, both as pets and for eggs, and a few had cows that provided milk. We know of no recipes directly recorded by keepers or their families, but this simple island recipe from Muskongus Bay could be made with just two of the available ingredients, in a hearth or on an open fire. —DL

1 cup lobster meat cut in small pieces

3 eggs well beaten mix with lobster and fry in a spider.

This will serve two people.

Sea Moss Farina

Frances Harlow Clukey • Bangor, Penobscot County

"I contributed this recipe to a Bangor/Eastern Junior League cookbook in 1980 because it was so 'Maine!' I made the sea moss farina with my grandmother, Josie Berry Harlow, at her summer cottage in Hancock. We still collect and dry the sea moss when we are on the coast, and the pudding is still a favorite at the hunting camp."

¼ cup dry sea moss*

1 quart milk

¼ cup honey

1 teaspoon vanilla

Any canned or fresh fruit for topping

*Gather Irish moss (carrageen) at the sea and dry it out, or buy agar-agar at a health food store.

Rinse sea moss to clean it. Soak in top of double saucepan with milk for a few minutes, then cook over boiling water for 20 minutes. Do not stir. Remove from heat. Strain milk off the moss.

Into the strained milk stir honey and vanilla. Pour into individual sherbet cups and let set; chill. Top with canned or fresh fruit. Makes 4 servings.

Portland, Me., Ram Island Ledge Light House.

Squash Muffins

Suzanne Trussell • Stetson, Penobscot County

"When I married my husband, Joe Stupak, in 1972, I met his delightful maternal grandmother, Glennora Moore. When Joe's mother, Celia, the oldest of Glennora's six children, was born in 1920, the family lived on a farm in Somerville. Later, they moved to Hallowell and eventually to Bath, where Glennora lived for many years in her home on Washington Street. It was a gathering place for her children and many grandchildren and great-grandchildren, especially on Sundays. This recipe appeared in the *Maine Rebekahs Cook Book* from 1964. Glennora was a proud member of the Maine Rebekahs. This recipe, although not her own, was one of Glennie's favorites. We continue to prepare it whenever we have leftover squash."

1 egg, beaten
4 tablespoons sugar
½ cup strained cooked squash
½ cup milk
¾ teaspoon salt

1¼ cups flour
1 teaspoon baking soda
2 teaspoons cream of tartar
4 tablespoons melted shortening

Beat together the egg, sugar, squash, milk, and salt. Add flour, baking soda, cream of tartar, and melted shortening. Beat together all ingredients. Put in warm greased muffin pans and bake at 400 degrees until toothpick comes out clean, about 20 minutes. Makes 12 large muffins.

Puff-In-The-Oven Pancake

Katina Stanwood • Ellsworth, Hancock County

"This quick and warming treat was a happy memory of my growing up in Maine. It wasn't until I was pregnant decades later that I craved the 'puff pancake' from my childhood. Although the humble pancake makes for an elegant dessert and is a healthy snack anytime of day, it was what I had for breakfast every day for the last four months of my pregnancy. This is a personal favorite for my son, now a teenager, as well."

2 tablespoons butter
2 large eggs, room temperature
⅔ cup milk
⅔ cup all-purpose flour
3 tablespoons sugar

Dash salt
Confectioners' sugar, for serving
Optional: Maine wild blueberry sauce,
maple syrup, fresh berries and other fruit

Preheat oven to 425 degrees. Place butter in a 10-inch ovenproof skillet; set pan in oven until butter is melted, 2 to 3 minutes.

Whisk eggs and milk in one bowl. In a second bowl, mix flour, sugar, and salt. Combine the two, and whisk until smooth. Pour into prepared skillet.

Bake until puffed and browned, 14 to 18 minutes. Dust with confectioners' sugar and serve with other toppings, if desired.

Maine Rebekahs, circa 1950: Glennora Moore is seated in the front row, third from the left.

Chanterelle Omelet with Fresh Chevre and Garlic Scape Pesto

Rob Dumas • Orono, Penobscot County

"To me, this dish is a true expression of the *terroir* of Maine. When I eat this, I remember the thrill of finding wild mushrooms in the woods, and the sun on my back as I harvest tender young scapes, the immature flowers of garlic plants, from my riotously green summer garden. You can substitute cultivated mushrooms for chanterelles, but I would encourage you to try wild ones at least once in your lifetime."

For each omelet:
4-6 wild chanterelle mushrooms
1 teaspoon canola oil
2 large eggs
1½ tablespoons butter

2 tablespoons plain crumbled chevre
    (fresh goat cheese)
1 tablespoon Garlic Scape Pesto
    (recipe follows)
Sea salt and freshly ground pepper, to taste

Preheat oven to 400 degrees. Clean chanterelle mushrooms thoroughly to ensure they have no dirt or forest detritus. Tear them into bite-size pieces. Toss mushrooms with canola oil and a pinch of salt, then spread out on a baking sheet and roast until lightly browned.

While mushrooms are roasting, assemble all of your remaining ingredients. Crack eggs into a small bowl, add a pinch of salt, and whisk until completely combined.

Place a 6- to 8-inch non-stick pan on medium low heat. Once the pan is fully heated, add your butter in two chunks and allow to melt completely before adding your beaten eggs. Stir immediately with a heat-resistant spatula, reduce heat to low, and continue stirring until the eggs begin to set.

Once the eggs begin to firm up, add the cooked mushrooms, the crumbled chevre, and the Garlic Scape Pesto. Roll your omelet to the front of your pan and allow the filling to heat through while very gently browning the edge of the omelet. (Some chefs will add another small bit of butter at this point.)

Before serving, invert your pan to roll the omelet onto a warm plate. Serve with a hearty piece of toasted local sourdough that has been smeared with fresh or cultured butter.

Garlic Scape Pesto

2 cups chopped garlic scapes
1 cup finely grated Parmesan cheese
1 cup mixed fresh soft herbs, such as basil,
    chervil, or parsley

¼ cup freshly squeezed lemon juice,
    or to taste
1 cup pine nuts, pepitas, or pecans
Olive oil, as needed

In a food processor, combine the scapes, cheese, herbs, lemon juice, and nuts or seeds. Blend until fully ground, while the processor is running, drizzle olive oil until you have a soft creamy pesto, adding more oil if you prefer a looser sauce. Adjust flavor with more lemon if desired.

Red Flannel Hash

Sylvia Sim • Liberty, Waldo County

"I was born in 1943 before the Baby Boomers. When I was growing up, my mother made this recipe when there was corned beef or ham leftovers, or the remnants of boiled dinner—whatever was available. Our neighbor, Clara Brewer, made the same recipe and used garlic vinegar, leaving out the garlic salt. Any way it was made, it was delicious and we cleaned our plates. My mother died in 1981 and I still use her recipes. I feel the current generation relies mostly on prepackaged foods and fast foods. It's becoming a lost art."

1 cup cooked carrots
¾ cup cooked turnip
¾ cup cooked parsnips
1 cup cooked shredded cabbage
2½ cups cooked potatoes
1 cup cooked beets
½ cup diced raw onions

½ teaspoon salt
½ teaspoon black pepper
½ teaspoon garlic salt
2 cups cooked meat (corned beef,
    ham, any leftovers)
4 teaspoons cider vinegar
⅓ cup water

Dice all vegetables and place in a black iron skillet. Sprinkle spices, meat, and vinegar over vegetables, then pour water over mixture. Cover and cook slowly. Stir occasionally until flavors are blended and it is thoroughly heated.

Squash Dinner Rolls

Linda Russell • Fryeburg, Oxford County

"When my children were young, I was a stay-at-home mom and listened to the Yankee Swap radio show where recipes where exchanged. I believe the Squash Dinner Rolls was called in by a nun. I have been preparing this recipe for over 25 years now and do not follow a recipe anymore. The rolls have been a favorite at family dinners, church suppers, and bake sales. I buy winter squash in bulk in the fall, cook and mash it, then freeze it in portions for one recipe. I always include the rolls in my family exhibit at Fryeburg Fair."

1 cup milk
½ cup margarine, plus more for brushing
1 cup cooked winter squash, mashed
3 to 4 cups flour

½ cup sugar
2 packages of rapid rise yeast
2 teaspoons salt

Heat milk with margarine until margarine is melted. Blend in winter squash, cool to lukewarm. In a large bowl, mix 1 cup flour with the sugar, yeast, and salt. Stir in milk mixture until smooth. Add remaining flour until dough is stiff. Knead in enough extra flour to make a smooth dough, about 5 minutes. Place dough in an oiled bowl, cover with plastic wrap and let rise for about 45 minutes or until doubled. Punch down and shape into rolls. Place rolls on greased baking dish and let rise 20 to 30 minutes. Bake at 350 degrees for 10 to 15 minutes or until golden brown. Brush tops of warm rolls with margarine when they come out of the oven.

Maine's Lemon Potato Nut Rolls

Carolyn Kelley • Caribou, Aroostook County

"Blue ribbon for a potato contest at the Fort Fairfield Potato Blossom Festival. If you love lemon you will love these rolls."

1 package dry yeast
⅓ cup sugar
⅓ cup oil
½ cup warm milk
½ cup mashed potatoes
1 tablespoon salt
1 egg

1 tablespoon lemon juice
3 tablespoons grated lemon rind, separated
3½ to 4 cups flour
¾ cup brown sugar
½ cup chopped pecans
Lemon Glaze (recipe follows)

Soften the yeast with ¼ cup warm water. Combine in bowl with the sugar, oil, warm milk, mashed potatoes, and salt. Stir together and add egg, lemon juice, and 1 tablespoon of lemon rind. Add enough flour to form a soft ball, and put on counter top or bread board to knead, adding flour, ¼ cup at a time, if needed. Cover and let rise for 1 hour. Roll out dough to a 12 x 16-inch rectangle, and brush with 2 tablespoons of melted butter. Combine the brown sugar, pecans, and 2 tablespoons of lemon rind, and sprinkle over dough. Roll as jelly roll, cut into sixteen 1-inch slices, and place cut-side down in greased pan. Cover to rise until doubled in size. Bake at 350 degrees for 20 to 25 minutes. Drizzle with lemon glaze before serving.

Lemon Glaze

½ cup confectioners' sugar
1 tablespoon lemon rind

½ teaspoon lemon juice
1 tablespoon milk

In a small bowl, beat all ingredients together until smooth. Drizzle over warm rolls before serving.

Swedish Pancakes (Svenka Plättar)

Christopher D'Amico • Brewer, Penobscot County

"This recipe comes to me from my mother from her mother and then her mother, who emigrated from Sweden to Massachusetts. So, it's over 130 years old, conservatively. From my earliest years, I remember my grandmother cooking them and I now use her plätt. They were a great treat that was very filling for us kids. To eat 'all seven' was an accomplishment! For over 65 years, my mother would cook these as a dessert option for her very special dinner party guests here in Maine, especially if she were serving as the traditional Smörgåsbord (buffet). We kids pilfered as many as we could sneak. As a cook, I can't hold a candle to my mother or grandmother, but I've still managed to make these as a Sunday breakfast for my two kids for over 30 years, and I'm introducing my three grandkids to them now."

6 eggs
1 cup flour
4 tablespoons sugar

½ teaspoon salt
2 teaspoons nutmeg (best if freshly grated)
3 cups milk

Begin preheat of Swedish plätt pan.

Meanwhile, in mixing bowl, whisk eggs and the rest of ingredients except milk until uniform. Gradually add portions of the milk and whisk until uniform and all the milk has been added.

Test temperature of pan by buttering one depression and ladling batter to just fill. Think of cooking eggs 'easy over/broken yolk' for cooking plättar; when batter is just about set, flip over with fork and butter knife. My technique is to ring the depression with the tip of knife to release the pancake, then slide it under and apply fork to hold pancake and flip into same depression. Allow any unset batter to slide off into depression and lay pancake atop.

When the pancake is fully set and the first side is starting to brown, it's done. Use the same fork and knife to remove pancakes to a warm plate kept in the oven. Adjust temperature as needed and butter each depression before you proceed with cooking rest of batter. Remix batter before ladling next batch onto plätt. (I use a cold stick of butter, with wrapper peeled back, to ring each depression with the end of the stick, before adding batter. I also daub each pancake again with butter, just before removing to warm plate. I keep throwing the stick of butter into the freezer between uses, to keep cold to minimize the buttery mess it would otherwise become by the end of the cooking.)

Serve warm with dollops of lingonberry jam on top of each to be authentic. But any jam, especially homemade, will be enjoyed. These are great for a breakfast or brunch or dinner or dessert. Makes about 35 of 3-inch pancakes.

Tea Rolls and Bread

Paula Hopkins Dayboch • Camden, Knox County

"My great-grandmother, Mary Lucretia Edes Hopkins, was born in Greenville in 1868, and died in Camden in 1959, a year before I was born. The Edes family were prolific and came to Maine in the 1700s via Charlestown, Massachusetts.

Being the oldest girl of eight children, Mary had to help raise her younger siblings after her mother's early death. Mary and her husband, Warren, went on to raise four children of their own and moved to Camden at the turn of the century to work in the woolen mills. According to family stories, Mary made these rolls/bread for an inn in Greenville. When they moved to Camden, Mary made this recipe for guests at the Mt. Battie Clubhouse, which stood atop the mountain in Camden. She taught the women in our family, and we still make this recipe to this day."

1 cup scalded milk
5 cups flour, separated
1 yeast cake dissolved in ¼ cup
   lukewarm water
2 eggs, beaten

¼ cup sugar
1 teaspoon salt
¼ cup melted butter
Pinch nutmeg

Warm milk to lukewarm. Add 2 cups sifted flour. Beat well. Add dissolved yeast. Let mixture rise 1½ hours, then add the beaten eggs. To this add sugar, salt, melted butter, and nutmeg. Add enough flour to make a soft dough, knead well, and let rise until doubled in size. Shape into rolls, put into a buttered pan, and let rise 1 hour. Bake about 15 minutes in a "quick oven" (400 degrees).

Photo: The three Greek Yia-Yias of Biddeford. See recipe on page 34.

Hester's Doughnuts

Hester Gilpatric • Minot, Androscoggin County

"I have fried doughnuts for over seventy-five years. My mother made them every week and I have continued the tradition. When we formed the Minot Historical Society in 2001, before the town's bicentennial year in 2002, our first fundraiser was a food sale at Hemond's Moto Cross. We have continued every year since. My niece's significant other was in upstate New York attending a race and talking to another attendee. The fellow asked Steve where he was from. When he replied, 'Minot, Maine,' the other fellow said, 'There is a lady there that makes the best donuts!' A Society member quilted the sign for me plus several signs for the Society."

2 eggs
1 cup sugar
3 tablespoons melted shortening,
  plus more for frying
1 teaspoon vanilla
1 cup buttermilk

3½ cups flour
½ teaspoon nutmeg
1 teaspoon salt
1 teaspoon baking soda
1 teaspoon baking powder
Sugar, for serving

Beat together eggs, sugar, melted shortening, vanilla, and buttermilk. Into a separate bowl, sift together the flour, nutmeg, salt, baking soda, and baking powder. Add dry ingredients to wet. Place batter in a covered container and store overnight in the refrigerator.

Roll out on a floured board to ½-inch thickness. Cut with floured doughnut cutter. Fry in deep melted shortening, heated to 370 degrees. Drain on paper towels. Sugar, or serve plain. Makes 24 doughnuts.

Chocolate Stout Donuts

Amber Lambke • Skowhegan, Somerset County

"These outrageously good donuts were developed at a past Kneading Conference by Jenn Sheridan, using Maine Grains flour and local stout. The Kneading Conference is an annual convergence of bakers, millers, oven builders, and grain enthusiasts in Skowhegan. Much magic is created, recipes are developed and shared, and good bread is had by all."

2 tablespoons butter
2 ounces semi-sweet chocolate
   chips or chunks
2 eggs
⅔ cups sugar
1 cup stout
1 teaspoon vanilla
3¼ cups flour (we use Maine Grains Sifted
   or Pastry Flour)
2 tablespoons cocoa powder

1 tablespoon
   baking powder
¼ teaspoon salt
Fat/oil for frying

Glaze:
8 ounces powdered sugar
3 to 4 tablespoons stout (or milk,
   buttermilk, or water)

Melt butter and chocolate together in microwave for 30 seconds, checking and stirring every 10 seconds.

Combine eggs and sugar in a large bowl, and stir till combined. Add stout, vanilla, and chocolate/butter mixture.

Combine all dry ingredients in a separate bowl. Add dry to wet ⅓ at a time. When batter forms, refrigerate for 10 to 20 minutes to help stiffen the dough.

In a fryer or deep pot, heat oil/fat to 370 degrees.

Generously flour your work surface, your hands, and a cutter and rolling pin. Place dough on your work surface, and gently roll out to ½-inch thickness. Cut donuts with floured cutter, using a 1-inch cutter for donut holes.

Gently place donuts/holes in fryer. BE CAREFUL of splatters! Fry for 45 seconds each side, flipping with tongs or a slotted spoon. The holes will generally turn themselves. Do not overcrowd or overcook—the dough is dark so it can be hard to tell.

If desired, mix together powdered sugar and stout (or other liquid) to form a glaze, and drizzle over donuts before serving. Enjoy!

Yia-Yia's Teganides Greek Fried Dough

Nikki Gregory Erdman • Biddeford, York County

"My Yia-Yia Stella was born in Kotronos, Greece. It's as far south in Greece as you can get. Her father's mission was to bring his family to the United States. He worked to pay for their passage, one by one. They would come over alone through Ellis Island and live with family and friends. They went to work immediately, and began their new lives.

My Yia-Yia Stella came to New Bedford, Mass., when she was 10 or 11. She eventually moved to Biddeford, where she found work at factories and mills making shoes. I remember shopping with her in later years, and she would always take me to the shoe department to examine the craftsmanship and stitching quality. I loved it!

When she wasn't working, Yia-Yia Stella babysat and volunteered at our church, cooking for all sorts of events, together with her friends. I called them 'Chefs,' but in reality they were housewives/mothers/grandmothers who cooked their entire lives for extended families and other newcomers to our area. They were also part of the early immigration from Greece and Turkey in the late 1800s and early 1900s. Their families were among the founders of the St. Demetrios Greek Orthodox Church in Saco. Food was always in the mix. Everyday immigrant women like my Yia-Yia contributed immensely to our history in Maine. They are our unsung heroes, and need to be recognized and praised."

3 teaspoons salt
4 packages dry yeast
4 tablespoons shortening
4 tablespoons vegetable oil
1 quart whole milk
Cooking spray
4 eggs, beaten
5 pounds flour, sifted
Vegetable oil, for frying

Mix 1 teaspoon salt with dry yeast in 1 cup water. Let stand 30 minutes. Melt shortening and add vegetable oil. Pour milk into a separate pan and heat until warm.

Spray cooking oil in a large mixing bowl. Pour warmed milk in prepared bowl. Add melted shortening and oil mixture to milk. Add remaining 2 teaspoons of salt, and mix. Stir in yeast mixture and eggs. Slowly add small amounts of flour and mix with hands until dough is formed. Dough will be a little bit sticky. Knead for 10 minutes. Cover bowl. Yia-Yia Stella would wrap a blanket around the bowl and put mixture in a turned-off oven overnight—this step would ensure there were no drafts!

Heat oil in a deep fryer. Mix dough a bit. Cut off a small lump (roughly 2-inch chunk), and roll out into a long rope, about 10 inches in length. Twist dough into a cruller or wreath shape and fry. Use 2 forks or a pair of chopsticks to turn once. Remove from oil and drain. Serve hot or cold with feta cheese and olives. Delicious!

Mom Tuscan's Double-Batch Maine Donuts

Sally Foster • Solon, Somerset County

"This recipe was originally my grandmother Marion Whipple Tuscan's recipe. She lived in Solon, and handed it down to my mother and then me. I have made many batches of these. They come out great!"

2 cups sugar
4 eggs
2 tablespoons shortening
4 cups flour
1 tablespoon baking soda
2 tablespoons baking powder

1 teaspoon salt
1 tablespoon nutmeg
2 cups sour milk
6 cups lard or vegetable oil for frying
Sugar, for serving (optional)

Mix sugar with eggs and shortening, and cream together well.

In a separate bowl, mix together flour, baking soda, baking powder, salt, and nutmeg. Add sour milk and dry ingredients to the sugar mixture, alternating in three parts. Blend all ingredients together well. If necessary, add more flour to the batter until it is firm enough to handle.

Begin to heat the lard or oil to a temperature of 360-375 degrees. While oil is heating, flour an area to roll out the dough. Pour out one portion of the batter at a time, and add flour to the top so that it doesn't stick. Roll out gently, and use a floured donut cutter to cut the donuts from the dough.

When the fat is hot enough, gently lower one uncooked donut at a time down into the hot fat. Use caution not to splash the fat/oil on you. After placing about 4 donuts in the pan of fat, allow to cook until golden brown on one side and then turn each one over with a fork to brown the other side. When done, remove from fat with a slotted spoon, and place on a pan lined with paper towels to drain. If desired, while still warm, roll donut in a bowl of granular sugar, or eat them plain. Delicious. Enjoy!

Martha's Peaks Island Donuts

Robert Bernheim • China, Kennebec County

"Baggies filled with warm cinnamon sugar, plain, and chocolate doughnuts lined the front of the kitchen counter, two deep. The screen window fronting the New Island Avenue was wide open without worry that flies, mosquitoes, or any other insects might intrude on the flurry of frying taking place in Martha Callow's kitchen on Peaks Island. Regardless of the weather, islanders made their way on foot from the ferry terminal and surrounding homes and summer cottages, as well as by bicycle or vehicle to purchase Martha's Homemade Doughnuts every day of the summer. The JJ Nissen bread man was always the first in line at her window after his early morning delivery run. Sometimes the line snakes through her yard and out to the quiet street at the top of the hill overlooking the ferry terminal.

A well-loved transistor radio with the crooked antenna sat perched on the windowsill. Strings of top 100 pop hits like "Band on the Run" by Paul McCartney and Wings and "The Night Chicago Died" by Paper Lace, or any number of country favorites from Portland's own WPOR, like John Denver's "Annie's Song" and Gordon Lightfoot's "Sundown" crackled out of the small speaker, the genre determined by which of Martha's six children controlled the radio dial in their scrambled efforts to help sell the fresh treats. No one paid any heed to the headlines of the morning edition of *The Portland Press Herald*, cast aside on the back of the dining room table, proclaiming Governor Ken Curtis' latest proposals before the Maine legislature and details about the growing Watergate scandal. Only later, doughnut in hand and coffee front-and-center, would anyone crack open the paper. That's how it was on Peaks Island in those days.

The origin of the recipe came from a longtime summer neighbor. He made Martha and her children swear that they would not publish the recipe in any Island collection or other cookbook until after he had died. He is long gone, but the recipe will remain a secret a bit longer."

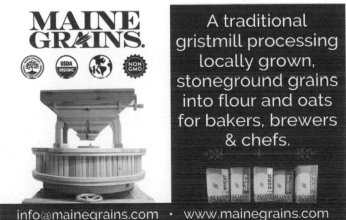

PRESERVES

Photo: Nancy McClaughlin getting ready to make
Stinky Foot Cranberry Apple Jelly. See recipe on the next page.

Stinky Foot Cranberry Apple Jelly or 'Aunt Martha's Special Berry' Jelly

Martha Hadley • Fort Fairfield, Aroostook County

"High bush cranberries are unique to northern climates like Maine, and even though cooking the berries to create the juice makes the whole house smell like stinky feet, the finished jelly is a wonderful addition to morning breakfast toast, as well as Sunday chicken dinner. My grandmother Mattie (Gould) Finnemore lived in rural Aroostook County, made 'Stinky Foot' jelly and added homemade apple juice to the recipe when berries were in short supply. She also used the leftover mash to make a special concentrate, used only twice a year in her holiday punch for Thanksgiving and Christmas dinners.

My mother, Nancy McClaughlin, makes 'Stinky Foot' jelly each year that she is able, and in 2019, I returned home when the berries were ripe to learn and prepare the family recipe. My great niece, Bailey, had tried 'Stinky Foot' jelly when she was four years old and did not like it. She is now seven years old, and I gave her a jar of 'Aunt Martha's 'Special Berry' Jelly,' which she tried and enjoyed. When we told her it was 'Stinky Foot' Jelly, she was delighted and proud that she now liked the jelly and could tell everyone! I look forward to teaching her how to make it when she is older, to keep the tradition and memory of her family alive."

2½ pounds tart apples
2 to 3 pounds ripe high bush cranberries

1 box Sure Jell pectin
9 cups of sugar

Prepare the apple juice:

Core apples, but do not peel, and cut into small pieces. Place in a large saucepan and add water to barely cover. Simmer for 10 minutes. Crush apples with a potato masher and simmer 5 more minutes. Strain through 3 layers of cheesecloth and allow juice to drip through, accumulating 3½ cups of juice. Do not press the pulp into the cheesecloth, as that will make the jelly cloudy.

Prepare the cranberry juice:

Pick high bush cranberries when they are at their ripest, before the frost, as the ripe berries contain the most natural pectin and the most juice. Remove the berries from the stems and place in a large saucepan. Add enough water to barely cover. Simmer for 10 minutes. Crush the cranberries with a potato masher to release the juice and simmer 5 more minutes. Strain through 3 layers of cheesecloth and allow juice to drip through, accumulating 3½ cups of juice. Do not press the pulp into the cheesecloth, as that will make the jelly cloudy.

Leftover pulp from apples and cranberries can be re-boiled, mashed, and strained (this time, squeezing the pulp) to make additional juice for punch or syrup.

Prepare the jelly:

Measure a total of 7 cups of juice into a large saucepan. Add 1 box of Sure Jell pectin. Bring mixture to a full rolling boil, stirring constantly. Stir in 9 cups of sugar all at once. Return to a full rolling boil, stirring constantly, and boil 1 minute. Watch the pot constantly as it can easily boil over and create a very sticky mess (even fire) and ruin all your hard work.

Remove from heat and ladle into prepared jars, leaving ½ inch of space at the top. If canning, process as you would any jelly.

I Wish I Had a Hot Dog

Ada Foss Cobb • Monson, Piscataquis County

"I don't think my sister Norma would forgive me if I didn't write of this little episode which happened during the Depression years, 1937 or 1938, while our family was living at the 'alley house.' Please remember that food was hard to come by and many meals consisted of potatoes, beans, canned mackerel, fried salt pork, and biscuits. Over and over again, potato with just plain milk, or salt pork with brown gravy with biscuits made our meals. There was no in between snacks like today, potato chips, pizza, Ritz crackers, or pretzels. I remember Norma and myself sitting with our feet in the oven (a habit formed with the wood stove), I reading as usual, and Norma just talking. She said, 'Don't I wish I had a hot dog,' and looked up at me. I remember saying, 'Make believe is the only way.'

She said, 'How?'

I got up, gave her and myself a slice of plain bread, put a dill pickle in it, and rolled it up like it was a hot dog in a slice of bread, and passed it to her. She looked up at me pitifully, and after taking the first bite said, 'Don't taste much like a hot dog, does it?'

To this day, if someone in the family doesn't really enjoy what's on the table, the phrase 'Don't taste much like a hot dog, does it?' comes to mind. Then the realization of how fortunate we really are, and the advantages of having such varied food in our cupboards and freezer to choose our menus from, makes us feel appreciative and humble."

See **Ada Foss Cobb's Grapenuts Pudding** recipe on page 227.

Pepper Relish

Donna Lambert • Pittsfield, Somerset County

"In the mid-1990s, I was teaching myself to make jellies and pickles and my aunt, Helen Seekins Gibbs, offered me this recipe from my maternal great-grandmother Etta Mae Nelson Libby's cookbook. My great-grandmother was an amazing woman. She was a nationally recognized rural letter carrier from 1903 to 1907. Her career was ended by the postal service when she married my great grandfather, because 'married women belong at home!' She kept her recipes in five composition books, either writing the recipes by hand—sometimes adding the name or initials of the person who gave her the recipe and the date—or by gluing in newspaper clipping.

This recipe was a favorite of my parents. They served it as a side dish with baked beans. The first time I made this, my father just happened to visit and when he saw the jars cooling on my counter, he asked 'Is this Etta's pepper relish? I haven't had this in years!' He then began picking up all the jars to take with him. In 1998, I changed it up a little and added some hot peppers. I submitted that relish to the Harmony free fair in 1998 and won a 2nd place red ribbon."

2 cups prepared peppers (see below)
7 cups sugar
1½ cups apple cider vinegar

1 bottle Certo liquid fruit pectin
(6 fluid ounces)

To prepare peppers, cut open about 1 dozen medium peppers and discard seeds. For best color, use equal amounts of green and red sweet peppers. Put through food chopper twice using finest knife. Drain pulp in sieve, and measure to 2 cups, packing it solidly into the cup until juices come to the top.

Measure sugar and vinegar into a large kettle. Add prepared peppers. Mix well and bring to a full rolling boil over hottest fire. Stir constantly before and during boiling. Boil hard for 2 minutes. Remove from fire and stir in Certo. Then stir and skim by turns for 5 minutes to cool slightly and to prevent floating peppers. Pack into prepared canning jars. If canning, process as you would any relish.

Cider Jelly

1877 • *Fish, Flesh and Fowl: A Book of Recipes for Cooking*
Ladies of State Street Parish • Portland, Cumberland County

Boxed gelatines were relatively new when *Fish, Flesh and Fowl* was published in 1877. This jelly combines the classic flavors of Maine apples and apple cider with this new product, allowing cooks everywhere to add a luxurious touch to meals. —DL

One-half box of gelatine with cold water sufficient to cover it, let it stand one hour, then add the grated rind and juice of one lemon, one half pint or little more of sugar, two thirds of a pint of cider, and a pint of boiling water, then strain into moulds.

Spiced Peaches

1885 • *Treasures, A Collection of Tested Recipes*
Experienced Cooks • Dexter, Penobscot County

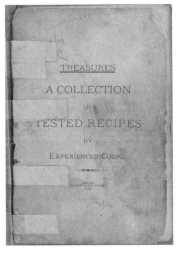

Preserves of all types allow us to save summer and fall harvests for nutrition and flavor deep into the winter months. Mainers are planting more peaches than ever, but they've long been a staple here. Opening a jar of spiced peach preserves in February takes us right back to the warm months. —DL

To nine pounds of peaches, add four and one-half pounds sugar, one pint vinegar, and cloves, cinnamon and mace, tied in separate cloths; core and halve the peaches, and put them in a jar; boil the vinegar, spices and sugar together, for a few minutes, and pour over the peaches, boiling hot; let them stand over night, and in the morning, put all in a kettle and boil ten minutes; take out the peaches, leaving the spice, and boil the vinegar till it begins to thicken, then pour over the peaches. Pears may be used instead of peaches.

Cranberry-Rhubarb Jam

Mark Messer • Ellsworth, Hancock County

"My great-aunt Frances passed her cranberry relish recipe along to me years ago. Not sure how many generations of our family used it, but it's a classic, for sure. I had a bumper crop of rhubarb one early summer and wondered what I'd do with it. I saw some cranberry relish in the freezer and started experimenting. I've also added dried fruit (blueberries, cherries) to good effect, but the original is just so darned good."

1 cup water
1½ cups plus 2 tablespoons sugar
2½ teaspoons triple sec
¾ teaspoon powdered ginger
1 pound clean, fresh cranberries

1 rough chopped navel orange (remove and dispose of thickest peel at top and bottom)
2 quarts chopped rhubarb
4 cups sugar

Bring water, sugar, triple sec, and powdered ginger to a boil in a 2-quart saucepan. Add berries, stirring until mixture returns to a boil. Reduce heat to a simmer, stir gently, until most berries have popped (cracked). Add orange, and stir occasionally for 5 minutes. If mixture is not at least 120 degrees, keep simmering and stirring. Remove from heat to cool.

Run cranberry mixture through a meat grinder or use a food processor to chop to the desired relish texture. If using a food processor, process the orange pieces separately first, then add the rest, to avoid over-processing the cranberries.

Makes nearly a quart of Aunt Frances' cranberry relish. Unless you have rhubarb handy, freeze this in an airtight container till rhubarb season.

To finish the jam, bring the frozen cranberry relish to room temperature. Combine rhubarb and remaining 4 cups of sugar in a medium saucepan. Let stand till the sugar is moistened by the juices in the rhubarb, 15 to 20 minutes. Boil mixture uncovered, stirring often, for 10 minutes. Add the cranberry relish and stir often until the mixture returns to a boil. Remove from heat and process as you would jam.

Riley Water Pickles

Sandy Oliver • Islesboro, Waldo County

"Two Ralphs and a bunch of cucumbers equal my introduction to Riley Water Pickles. The first Ralph, Ralph Gray, liked his Saturday night ham and beans with 'Riley Water' pickles, especially if his sister Edna Durkee made them. The other Ralph, Ralph Pendleton, called me up last summer and said, 'Do you have a large jar I could use to make Muddy Water Pickles in?' I said sure. Until I heard Ralph P. attach the word Muddy to these pickles, I thought Riley was someone's name. What Ralph needed, of course, to satisfy what one wag called his 'sour tooth,' was a one gallon glass jar.

Ralph Gray's sister-in-law Ruth Hartley used to have Ralph and Riley Water Pickles over for supper on Saturday night. Ruth would say to Ralph, 'Do you want to have supper with us on Saturday,' and he'd say 'Are you having beans?' because Ralph ate *only* baked beans at Saturday supper. Ruth provided ham, hot dogs, or meatloaf, made home-made baked beans and some biscuits. 'He always had to have brown bread,' said Ruth, 'he'd bring it, canned, sometimes with raisins, sometimes plain.' There was usually coleslaw.

'Then,' said Ruth, 'Ralph would say, `I've got some of Edna's Riley Water Pickles,' and he'd bring those. We always had to have the Mrs. J. A. P. Cake, named for Luella, Mrs. Joe A. Pendleton, a simple one egg chocolate cake, with butter and confectioners sugar frosting. That was dessert.'

'Supper was laced with tales of yore,' said Ruth, and with the zip of the pickles.

Now this bit about the riley or muddy water needs some explanation. One American colloquialism is to describe something or someone disturbed as riled up and often when water is riled up it is also muddy. These pickles are made with dry mustard powder in the brine, and they look like the very dickens, a mucky looking mess in a jar.

I poked around a little in my older Maine cookbooks to see if I could find any other simple pickles named muddy or riley or made with dry mustard powder. I did, but it appears that when people want to put a recipe in print they want to sound more refined than Riley Water implies. So in Marjorie Standish's *Cooking Down East*, there they are on page 231 named 'Old Fashioned Sour Cucumber Pickles,' using twice as much mustard and half as much sugar as the recipe which follows. The Pastor's Aid Society of Knight Memorial Methodist Episcopal Church of Calais, Maine, emitted a cookbook in 1922, which gives a recipe at the opposite end of the scale from Mrs. Standish's: 'Sweet Cucumber Pickles,' same procedure with dry mustard powder but *three* cups of sugar.

The *Bingham Grange Cook Book* printed in 1922 show these pickles by the name 'Sour Cucumber Pickles.' The Ladies' Society of the First Universalist Church in Machias, issued a cookbook, *Machias Cookery*, in 1909, revised in 1926. They called them 'Saco Pickles,' but the Saco *Women's Educational and Industrial Union's Cook Book*, from 1923, doesn't mention them at all.

Ralph Gray's daughter Susie Wilbur gave me the recipe which follows. She got it from her Aunt Edna, the same Edna Ralph mentioned above. Susie says, 'Aunt Edna and I used to eat a chunk or two of Riley Water Pickles with the salmon sandwiches we had as a snack whenever I was up there tying quilts.'

One reason Susie really appreciates these pickles is what she calls the 'Effort Factor.' Some things, she reports, taste better in proportion to how little effort is required to make them. They have a sour saltiness, a real zippy 'twang,' said Susie. These do not require canning. They turn olive green when they are ready to eat, and have a firm but not crisp texture. The cucumbers need to be put in the brine whole, and when you want some just cut off a chunk, 'an inch or larger,' says Susie.

Islesboro's Ralph Gray died last month, his sister Edna a couple years ago. Goodness knows how much his neighbors and family will miss Ralph, as they have already missed Edna. Maybe that next generation coming up, folks like Susie and the other Ralph, will at least keep the Riley Water Pickle tradition going strong."

Riley (or Muddy) Water Pickles

To a gallon of vinegar use:
1 cup of salt

2 cups of sugar
½ cup dry mustard

Pack small, fresh cukes into a sterile jar. Pour in the juice and close it up. It will be ready in a couple weeks or longer. Keep cool.

Etta's Hot Dog Relish (Chow-Chow)

Caryl McIntire Edwards • Harrison, Cumberland County

"Etta Pratt McIntire was a wonderful cook! She made wonderfully tasty food out of very little. She grew up in Wilton, went to York to teach, met Claude McIntire at a Grange play, and married him. She made this relish for her family (six children) and later for all of her sixteen grandchildren. Etta was my grandmother and she inspired me to become a teacher, too. Her cooking is one of the many things I admired and loved about her."

1 peck green tomatoes
1 cabbage (3 to 4 pounds)
1 cup salt
8 large onions, finely chopped
3 or 4 red onions, finely chopped
3 red or green peppers (or mix for color)
1 quart cider vinegar

3 pounds brown or white sugar
   (Etta used brown)
1 tablespoon dry mustard
2 tablespoons turmeric powder
   (Etta used 1 or 2 teaspoons)
2 tablespoons cinnamon
2 tablespoons ginger
1 tablespoon cloves

Chop tomatoes and cabbage—you can grind in a food processor or use a meat grinder, as Etta did. Vegetables should be ground fine. Cover with the salt. Let stand overnight.

Drain in the morning. You may want to rinse off some of the salt, as well. Add chopped onion and peppers. (Again, Etta used the meat grinder, but using a food processor for this would be fine.)

Put the cider, sugar, mustard, and turmeric powder in a saucepan. Place the

cinnamon, ginger, and cloves in the center of a piece of cheesecloth and bring up the corners to tie them into a bag. Add the spice bag to the saucepan and bring mixture to a boil. Add the chopped vegetables to the pot, and cook about 30 minutes, being careful not to let it scorch. Remove spice bag. Place relish in sterilized jars. If canning, process as you would any relish. Makes 15 pints.

Martha Ballard:
A Woman's Place on the Eastern Frontier

Nancy Harmon Jenkins

*"Snows & Blows but we are able to Make a fire and have food to Eat,
which is a great Mercy for which I wish to thank ye Great Doner."*
—April 1, 1807

Martha Ballard was just shy of 50 in January of 1785 when she began her diary. From then till her last entry on May 7, 1812, shortly before she died, not a day seems to have passed without a comment of some kind, even just a note about the weather or a birth or death in the Maine frontier community that she served as midwife and visiting nurse.

Mrs. Ballard came to the Kennebec valley in 1777 from Oxford, Massachusetts. Her husband Ephraim, a miller, had arrived two years earlier. After his wife and five children joined him, Ephraim settled his family along the banks of Bowman's Brook where it empties into the Kennebec in Hallowell. There he set up a gristmill and saw mill and Martha raised their children, planted her gardens, gathered herbs like balm o' Gilead, buckthorn and mallow, and composed her diary. The Ballards were residents of this river community throughout the 27 years of the diary.

Food historians examining the diary have to read between the lines for information. There's not a recipe to be found, nor any instructions as to how she prepared the cornmeal and wheaten flour ground in Ephraim's mill, the fruits and vegetables from her garden, the veal calves and pigs that were slaughtered on a regular basis. But she notes what she planted, when she harvested, days of brewing and baking, of churning and cheese-making, and, though cooking was a minor interest in her busy life, when guests arrived for tea, coffee or chocolate, "roast chickins" or a "line of veal."

Martha kept poultry for meat, eggs, and feathers, milked and pastured cows, made butter and cheese for the family larder and for sale, spun flax and wool and wove fabric, kept vegetable and herb gardens, and produced pickles and pantry staples for the winter. But the Ballards were not totally self-sufficient, and both cash and barter went for coffee and tea, molasses, pepper and salt, garden seed, tobacco, sugar, and fish. Hallowell was within the tidewater of the Kennebec, and the Ballards had good access to fresh and salt cod, smelts in season, and smoked herring. Commodities like flour, apples, potatoes, wheat, and corn were common purchases, even though they were all produced by the family or neighbors. Martha frequently mentions making cheese, but almost as frequently she speaks of buying it at one of the stores in the community.

"The girls Baked & Brewed," she says on many occasions, indicating either her own two daughters or, after they married and moved on, the hired girls who helped out. From this we understand the intimate yeasty connection between baking bread and brewing beer—but we don't know whether the girls were making corn bread, wheat bread, or—most likely—the mixture that thrifty New England housewives called thirded bread, a third cornmeal, a third rye, a third wheaten flour.

Baking was a regular activity in the Ballard household, often accompanied by brewing, since similar yeasts were used for both bread and beer. Even the humblest European-American home had a hearth of some sort, but not every home had a bake oven. Many of Martha's neighbors brought bread and pies to bake in her oven from time to time, exchanging oven use for other goods and services.

What about leaven for the bread? Cooks could rely on a type of sourdough, keeping back part of the dough from each baking to start the next batch, but in households like Martha's where beer was produced, barm, the frothy residue kicked up when brewing, was also used to raise bread. There were other leavens made with hops and/or potatoes to entice wild yeasts drifting on the air.

Along with apple and mince, pumpkin pies were favorites in the Ballard household. Not a baking day went by, it seems, without pies being put in the oven. Were they eaten as dessert at the end of the meal or were they sometimes a main course for supper, with a piece of cheese on the side—as they still were in old-fashioned homes in my Maine childhood?

Most of what Martha grew in her garden is easily recognizable today (carrots, onions, beets, parsnips, radishes), but some have fallen out of favor or fashion—broad beans, the old-fashioned name for fava beans, and Jerusalem artichokes being notable. Martha also grew peppers and garlic (for cooking or medicine— possibly both), and she mentions plums, quinces, gooseberries, damsons, and cherries. Rhubarb was a familiar fruit that grew well in our northern climate, though it too may have been more for medicinal than for culinary purposes. Twentieth-century gourmets who delight in "discovering" new varieties should note that Martha mentions blue potatoes and both purple and sweet corn flourishing in her garden. Because she was a midwife, which meant that she also served as something of a paramedic, particularly for the women of her community, she grew a great variety of medicinal herbs, some of which may also have been used in cooking—coriander, anise, mustard, and camomile. Surprisingly, she speaks several times of harvesting saffron or providing it as a medicine.

Day by day, in the month of May 1809, here's what Martha did in her garden: set turnips and cabbage stumps; planted cucumbers and three kinds of squash; again, planted squash and cucumbers; prepared a bed and planted more squash seeds; again, planted squash, also cucumbers, muskmelons and watermelons; planted "long" squash; dug holes and planted three quince trees; planted two more quince trees and an apple tree; planted potatoes; set out lettuce plants and strawberries (the squash and cucumbers planted on May 15 were already up a week later, she noted); sowed "string peas"; planted "crambury," brown, and hundred-to-one beans; set out—that is, transplanted—squash plants; again, set out squash plants and cucumbers. Mr. Ballard helped with the digging and set the poles for Martha's hop plants, but Martha did everything else. While doing so in that month of May she also tended a sick neighbor, delivered four babies (including one of her own granddaughters), brewed ale, baked bread, boiled soap, ironed, and did the normal run of housework. That year she was 74 years old.

We don't have many details of what Martha put on her table; the diary lacks the kind of notes about seasoning or cooking time that can help a skilled cook reconstruct a recipe. Despite many notations about cooking and sharing food, about extra mouths at the table, guests who came for a meal or to spend a few days, we don't even know if Martha was a good cook. Did friends and family look forward to her roast chickens, her loin of veal? Alas, we'll never know because not once does she provide us with a reference to cooking procedures, a suggestion of flavoring, let alone a recipe. Yet it's impossible to read Martha Ballard's diaries without coming away with a sense of the overwhelming importance in Maine's earliest days of women's role as providers of food, a role that gave recognized value and dignity to the lives of women, not just in Maine frontier villages but throughout the young republic.

Brenda   Diane   Barbara

Merry Christmas
— and a
Happy New Year

APPETIZERS, DIPS & SAUCES

Photo: The Kerr girls: Brenda, Diane, and Barbara.
See Kerr family recipe for Cereal Stuff on the next page.

Cereal Stuff

Brenda Kerr • Durham, Androscoggin County

"I grew up in Oakland and never lived more than a mile from my Gramma Kerr. She was a constant and fearless cook, but her traditions were engrained. Stewed beans and Johnny cake on Thursdays, baked beans and yeast rolls on Saturday. Even today, a Saturday family dinner with my two sisters, Dodie (Diane) and Barbara, and all the 'kids' is still baked bean and yeast rolls. Maine comfort food.

My Gramma Kerr would make 'Cereal Stuff' each year for Christmas, and ONLY for Christmas! The first batch would be delivered on the Friday after Thanksgiving, and then occasionally until Christmas, which is generally when the boxes of cereal would be gone.

After Gramma passed, I became the very proud recipient of one of her hand-written 'cookbooks.' It's a steno notebook, and many of the recipes within were copied from TV.

I believe I found the origin of 'Cereal Stuff', in her 'TV - Tid Bits' recipe. From this base, over the years, Gramma created her version. I remember when Crispix was introduced in the early 80's, and my 80+ year old Gramma decided to modify her recipe once again to add this 'new' cereal.

I must admit that the Christmas-only rule was broken just one year, 2001, when I was thru-hiking the Appalachian Trail and decided Cereal Stuff was perfect Trail food!"

2½ cups Rice Chex	1 cup butter
2½ cups Wheat Chex	1 scant teaspoon celery salt
2½ cups Corn Chex	1 scant teaspoon onion salt
2½ cups Cheerios	1 scant teaspoon garlic salt
2½ cups Crispix	6 dashes Tabasco or Secret Aardvark
2½ cups Kix	hot sauce
2½ cups pretzel sticks	1½ tablespoons Worcestershire sauce
1 cup mixed nuts	

Preheat oven to 200 degrees.

Toss cereals, pretzels, and nuts in a large roasting pan. Melt butter. Add spices, hot sauce, and Worcestershire sauce. Stir until well mixed.

Use a wooden spoon to toss the dry ingredients with the butter sauce to coat well. Bake for 2 hours, stirring every 30 minutes.

Mamie Berry's Cranberry Sauce

Peter Berry • Bridgton, Cumberland County

"I helped my mother, Mamie Berry, make this when I was a kid at our home in Bridgton in the 1940s. She made it with her mother in Caribou in the 1920s, and she got the recipe from her mother who had emigrated from New Brunswick, Canada in the 1890s. When I had a family of my own in the 1960s my kids helped me make it. I have passed it on to them. It has been a part of our family's Thanksgiving for well over a 100 years."

1 cup water
¾ cup sugar
12 to 16 ounces cranberries
Zest and juice of 1 orange

1 pear, cored and diced
½ cup maple syrup
1 or 2 teaspoons cinnamon, to taste

Heat water and sugar in small pot until it begins to darken. Wash cranberries and place in large pot. Add sugar water. Bring mixture to a boil, then reduce to simmer. Add zest and juice of orange. Add pear, maple syrup, and cinnamon, to taste. Stir and pop berries until sauce thickens. Remove from heat and let stand until cool. This makes a tart sauce.

Best Barbecue Sauce

Sally Trice • Portland, Cumberland County

"This is a recipe that my mother made and now I am using—it simply enhances the flavor of anything you put it on: chicken, beef, or pork."

½ cup olive oil
1 cup finely chopped onions
1 cup catsup
1 tablespoon honey
1 tablespoon chili powder

2 tablespoons Worcestershire sauce
1 teaspoon sea salt
⅛ teaspoon ground black pepper
Dash of Tabasco sauce (optional)

Heat the oil in a saucepan over medium heat. Add onions and sauté until tender, about 5 minutes. Stir in remaining ingredients and simmer for 5 to 10 minutes.

Blueberry Balsamic Barbecue Sauce

Patty Pendergast • Thorndike, Waldo County

4 cups wild Maine blueberries, fresh or
Wyman's frozen
⅔ cup balsamic vinegar
½ cup maple syrup
1 tablespoon plus 1 teaspoon of
smoked paprika

1 tablespoon grated ginger
¼ teaspoon ground black pepper
⅛ teaspoon cayenne
1 teaspoon vanilla

Put all ingredients in a skillet and simmer until thick, stirring frequently. Use a hand emulsifier to blend until smooth. Good with chicken, salmon, or pork. Easily canned with hot water or steam bath.

Maine Wild Blueberry Salsa

Ellen Farnsworth • Machias, Washington County

"I live in Berry Township, a suburb of Machias, and have been a Chairperson for the Machias Wild Blueberry Festival for many years. I developed this recipe to enter in the cooking contest that is held every year during the festival, and I was honored to have this dish awarded Best Overall Entry."

2 medium heirloom tomatoes
¾ cup chopped sweet onion
1 jalapeño pepper, seeded and finely
chopped
½ Hungarian pepper, seeded and finely
chopped
1 cup wild Maine blueberries, fresh or
Wyman's frozen

2 cloves garlic, minced
2 tablespoons chopped cilantro
2 tablespoons chopped Italian parsley
2 tablespoons rice vinegar
2 tablespoons extra-light virgin olive oil
Salt and freshly ground pepper to taste

Score the bottom of the tomatoes by slicing a small cross just through the skin. Immerse in boiling water for 15 seconds, then immerse in bowl of cold water. Peel off tomato skins. Cut tomatoes in half; seed and chop the tomatoes. Discard seeds.

In a medium bowl, combine tomatoes, onion, and chopped peppers. Fold in the blueberries. Add garlic, cilantro, parsley, vinegar, oil, salt, and pepper. Mix gently.

Store in the refrigerator overnight to allow the flavors to meld. You may wish to drain the salsa slightly before serving if the tomatoes are very juicy.

Lancey House Dip

Susan Koch • Scarborough, Cumberland County

"When I was a young child growing up in Pittsfield, my family owned the Lancey House for a brief period of time. The Lancey House, originally built in 1868, and rebuilt in 1911, was a beautiful old hotel with an elegant dining room. It burned down in 1965 and was not rebuilt. I have fond memories of going there with my family for dinners. The Lancey House Dip was served to every table in the dining room as soon as guests were seated.

My mother continued to make this dip for parties and family events her whole life. My kids love it and I still make it today, as do many other people who grew up in Pittsfield. It seems that everyone who tries it, loves it, even people who say they don't like blue cheese!"

1 small green pepper, diced
½ onion, diced
1 ounce pimentos, chopped
4 ounces blue cheese
½ pound sharp cheddar cheese, shredded
¼ pound cream cheese, room temperature

1 pound cottage cheese
A few dashes of Tobasco sauce
A few dashes of Worcestershire sauce
½ teaspoon garlic salt
Salt and pepper to taste

Mix all ingredients together by hand until well blended. Serve with crackers and/or sticks of carrots, celery, and cucumber.

Riverhouse Scallops "Benedict"

Paul Denckla • Camden, Knox County

"Some of my best recipes start with ideas that I have 'borrowed.' I'll have an amazing meal and ask the chef to come out and talk with me. On some occasions I have gotten permission to go in the kitchen, much to the embarrassment of my wife and children. Having gotten the recipe, I'll take it home, tweak it and personalize it, as I did with these delicious scallops."

1 lemon
4 diver scallops
2 ripe avocados

Hot sauce (I like Chip's Sweet Heat)
1 sprig fresh dill

Squeeze the juice of a lemon into a cereal bowl. Using a sharp boning knife, slice each of the raw scallops horizontally into 3 wafer-thin slices. Make sure to slice cleanly, and not to "saw" or pull the knife blade back and forth.

Place scallops in bowl with the lemon juice, making sure they are completely covered by the juice. Slosh around a little, if necessary.

Slice each avocado in half and remove the pits. Place one of the halves on a cutting board, face down. Cut it into thin slices (⅛ inch) and arrange them on your serving plate. Try to avoid cutting slices from the hollowed pit area as much as possible, so you get fully round slices. You will need one slice for each scallop wafer.

Place one scallop slice on each slice of avocado. Shake 3 drops of hot sauce on each scallop to create the "Benedict" poached egg effect. Top each scallop with a tiny frond of dill. Refrigerate until ready to serve. Makes 4 servings.

Crab Dip

John Bennett • Portland, Cumberland County

Oakhurst Dairy, the largest dairy producer in Maine and once the largest independent dairy in northern New England, was founded in 1921 and was owned and operated by the Bennett family for over 90 years. At one time, six Bennett family members all held important roles at the dairy. Before rejoining the family dairy business, current President and General Manager John Bennett owned a successful wholesale seafood business on the Portland waterfront called Port Quality Shellfish. This delectable family recipe originated from John's seafood routes as a way to help promote quality local products.

1 pound crabmeat

8 ounces cream cheese

8 ounces Oakhurst Sour Cream

¼ cup minced white onion

1 tablespoon Dijon mustard

1 tablespoon Worcestershire sauce

Dash of Tabasco

Paprika, for sprinkling

1 tablespoon chopped fresh chives, for serving

Thoroughly mix the above ingredients. Bake in medium size casserole dish for 30 minutes at 350 degrees. Sprinkle with paprika if desired before baking. Sprinkle with chopped fresh chives before serving.

Maple Bourbon Candied Bacon

Jason and Lori Candelora • Lovell, Oxford County

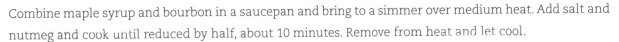

Sponsored by
Maine Credit Unions

"I was born in New Haven, Conn., but have lived in Maine since I was 7. My wife and I really enjoy cooking and entertaining and were looking for something new to make for our friends when I came across a recipe for candied bacon. We were hooked as soon as we tried the first batch. This recipe is an evolution of the original."

1 cup maple syrup

⅓ cup bourbon

1 teaspoon salt

½ teaspoon nutmeg

½ pound thick-cut bacon

1 cup brown sugar

1 teaspoon cinnamon

Combine maple syrup and bourbon in a saucepan and bring to a simmer over medium heat. Add salt and nutmeg and cook until reduced by half, about 10 minutes. Remove from heat and let cool.

Arrange bacon in a shallow baking dish and pour cooled syrup mixture over it. Let stand in fridge for 30 to 60 minutes.

Preheat oven to 350 degrees.

In a small bowl, mix brown sugar and cinnamon. Arrange bacon on foil-lined rimmed cookie sheet and coat with brown sugar mixture. Bake until bacon is at desired doneness (15 to 20 minutes), sprinkling with brown sugar mixture every few minutes.

Sambusa

Gamana Yarow • Lewiston, Androscoggin County

Gamana Yarow is a member of the Somali Bantu community in Lewiston, and is a farmer and food enthusiast. As a producer, she attends two farmers' markets, selling seasonal produce. Sambusas are stuffed Somali dumplings, filled with meat or vegetables and fried until crisp. They're a popular celebration food, eaten at special events and holidays, and make a great portable snack.

Dough:
3 cups all-purpose flour
½ teaspoon salt
2 tablespoons vegetable oil

Filling:
3 tablespoons vegetable oil, separated
1 small onion, finely chopped
1 clove garlic, minced or pressed

2 tablespoons curry powder
1 pound ground beef
1 teaspoon salt
½ teaspoon black pepper
¼ cup shredded cabbage
¼ cup shredded carrots
2 tablespoons chopped cilantro
Oil for frying

To make the dough, mix together flour and salt in a large bowl. Add vegetable oil, and toss with a fork. Add 1 cup warm water and slowly knead until dough forms. Cover and let rest 10 to 15 minutes.

While dough rests, make the filling. In a large skillet, heat 2 tablespoons of the oil and sauté the onions, garlic, and curry powder. Add the ground beef and brown, stirring regularly until meat is cooked. Add salt and pepper. In a separate smaller skillet, heat the remaining tablespoon of oil and sauté the cabbage and the carrots until tender, 5 to 7 minutes, stirring frequently. Add the vegetables to the cooked beef, and stir in the cilantro. Taste, and adjust seasoning. Remove mixture from heat and let cool until it can be handled.

While mixture is cooling, lightly flour a clean countertop. Divide dough into four pieces and roll into thin sheets, roughly 12 x 12 inches. Using a knife, cut dough into squares about 6 x 6 inches, then cut these in half diagonally, to make triangles of dough. Place a mound of filling in the center of each triangle, and fold the dough over it, making a smaller triangular packet. Seal by firmly pressing the edges together, moistening the edges with a little water, if necessary.

Line a baking sheet or serving dish with paper towels. In a large skillet, heat 1 inch of oil until it sizzles (or a thermometer reads 370 degrees). Place the sambusas in the oil in batches, making sure not to crowd the pot. Cook for 2 minutes on one side, then flip over using a slotted spoon, and cook for 2 more minutes on the other side. Sambusas should be golden brown on each side. Drain briefly on paper towel before serving hot.

Maple Chili Shrimp in Blankets

Louisa Edgerton • Bath, Sagadahoc County

"I was born and raised on the coast of Maine, and spent summers at Ocean Point, which I credit for my love of fresh seafood. I'm always tinkering and experimenting with new recipes and holding themed dinner parties for friends and family to test new dishes, which is how this shrimp recipe came to life. I'm a manager at Now You're Cooking in Bath, where I also teach cooking classes. This recipe is part of a Maine seafood class I'm currently developing."

1 teaspoon smoked paprika
½ teaspoon chili powder
3 garlic cloves, minced
¼ teaspoon salt
¼ teaspoon pepper
2 tablespoons olive oil

1 tablespoon maple syrup
1 pound shrimp, peeled (26-30 small shrimps)
1 package puff pastry, thawed
1 recipe Maple Chili Sauce (recipe follows)

In a large bowl, combine spices, olive oil, and maple syrup, whisking until thoroughly incorporated. Add shrimp, and toss until everything is coated. Cover bowl and set aside at room temperature for 30 minutes to 1 hour.

Preheat oven to 400 degrees. Take thawed puff pastry out of the box and roll thin with a rolling pin. Use a pastry cutter to slice strips about 1 x 4 inches.

Place a shrimp on each strip of puff pastry and roll up. Arrange rolled shrimp on a lined baking sheet and bake for 15 to 18 minutes, until pastry is golden brown.

Serve hot or at room temperature with Maple Chili Sauce.

Maple Chili Sauce

2 tablespoons olive oil
3 garlic cloves, minced
2 teaspoons smoked paprika
1 teaspoon chili powder

½ teaspoon salt
½ teaspoon pepper
2 tablespoons maple syrup

Heat oil in a small saucepan over medium heat. Add garlic and stir for about 20 to 30 seconds, but don't allow to brown. Stir in all other ingredients and cook for 2 to 3 minutes on low heat. Serve warm.

Meat Knish

Karl Schatz • Gray, Cumberland County

"My great-grandmother Sadye Schatz ran a boarding house in Old Orchard Beach and later went on to be one of two Kosher caterers in Portland in the 1940s and '50s. Her grandkids called her 'Nana' but to us great-grandkids she was 'Cookie Nana,' because there were always cookies whenever we would visit. She provided many recipes to a number of different Portland Jewish community cookbooks. This recipe appeared in *Requested Recipes*, printed in 1963 by the Temple Beth El Sisterhood in Portland. The recipe is attributed to Tyna Merdek, but in the margin next to the recipe, Cookie Nana scribbled 'mine,' underlined twice."

Pastry:
4 cups flour
1 tablespoon baking powder
1 teaspoon salt
1 teaspoon sugar
1¼ cups shortening
1 beaten egg

Filling:
2 or 3 onions, chopped
2 tablespoons chicken fat or vegetable oil
3 pounds cooked meat
Salt and pepper, to taste

To make the pastry: Sift together the dry ingredients. Blend the shortening into this, as for pastry. Add the beaten egg and 1½ cups water, and mix well. Cut dough into quarters and roll each piece into a thin sheet.

To make the filling: Steam the onions in fat or oil, and grind with the cooked meat. Season with salt and pepper to taste.

Put the meat mixture onto the rolled dough, roll filled dough into a long tube, and cut into 2-inch pieces. Fold dough over each end of each piece, seal both ends by pinching the dough together, and brush with melted shortening. Bake in a 400-degree oven until brown.

Potato Knish

Elise Richer • Portland, Cumberland County

"Knishes are not fancy food, and the measurements of everything are approximate. The recipe should work well even with some variation, so use what you have on hand. Just avoid having the filling become too wet. And no bacon, please! At my shop, Tin Pan Bakery, we make our knishes large. Each one weighs 7 ounces, or almost a half-pound. But they can be made in any size you like using the same method; you will just need to adjust the cooking time to avoid over cooking them."

Dough:
7 tablespoons butter
2 tablespoons olive oil
¼ teaspoon salt
2¼ cups flour

Potato Onion Filling:
2 large onions

1 tablespoon vegetable oil, for frying
2 pounds Maine potatoes, peeled and cut
  into chunks
4 tablespoons butter
Salt and pepper
3 tablespoons butter, melted
1 egg, beaten

To make the dough: Place ½ cup warm water, butter, olive oil, and salt in a medium saucepan, over medium heat. Heat until butter has melted. Remove from heat and stir in the flour. Dump the mixture out onto a clean countertop and fold the dough over itself 5 to 10 times, until smooth. Wrap dough in plastic and let chill in refrigerator until ready to use.

To make the filling: Chop onion roughly and fry in oil over medium high heat until dark brown but not scorched. Onion should be fried, not caramelized.

While onion cooks, place potatoes in a saucepan and add enough cold water to cover. Boil until tender, drain off water, and mash. Add butter and salt and pepper, to taste. Stir in the fried onions.

To assemble: Preheat oven to 400 degrees. On a floured surface, roll out dough to make a rectangle 2½ feet long by 6 inches wide. If the dough springs back, let rest 5 to 10 minutes before continuing to roll.

Spread potato/onion filling down the center of the dough (the long way) in a line about 2 inches wide. Brush melted butter onto the dough on either side of the filling. Pull each side of the dough over the filling, so that the filling is completely covered, and press together gently to seal. You will have a long "snake" of filled dough.

Cut the "snake" into eight even pieces. Set each piece on its side on a parchment-lined rimmed baking sheet. Tuck the dough, gently smush the knish down a bit, and pinch the top to seal. Brush the beaten egg over the top, if desired. Bake for 25 minutes. Best served warm.

SOUPS & CHOWDERS

Photo: Chef Sav Sengsavang cooking at home in Bethel.
See his recipe on the next page.

Chilled Green Curry and Asparagus Soup with Lobster

Sav Sengsavang • Bethel, Oxford County

"I'm a first generation American; son of Laotian immigrants, born in New York and raised in Virginia. I fell in love with a native Mainer and followed her north where we landed and grew our business out of a humble food trailer. At Le Mu Eats we serve up what is best described as Laotian-American Comfort Food, a blend of multiple influences, including South East Asian flavors, local Maine produce, and nods to Southern cuisine. I grew up in a Laotian household, dedicated to traditional Lao foods, flavors and cooking techniques. However, anytime I stepped out of my household, I was exposed to the world of American foods. I love taking in the food scene around me, playing with the traditional Lao dishes I grew up with, and finding a way to add my own signature to foods that seem familiar and comfortable."

8 tablespoons olive oil, divided
1 onion, chopped
1 ounce ginger, chopped
2 stalks celery, chopped
3 cloves garlic, smashed
3 stalks green onion
1 stalk lemon grass, chopped
2 Thai lime leaves
1 quart water

1 pound lobster, live
2 pounds asparagus, cut into ½-inch pieces
    (8 to 10 tips reserved)
3 tablespoons sugar
4 ounces green curry paste
16 ounces coconut milk
Salt and pepper, to taste
1 radish, sliced into thin wafers, for serving

Heat 4 tablespoons olive oil in a large pot over medium-low heat. Add onions, ginger, celery, garlic, green onion, lemon grass, and Thai lime leaves. Cook, stirring occasionally, until ingredients become translucent. Add water, increase heat, and bring to a boil. Place lobster in boiling broth and cook for 12 to 15 minutes. While lobster is cooking, grab a bowl of water and ice, and have it ready. Transfer cooked lobster to the ice bath to cool down. Lower pot's heat to a simmer.

Remove lobster from the ice bath and break it down, pulling out the claw and tail meat. Set the meat aside in the fridge, and return the shell to the pot, allow to cook for 15 more minutes at a simmer, occasionally skimming scum from the top. This will make a nice lobster stock. Once the stock has finished cooking, let it cool slightly, then strain it out of the pot into a bowl, using a fine mesh sieve. Set stock to the side.

In a large pot, heat remaining olive oil over medium heat. Add green curry paste and stir for 2 to 3 minutes, allowing the paste to "bloom." Add your asparagus stalks to the pot and cook with the curry paste, stirring occasionally until asparagus are bright green and tender, 4 to 5 minutes. (Reserve tips for garnish.) Add sugar, and continue to stir. Add reserved lobster stock and increase heat until pot comes to a boil. Reduce heat, add coconut milk, and simmer for 10 to 12 minutes. Turn off heat and allow to cool slightly.

Set a fine mesh sieve in a large bowl. Working in batches, puree soup in a blender until very smooth, then strain through sieve. Once all the soup is pureed and strained, season to taste with salt and pepper. (Season a little heavily, since cold dishes tend to dull the saltiness.) Cover and chill for at least 4 hours.

Right before serving, bring a small pot of water to a boil, and prepare a bowl of ice water. Blanch the reserved asparagus tips for 20 seconds, immediately plunge into the ice bath, and pat dry.

Take out reserved, chilled lobster meat and cut into chunks. Divide lobster between bowls. Pour chilled soup into each bowl around the lobster. Finish by placing two asparagus tips across the lobster and sprinkling with radish slices. Makes 4-5 servings.

Carrot Ginger Soup

Susan Spector • Portland, Cumberland County

"I created this recipe for a small natural foods market and cafe that my husband and I used to own. This is a great soup for dinner with a salad!"

3 pounds carrots
2 large potatoes
1 large sweet Vidalia onion
1 large sweet potato
3 tablespoons chopped candied ginger
2 boxes low-sodium vegetable broth
1 teaspoon salt
2 to 3 shakes Montreal steak seasoning
1 tablespoon cinnamon

½ cup peanut butter
1 tablespoon dried parsley
3 to 4 tablespoons coconut aminos
½ teaspoon black pepper
Two pinches cayenne pepper
2 tablespoons honey

Cut carrots, potatoes, onion, sweet potato, and crystalized ginger into bite-sized pieces. Cover with vegetable broth and bring to a boil. Add salt, Montreal seasoning, and cinnamon and simmer until carrots, onion, and potatoes are fork tender. Cool to room temperature and add peanut butter, dried parsley, coconut aminos, black pepper, cayenne pepper, and honey. Using an immersion blender, blend all ingredients together. Adjust seasonings according to taste with salt and pepper.

Dinner Chowder

Marilyn Meyerhans • Fairfield, Somerset County

"My Mom got this recipe from her mother-in-law, Mary Hanson from Sanford. It is an old family recipe using all the ingredients one would have on the farm in the winter. In my mind, this is the perfect comfort food, great the day it is made and great as leftover."

4 or 5 medium potatoes, cubed
2 medium carrots
1 big onion, chopped
¼ head green cabbage, sliced
3 stalks celery, chopped (optional)
½ cup butter

½ cup flour
2 cups milk, or thereabouts
1 cup sharp cheddar, shredded
1 teaspoon white pepper (black is OK)
1 teaspoon dry mustard (or not, to taste)
1 large can crushed tomatoes

Place 4 cups water in a big pot, and add potatoes, carrots, onions, cabbage, and optional celery. Cook the vegetables till tender, adding more water if necessary. In a separate smaller pot, melt butter over medium-low heat, and whisk in flour. Pour in milk, stirring constantly, to make a white sauce. Stir in cheese, pepper, and optional dry mustard. Add the white sauce to the big pot full of veggies, turning the heat off so it is not boiling. Add the tomatoes to the mix, stir up and enjoy!

Rockport Fishermen's and Farmers' Seafood Soup

Robert Kollmar • Rockport, Knox County

"This is simple country cooking using as many homemade and homegrown items as possible for the home cook to enjoy. This soup may be seasoned to taste, and may be tailored to any fresh seafood."

1 pound medium-sized shrimp, cooked
   and hulled
¼ teaspoon Old Bay seafood seasoning
¼ pound smoked sausage, cut into
   ½-inch cubes
½ teaspoon black pepper
3 garlic cloves, minced
3 strips bacon, diced
2 medium yellow onions, diced
1 red bell pepper, diced
2 tomatoes, diced

1½ cups cocktail sauce
   (homemade or purchased)
1 quart spaghetti sauce
   (homemade or purchased)
3 bay leaves
3 teaspoons Worcestershire sauce
4 teaspoons lemon juice
4 mushrooms, cleaned and diced
½ pound salmon, diced into ½-inch cubes
½ pound haddock or pollock, diced into
   ½-inch cubes

Place shrimp in a medium-sized bowl and sprinkle with Old Bay. Set aside.

In a separate small bowl, combine cubed smoked sausage, black pepper, and minced garlic. Set aside.

Heat a medium-sized stock pot on medium heat. Add bacon to the pot and sauté until lightly browned. Add onions and pepper, and lightly stir until softened. Add smoked sausage mixture and continue to lightly stir. Add the tomatoes, cocktail sauce, spaghetti sauce, bay leaves, Worcestershire sauce, lemon juice, mushrooms, salmon, and haddock or pollock. Cook, stirring gently to maintain the integrity of the fresh fish. Cover the pot, lower the heat to low, and cook for 25 minutes.

Add the shrimp and cook for 1 more minute. Remove the bay leaves before serving.

Haddock Chowder

Jeff Holden • Cape Elizabeth, Cumberland County

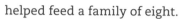

"My father, Richard, lobstered right off Portland Head Light as a summer job through high school in the late 1930s. He joined the military and served in the Air Force during World War II, and attended Bowdoin on the GI Bill. Every summer he got back on the water hauling traps. He went into the insurance business but continued to fish recreationally his whole life. One of six children, I fell in love with the ocean on fishing trips with my dad, and we ate fish constantly growing up. A favorite dish was my mom's haddock chowder—a simple pot of Maine potatoes, onions, half and half, butter and flaky white fish—that

helped feed a family of eight.

In high school I followed in my dad's footsteps, getting a summer job as a sternman on a lobster boat and eventually built a 31-foot fiberglass lobster boat and started hauling my own traps. I sold the boat and started a little fish market on top of Munjoy Hill, selling live lobster and crab, cutting fish, and picking crab meat, all out of a single room. In the 1980s, I became the state's first licensed lobster processor.

I have three sons, and my eldest, Luke, has followed the family tradition, lobstering as a summer job in high school and college, and eventually founding Luke's Lobster. The flagship Luke's Lobster overlooks Portland Harbor from the end of Portland Pier, the same waters our family has fished for almost 100 years."

1 pound Yukon potatoes
4 tablespoons (½ stick) butter, separated
1 pound yellow onions

1 pound boneless haddock fillet,
 fresh or frozen
1 quart half and half
Salt and pepper, to taste

Peel potatoes and cut in ½-inch cubes. Place in a deep pot and cover with water. Boil until fully cooked, remove from heat, drain, and cool under cold water to stop cooking. Place potatoes in a dish and reserve pot for fish.

In a saucepan, melt 2 tablespoons of butter on low heat. Peel onion, and cut into large slices. Place slices in pan, cover, and cook over low heat until tender. Remove from heat.

Pour 4 inches of water into the reserved deep pot. Add haddock fillets, and cook over medium heat until fillets are opaque and flake easily with a fork and are cooked to an internal temperature of 145 degrees. Remove from heat, and drain water from pot.

Add cooked potato, onion, remaining butter, and enough half and half to cover the ingredients. Stir and add salt and pepper, to taste. Add additional half and half, as desired, and continue to mix gently. Taste, adding additional salt and pepper in equal parts, as desired. Cook until piping hot (185 degrees). Chowder can be served immediately, or cooled and reheated.

Stutzman's Chicken Pot Pie Soup

Arlene Goldstein • Sangerville, Piscataquis County

"This recipe is one of the most popular soups at Stutzman's Brick Oven Farm to Table Cafe, owned by my friends and employers Sid and Rainey Stutzman. Their farm is still vital and relevant after over a century and three generations. They are the embodiment of the Maine farm family's love of the land and community. This soup is among the simplest recipes ever, made even more delicious when the veggies are all grown on the farm."

1 large yellow onion, diced
6 celery stalks, diced
6 carrots, sliced in coins
1 tablespoon Bell's Seasoning, or 1 teaspoon
    ground sage and 1 teaspoon thyme
5 quarts chicken stock or broth

3 cups boneless cooked chicken, diced
1 pint heavy cream
1 cup potato flakes or 2 large russet
    potatoes, boiled and mashed
1½ cups frozen green peas
Salt and pepper, to taste

In large heavy-bottomed pot, combine veggies, herbs, and stock. Bring mixture to a boil and simmer until veggies are tender. Add chicken meat and cream. Return to simmer and slowly whisk in potato flakes or mashed potatoes, peas, and salt and pepper. Adjust seasoning and enjoy.

Chicken Tortilla Soup

Mary Herman • Brunswick, Cumberland County

"I grew up in a large Jewish family in Milwaukee. Every Sunday after Sunday school (yes, we called it that, not 'religious,' or 'Hebrew' school, because 'Hebrew School' was on TUESDAY, and two days a week was too much...) we gathered at my grandfather, Papa's, home. He watched 'Meet The Press,' 'Hallmark Hall of Fame,' and other serious shows while kids played cards, games, and generally ran around. Often my grandmother made 'Chicken in the Pot,' for all of us.

Fast forward to today. Every Sunday afternoon, September through the Superbowl, is 'Football Sunday.' My husband, [Senator] Angus [King], and I gather with our grown kids and grandkids for games and dinner. I usually make football munchies and a soup. Chicken Tortilla Soup is my modern-day version, kinda, of Chicken in the Pot. It's hearty and appeals to three generations!"

1 large onion, chopped
2 tablespoons olive oil
2 to 4 cloves garlic, minced
2 teaspoons oregano
2 teaspoons cumin
2 teaspoons chili powder
2 to 3 jalapenos, diced (optional)
28-ounce can diced tomatoes
    (I prefer fire-roasted)
6 cups low-sodium chicken broth
1 can black beans, drained and rinsed
1 can corn kernels, drained and rinsed

1 tablespoon lime juice, or more to taste
Salt and pepper, to taste
1 rotisserie (or home-roasted) chicken

For serving:
2 avocados, cubed
Grated cheddar or crumbled Mexican
    cojita cheese
Lime wedges
Chopped fresh cilantro
Crushed tortilla chips

In a large soup pot over medium heat, soften onion in olive oil, 2 to 4 minutes. Stir in garlic, oregano, cumin, and chili powder. Add jalapenos, if using.

Stir in canned tomatoes and chicken broth. Add black beans and corn. Stir in lime juice, salt and pepper, and adjust seasonings to taste. (You may want to add cinnamon and/or sugar—years ago a friend with Mediterranean ancestry taught me always to add cinnamon to tomato-based recipes.)

Simmer soup on the stove while you shred the chicken. (It's prettier shredded, and I think it tastes better.) Add the chicken to the soup and keep tasting.

Before serving, arrange avocados, cheese, lime wedges, cilantro, and tortilla chips with a stack of bowls and spoons. Let each person make their own bowl!

Slovak Sauerkraut Mushroom Soup

Susan Vayda • Falmouth, Cumberland County

"My parents were both born in Czechoslovakia, in 1915 and 1922. My mother made traditional Slovak recipes all her life, and this recipe is what we ate every Christmas Eve. It is simple, yet very savory—what I have come to describe as the Slovak umami! In Slovakia, cabbage and mushrooms are mainstay ingredients. My mother, Suzan Vayda, loved Maine as it reminded her of Husak, Czechoslovakia, where she was born. My parents are both deceased, but we continue to serve this wonderful soup every Christmas Eve."

3 ounces dried porcini mushrooms
5 cups water, divided
1 whole medium onion, peeled
1 cup sauerkraut juice (drained from 2 pound package of sauerkraut)

2 pounds sliced fresh mushrooms
¼ cup butter
¼ cup all purpose flour
Kosher salt and fresh ground pepper

In a medium saucepan, put dried porcini mushrooms in 2 cups warm water. Simmer on stove for 15 minutes. Strain out rehydrated mushrooms, reserve, and gently pour "mushroom liquid" into a large soup pot, being careful not to disturb the sediment on the bottom. Chop reserved rehydrated mushrooms and add to soup pot. Pour in remaining 3 cups of water and add whole onion, and bring to a boil. Reduce heat, and simmer for 2 hours.

Remove onion and add sauerkraut juice and sliced mushrooms to the pot. Simmer for 15 minutes.

In a small skillet, melt butter and add flour, whisking until it becomes light brown. Temper the mixture by adding ½ cup hot soup to it, whisking until smooth. Pour tempered mixture in the hot soup, stirring the soup constantly for 10 minutes. Turn off heat. Add salt and pepper to taste.

Soup is ready to be served, or it can be refrigerated and reheated for up to 1 week. Soup improves in flavor as it ages.

Pullen Sisters' Recipe Box

Ruth Ristich • North Yarmouth, Cumberland County

"My great-grandmother Josephine Ruth Curtis Pullen was the daughter of a merchant clipper ship captain, Joseph Russell Curtis. She was born in 1852 and raised as one of eight children in Yarmouth, Maine. She married Warren Winfield Scott Pullen, who was born in Leeds, Maine in 1852. They bought a farm on Sligo Road in North Yarmouth and raised their thirteen children there. This photo of the Pullen sisters was taken in the fall of 1900: Maude, Eliza, Grace, Josephine, and Lydia. Josephine and Eliza both taught Home Economics (sewing, cooking, and homemaking skills) in a one-room schoolhouse in York, Maine, then in Marblehead and Beverly, Mass. My mother, Ruth Elizabeth Pullen Ristich, followed in her aunts' footsteps and also taught Home Ec for her entire teaching career.

In addition, my mother did something unique in the family by joining the first company of the Women's Auxiliary Army Corps during World War II. She went into Officer's Training, including Bakers and Cooks School, and became a 1st Lieutenant of the 'mess.' I have some wonderful photos of her during her Army cooks' training, plus some large quantity recipes, such as Lemon Meringue Pie to serve 250, with details about how many women are needed to crack and separate 'x' dozen eggs! She traveled to Fort Bragg, North Carolina; Fort Riley, Kansas; Pope Field, Des Moines, Iowa; and finally to Hamilton Field in Bermuda, where she met my father, who was a celestial navigator in the Army Air Corps. I am one of five children (four girls and one boy), and we all learned to cook and sew.

At the farm in North Yarmouth, great-grandfather Warren Winfield Scott Pullen grew tomatoes, cucumbers, buckwheat (to feed the horses and cows), potatoes, peppers, beans, onions, and many other crops. My great-aunts picked blackberries and blueberries, and they had wild cranberries in the adjacent fields (still do). We still have the blackberry canes and wild blueberries at the farm. My mother used to tell us that her grandmother, Josephine Ruth, used a barrel of flour a week to make biscuits, bread, doughnuts, cookies, and cakes.

We found an old wooden recipe box at the farm. I believe the recipe box belonged to my great-aunt Eliza. We also found an old line-a-day diary from their mother Josephine (my great-grandmother) that spanned the years 1929-1933. She and her husband were married for 65 years and lived and worked as farmers. Their home had no electricity but they did get a telephone in 1929. Sample diary entry: January 12, 1919 'Snowed in…. bake bean day.' April 16, 1929 '…Got the buckwheat cut and fried the bacon.' April 25, 1929 'Only churned 11 lbs of butter, one lb less than last week.'"

Lobster Stew for 50

Eliza Pullen
S.D.S. 1917

10 lb. of lobster meat (cut in $\frac{1}{2}$ in pieces)
12 qts. of milk
2 lbs. butter
Salt + pepper to taste

5 lobsters
yield 1 lb. meat

Melt butter add lobster meat. Sauté 20 min. but do not use high enough heat to brown butter.

To make liquid for stew add lobster shells to 2 qts. cold water. Boil 20 min. Strain add the milk which has been scalded. Add sauté'd lobster meat. Season - Let stand $\frac{1}{2}$ hr before serving to bring out flavor.

Oyster Stew for 60

Eliza Pullen

2 gal. oysters
2 gal milk
2 tbs. salt
2 qts water
2 lb. butter
$\frac{1}{2}$ ts. pepper

Put oysters in colander, pour the cold water over them (reserve this liquid) Heat liquid to boiling point, add oysters, cook on low heat till oysters curl. Add heated milk, butter + seasoning.

Place several oysters in each bowl for serving. Add hot stew — Serve at once

Potato and Leek Soup with Chive Oil

Kathy Gunst • South Berwick, York County

Kathy Gunst, Maine food writer and contributor to NPR's Here and Now, originally featured this recipe in her book *Soup Swap* (Chronicle Books). "A thick, creamy soup, this is one of my favorite comfort foods. On a cold winter day there are few soups more soothing. But on a humid summer Maine day there are few soups more refreshing. Served cold this soup is known as Vichyssoise. If you're serving the soup cold, plan on letting it chill for 4 to 6 hours. The soup and the chive oil can be prepared up to 24 hours ahead. Use a good, fresh Maine potato! The emerald-green chive oil adds a subtle onion flavor and gorgeous color to vegetable and seafood soups. I like keeping it in one of those squeeze bottles that diners use to serve mustard and ketchup."

8 medium leeks
1½ tablespoons olive oil
2 tablespoons minced chives, plus more
    for garnish
1 tablespoon chopped fresh thyme
5 large medium-starch potatoes, like
    Russets or Yukon gold, peeled and cut
    into 2-inch pieces

8 cups chicken stock, vegetable stock,
    or low-sodium canned chicken
    or vegetable broth
Sea salt
Freshly ground black pepper
½ cup plus 2 tablespoons heavy cream
Chive Oil (see next page)

Trim off the dark green section of the leeks and save for making stock. Halve the pale green and white sections lengthwise, rinse under cold running water, and pat dry. Cut crosswise into 2-inch pieces.

In a large stockpot over low heat, warm the olive oil. Add the leeks, 2 tablespoons chives, and thyme; cover; and cook, stirring occasionally, for 10 minutes. Add the potatoes, stir well, and cook for another 2 minutes. Add 7½ cups of the chicken stock, season with salt and pepper (if using canned chicken broth, be careful not to oversalt the soup), and bring to a boil over high heat. Turn the heat to low, cover, and simmer for 15 to 20 minutes more, or until the potatoes are tender. Remove from the heat and let cool slightly.

Using a food processor or blender, and working in batches or using a handheld immersion blender, purée the soup until smooth. Return the soup to the pot. If the soup is too thick, add the remaining ½ cup stock and the cream and stir until blended. Taste and adjust the seasoning, adding more salt and pepper if needed, and bring to a simmer over low heat or cover and chill for 4 to 6 hours.

Ladle the soup into mugs or bowls and serve, hot or cold, with a generous teaspoon of the chive oil swirled into each and a sprinkling of minced chives.

Chive Oil

¾ cup packed chopped fresh chives
¾ cup olive oil

Sea salt
Freshly ground black pepper

Using a food processor or blender, purée the chives and olive oil; season with salt and pepper. Store in a covered container in the refrigerator for up to 1 week. Bring to room temperature before serving. Makes about ¾ cup.

Tomato Stew

Stephen Dunham • Lewiston, Androscoggin County

"I want to honor my grandmother Arline Dudley and family for sharing these recipes and a love of cooking with me over the years. There were at least five hard working generations of my family all from central Maine. There is a long tradition of wonderful cooking and baking recipes in the family history. This is one of the many recipes my grandmother taught me when I was a child, and I've been making them for 60 years. This was always a family favorite."

3 cups diced fresh tomatoes
⅛ teaspoon baking soda
2 cups whole milk
2 cups evaporated milk
Salt to taste

Pepper to taste
Garlic powder to taste
1-1½ tablespoons sugar
¼–½ stick butter (2-4 tablespoons)

Cook tomatoes in saucepan on medium heat for 15 to 20 minutes, and let cool slightly. Add the baking soda.

Combine the milks and scald in a separate saucepan. Add scalded milk to tomato mixture. Add salt, pepper, garlic powder, and sugar, to taste. Stir well.

Place pats of butter on top to melt, and serve. Stew improves with age.

Cullen Skink
(Smoked Haddock Chowder)

Jennifer Scism • Kittery, York County

"I was a chef and restaurant owner in New York City when I pulled up my city roots and moved to Maine for good in 2010. I was completely won over by its beautiful coastline and delicious lobster rolls, so I just kept coming back. Once I moved to Maine, I started a small catering company. For an event with the Old York Historical Society, I was asked to make Cullen Skink. I had no idea what it was or how to make it! I learned that it was a traditional Scottish chowder, made with smoked haddock. The chowder itself is fairly simple, but the smoked fish imparts a richness that I would normally achieve using bacon. It only took me one time to make this meal to become a convert. It warms you through and through on a cold wet Maine winter's night."

2 large potatoes
7 cups whole milk
½ bunch of flat leaf parsley, washed, leaves picked, stems reserved
2 sprigs fresh thyme
2 bay leaf
1 pound smoked haddock fillet, bones and skin removed

4 tablespoons butter
2 large onions, chopped into ¼-inch dice
1 cup red potatoes, cut into ¼-inch dice
1 cup fresh sweet corn
Salt and pepper

Peel potatoes and cut into large dice. Bring a large pot of boiling water to the boil, and cook potatoes until soft. Drain and cool slightly, then put through a food mill.

Pour the milk into a large saucepan. Tie the parsley stems and thyme together into a bundle and add to the milk. Finely chop the parsley leaves, and keep to one side. Add the bay leaf and the smoked haddock to the milk.

Bring the milk to a gentle boil and cook for 3 minutes. Remove saucepan from heat, and leave for 5 minutes for the herbs to infuse their flavor. Remove the parsley stems from the milk with a slotted spoon, and use the same technique to strain out the fish. Place fish on a platter and reserve.

Melt butter in another saucepan, over medium heat. Add onions and cook gently until translucent, about 5 minutes, being careful not to overcook. Add the infused milk to the onions, then add

the mashed potato, and stir until totally incorporated into the milk. The soup should be a thick, creamy consistency. Add the diced potato and corn, and cook for 4 to 5 minutes.

Using a fork, flake the smoked haddock into meaty chunks, taking care to remove any hidden bones you may find. Add fish to the soup. Stir in the chopped parsley leaves and bring to a gentle simmer, cooking for a further 4 to 5 minutes. Do not over stir. If you stir too frequently, you will break up the fish.

Taste the soup, and add salt and pepper as needed. Be careful with the salt, as the fish will impart quite a salty flavor all on its own. Serve piping hot. Makes 4-6 servings.

Potpourri Soup

Randy Hatch • Bangor, Penobscot County

"Winifred Hatch was my grandmother. She was born in Dexter in 1898. She was quite a good cook, generally making more sophisticated things than this soup. Our family loved her soup because, at the time, it seemed very spicy and exotic. She did not use tripe, which I guess is the Philly version of pepper pot. The only reason I have this recipe is it was published in a Dexter, Maine cookbook. Most of Winnie's recipes are lost to me."

¾ pound hamburg
4 tablespoons butter
3 onions, sliced
⅓ cup barley
20 ounce can tomatoes
½ teaspoon whole black peppercorns

½ teaspoon ground black pepper
3 sliced carrots
3 diced potatoes
3 stalks celery, diced
1 teaspoon Worcestershire sauce

Cook meat in butter 2 to 3 minutes. Crumble with fork. Add onions; cook 5 minutes. Add barley, tomatoes, water, salt and peppers. Cover and simmer gently over low heat for 1 hour. Add vegetables. Cover and simmer gently for 1 hour longer.

VEGETABLES

Photo: Jules Arsenault displays a giant foraged turnip.

Creamy Mashed Turnip

Jamie Gordon • Bradley, Penobscot County

"This vegetable dish was a favorite of customers and employees at my friend chef Leslie Thistle's Dover-Foxcroft and Bangor restaurants. Lucky for me she was willing to share. Thank you, Les!"

4 or 5 pounds turnips, fresh or frozen,
    peeled and cubed
Salt and pepper, to taste
8-ounce package cream cheese
½ cup butter

¾ cup grated Parmesan cheese
½ to 1 cup cream, to taste

Place turnips in a large pot, cover with water, and cook until tender. Drain, and combine with the other ingredients. Puree in small batches until well combined. This recipe makes a large amount. A crock pot works well for keeping warm or reheating.

Hearty Layer Casserole

Martha Speed • Edgecomb, Lincoln County

"This casserole is vegetarian, but one could add meat to a middle layer."

1 potato, thinly sliced
1 onion, thinly sliced
1 clove garlic, minced
¼ cup raw (uncooked) rice
1 ounce Swiss cheese, shredded
16-ounce can stewed tomatoes
    with juice

1 tablespoon brown sugar
1 teaspoon dried basil
1 teaspoon dried oregano
Thinly sliced vegetables: pepper,
    mushroom, celery, zucchini

Place ingredients in 9 x 13-inch casserole dish in the order listed above, leaving the potato on the bottom. Sprinkle the brown sugar over the stewed tomatoes, before sprinkling on dried basil and oregano. Layer everything, ending with a variety of vegetables on the upper layer. Pour water into the casserole, until you can see it through the vegetables. Cover pan with foil and cook at 350 degrees for 1 hour 15 minutes, then cook uncovered for 45 minutes more.

Chick Pea Salad

Ulla Meir • Caribou, Aroostook County

Astronaut Jessica Meir credits her interest in space to the clear view of stars from her childhood home in Aroostook County. Meir's mother, Ulla, came to Maine from Sweden with her late husband, Josef, who was of Iraqi-Jewish descent. They raised their five children in Caribou, and while Meir has gone on to work as a scientist all over the world—and beyond—she still considers Maine her home. So much so that when she went into space, she took a state flag with her. This salad was a family favorite in the Meir home.

2 teaspoons Dijon mustard
½ teaspoon salt
¾ cup good quality olive oil
½ cup freshly squeezed lemon
¼ teaspoon freshly ground pepper
2 large cans garbanzo beans, drained and rinsed

1 red onion, sliced in thin rings
4 to 6 ounces feta cheese, cut into cubes
½ European cucumber, cut into ½-inch rods
1 box cherry tomatoes, rinsed and cut in halves
½ bunch parsley, cut and chopped

Whisk together mustard, salt, oil, lemon, and pepper. Mix beans and onion and pour dressing over, stirring to blend well. Let rest covered in the fridge, preferable overnight but minimum 1 to 2 hours before serving. The longer the better.

Before serving mix in feta, cucumber, tomatoes, and parsley. Enjoy like the Meir children. Makes 8 to 10 servings.

Pumpkin Seed Croquettes with Shiitake Mushroom Gravy

Avery Kamila • Portland, Cumberland County

"Maine has a rich vegetarian tradition. In the 1800s, Maine native Ellen G. White, who founded the Seventh-day Adventist Church, advocated that church members follow a vegetarian diet, and it is estimated that today roughly half of the Christian denomination's 18 million followers worldwide eat meat-free. In the 1970s, Maine's back-to-the-land movement was influenced by prolific authors and prominent vegetarians Helen and Scott Nearing. Today, vegetarian eating in Maine has moved out of the counterculture and into the mainstream, with many of the state's top chefs creating innovative plant-based dishes and menus.

I created this recipe to capture the classic flavors of of the Maine harvest season in a hearty entree dish that is totally vegan. Each year, I make the dish for Thanksgiving, and I always hope for leftovers since the croquettes are the perfect sandwich filling when topped with vegan gravy and cranberry sauce."

Croquettes:

3 cups grated organic carrots

2 cups raw or roasted pumpkin seeds

3 tablespoons extra virgin olive oil, plus extra to sauté onions

2 gloves garlic, finely chopped

1 tablespoon tamari or soy sauce

1 teaspoon toasted sesame oil

3 cups cooked sweet brown rice

3 tablespoons fresh sage, finely chopped

1 teaspoon sea salt

1 teaspoon dried celery seed

1 teaspoon dried basil

1 medium onion, diced

Gravy:

1 medium onion, finely diced

3 tablespoons extra virgin olive oil

2 to 2½ cups shiitake mushrooms, finely diced

¼ cup tamari or soy sauce

1 cup hemp milk or other nondairy milk

2 tablespoons fresh sage, finely chopped

1 teaspoon garlic powder

1 teaspoon dried thyme

1 teaspoon dried basil

¼ cup whole grain flour, such as spelt, rye, or wheat

Baste:

½ cup extra virgin olive oil

½ cup tamari or soy sauce

Preheat oven to 400 degrees. Grate carrots. Add pumpkin seeds to food processor and pulse a few times until coarsely ground. Then add olive oil, garlic, tamari, sesame oil, and ½ cup water to the food processor. Process until the mixture has a creamy texture. If it's too sticky, add more water. Add pumpkin seed mixture to a bowl with brown rice, carrots and seasonings. Mix together until well blended. Sauté onion until caramelized and add to mixture in bowl.

Oil a large casserole dish or baking pan. Take roughly ½ cup of the mixture into your hands and form a ball. Then roll it into a slightly oval or oblong croquette. Press the croquette onto the oiled baking pan. Repeat until the pan is full.

Whisk together the baste ingredients and brush it over each croquette. Place the pan in the oven and bake 50 to 60 minutes until the croquettes are crispy on the outside. Baste the croquettes again after 20 minutes.

Serve with vegan gravy and cranberry sauce. Makes 20 to 24 croquettes.

To make the gravy: Heat a heavy bottom saucepan and sauté the onions in olive oil until they begin to brown. Add mushrooms and sauté for 5 to 10 minutes. Then add tamari, hemp milk, and ½ cup water. Stir until well blended. Mix in seasonings and allow to simmer for 15 to 20 minutes. Slowly add flour until the gravy is thick and doesn't easily run off a spoon. Serve hot. Leftover gravy can be kept in refrigerator and reheated for up to a week. Or freeze leftovers and when you thaw and reheat, add extra hemp milk and water to thin the gravy.

Shaker Stewed Tomatoes

United Society of Shakers • New Gloucester, Cumberland County

This nineteenth-century Shaker recipe originated with the Shakers at Mount Lebanon, New York, but was shared with all the Shaker communities. It was especially popular among the Maine Shakers and is still a favorite today! Note: Shaker Bouquet Garni is a classic French blend of rosemary, thyme, marjoram, basil, and chervil.

1 quart stewed tomatoes	1 tablespoon sugar
½ cup light cream or whole milk	¼ teaspoon Shaker Bouquet Garni or
¼ teaspoon baking soda	provencal herb blend
¼ cup crushed crackers (Saltines)	1 tablespoon butter or margarine

Heat tomatoes, and add the cream and baking soda. Allow to simmer several minutes. Add the cracker crumbs. Simmer until cracker crumbs have swelled. Add the sugar and Shaker Bouquet Garni. Just before serving, add the butter; allow to melt. If you wish, you may add a dollop of ketchup and salt to taste.

Twice-Baked Potatoes

Katherine McGee Wilson • Fort Fairfield, Aroostook County

"I grew up in Fort Fairfield, a small town nestled along the Aroostook River as it flows into Canada. My grandparents were potato farmers. In the 1920s my grandfather, Thurber Eugene Holt, cleared the land using big draft horses and planted potatoes.

The whole culture of the community centered on the growing and harvesting of potatoes. Even as children we were involved. Many of us participated by cutting up seed potatoes for planting in the spring and pulling mustard and other weeds in the fields during the summer growing season. In late July, the fields of potatoes put out their sprinkling of white and pink blossoms. Come fall, everyone (and I do mean everyone!), worked during the harvest. The harvest, known as 'Diggin',' was so important that schools were closed for three weeks or more, so that everyone could help.

We ate potatoes every day, and sometimes we ate potatoes at more than one meal. We ate baked potatoes and mashed potatoes. We had home fries, which we called 'hash,' for breakfast. We had potato salad for lunch, and on special occasions we had baked, stuffed potatoes. When potatoes were not featured as themselves, they were usually included somewhere in other dishes, such as casseroles and stews."

6 medium or 3 large potatoes	Salt and black pepper
½ cup milk	1 cup shredded cheddar cheese
2 tablespoons butter	Paprika, for sprinkling

Preheat oven to 350 degrees. Prick potatoes all over with a fork, wrap each one in foil, and bake until soft, 60 to 70 minutes. Remove from oven and unwrap.

When potatoes have cooled just enough to handle, slice the potatoes in half lengthwise. If they are very large, slice them again lengthwise, into wide quarters. Using a teaspoon, scoop out the potato flesh into a bowl, leaving potato shells about ¼-inch thick.

Mash the potato in the bowl along with the milk, butter, and salt and pepper. Use a bit more milk if the mixture seems too dry. Blend in half of the shredded cheese.

Spoon the mashed potato mixture back into the shells. Arrange on a rimmed baking sheet. Sprinkle with the rest of the shredded cheese. Dust lightly with paprika.

Raise oven temperature to 400 degrees, and bake for 15 minutes, or until heated through and the cheese is melted. Makes 6 servings.

Chestnut and Winter Squash Tart

Vanessa Seder • Portland, Cumberland County

"I started making this recipe years ago and it has become a staple at holiday family meals and potlucks. The tart is both savory and slightly sweet, due to the chestnuts in both the crust and filling. We eat a lot of squash in our family, and this recipe makes good use of the winter squashes found locally at the farmers' markets. The finished tart looks beautiful and is a very portable option to bring to any gathering."

Crust:

1¼ cups all-purpose flour

½ cup chopped jarred chestnuts

½ teaspoon sea salt

½ cup (1 stick) cold unsalted butter, cut into small pieces

3 to 5 tablespoons ice water

Filling:

2-pound winter squash such as red kuri, kabocha, delicata, or butternut, seeded, peeled and sliced into ¼–inch-thick wedges

3 tablespoons plus ½ cup extra virgin olive oil

Sea salt and freshly ground black pepper

1 to 2 teaspoons thinly sliced red jalapeño

1 tablespoon unsalted butter

½ pound shallots, peeled and sliced thin

4 cloves garlic, peeled and chopped

1½ cups chopped jarred chestnuts

12 fresh sage leaves

2 tablespoons pomegranate seeds

To make the crust: Combine all-purpose flour, chestnuts, and salt in the bowl of a food processor. Pulse until the mixture resembles a coarse meal. Add butter and pulse until butter is the size of small peas. Add 3 tablespoons ice water and pulse a few times. Mixture will look sandy. Take a bit of the mixture and press it together in your hand. If it sticks together and forms a dough, it is ready. If it still crumbles, pulse in more ice water, 1 tablespoon at a time. Wrap dough in plastic wrap and refrigerate at least 1 hour, or overnight.

Roll dough out onto a lightly floured surface into a rectangle about ⅛-inch thin. Press crust in a 14 x 4-inch rectangular tart pan with removable bottom, trimming the edges. Pierce crust all over with the tines of a fork. Cover and refrigerate for about 10 minutes.

Preheat oven to 375 degrees with oven racks on upper and lower thirds. Place a piece of parchment over the tart dough and cover with pie weights. Bake crust on lower rack until beginning to firm, 10 to 12 minutes. Remove parchment and pie weights and continue to cook until crust is golden and set, about 20 minutes. Transfer crust to a cooling rack and allow to cool to room temperature.

To make the filling: Increase oven heat to 425 degrees. Place squash in a large bowl and gently toss with 2 tablespoons oil, 1 teaspoon salt, ½ teaspoon pepper, and jalapeño slices. Divide mixture between two parchment-lined baking sheets. Roast squash, tossing and rotating pans halfway through cooking, until tender and slightly caramelized, 30 to 35 minutes.

Meanwhile, melt butter and 1 tablespoon oil in a medium skillet over medium-low heat. Add shallots and garlic and cook, stirring occasionally, until very soft and slightly caramelized, about 20 minutes. Mix in chestnuts and heat through. Season to taste with salt and pepper.

In a small skillet, heat remaining ½ cup olive oil over medium heat until shimmering. Have a paper towel-lined plate ready. Add a few sage leaves at a time to the hot oil, and fry until crisp but still very green, about 10 to 15 seconds. Transfer with a slotted spoon to the paper towel–lined plate and sprinkle with salt.

To assemble tart: Spread the shallot-chestnut mixture over the bottom of the crust. Top with the roasted squash and garnish with fried sage leaves and pomegranate seeds. Serve warm or at room temperature.

Baked Beets

JeanAnn Pollard • Winslow, Kennebec County

"This beet recipe was originally published in my cookbook, *The Simply Grande Gardening Cookbook,* now out of print. My husband grew all of our organic vegetables in our big gardens while I cooked everything. Beets are often overlooked, but are a truly wonderful vegetable!"

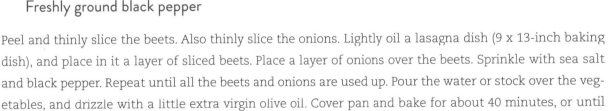

4 to 5 large beets
2 to 3 large onions
Sea salt
Freshly ground black pepper

¾ cup water or vegetable stock
Extra virgin olive oil, for drizzling

Peel and thinly slice the beets. Also thinly slice the onions. Lightly oil a lasagna dish (9 x 13-inch baking dish), and place in it a layer of sliced beets. Place a layer of onions over the beets. Sprinkle with sea salt and black pepper. Repeat until all the beets and onions are used up. Pour the water or stock over the vegetables, and drizzle with a little extra virgin olive oil. Cover pan and bake for about 40 minutes, or until beets are tender. Check by pricking with a fork. Serve hot.

And do note: Leftovers can be whizzed in a blender with milk or cream plus a sprinkling of tarragon to make a thick, fuchsia-colored soup that's about as tasty as possible.

Claptrap

Mary Drymon DeRose • South Portland, Cumberland County

"My grandmother made claptrap, and this is her recipe. Claptrap is a mix of three winter root crops that have interesting histories. The potato was brought from South America to Europe by early sixteenth-century explorers. The use of orange carrots was popularized in the early eighteenth-century by the followers King William of Orange, the Dutch prince who battled for and won the throne of England at the Battle of the Boyne in Ireland. Some of the 1718 settlers of Maine had fought in his army or participated at the Siege of Londonderry. Rutabaga is also called 'swede.' It was brought into England and Ireland by Viking invaders. Mix them together and you get a real bowl of history."

1 teaspoon sea salt
4 large white potatoes
4 large orange carrots

1 small rutabaga
2 tablespoons butter
2 tablespoons cream

Peel and cut the vegetables into about 1-inch chunks. Place in large pot and cover with cold water. Add salt and boil until everything is fork tender. Drain and mash together in the same pot. Add butter and cream and return to low heat, mixing in butter until it melts.

Nana Malone's Potato Salad

Danielle and Paige Perry • Portland, Cumberland County

"Potato salad isn't the most exciting food, except when it's our Nana Malone's Potato Salad! Any time we had family get togethers, my Nana was *always* asked to bring her potato salad. It went something like this, 'Bea, you are bringing your potato salad, right?' We asked Nana how she came up with the recipe and she said it was actually her mother-in-law's recipe, who was ALSO known as Nana Malone to our mom and her many, many cousins. We are now old enough to start bringing this family recipe to our friends/family gatherings in the hopes that they enjoy it as well."

2½ pounds red potatoes
1 tablespoon kosher salt
½ cup prepared mayonnaise
   (Nana used Hellman's)
⅛ cup sugar

3 tablespoons distilled white vinegar
1 teaspoon onion powder
   (or substitute chopped onions)
½ teaspoon salt
Sweet paprika, for serving

Cut potatoes into rounds approximately ½-inch thick, and then into 1-inch chunks. (Nana Malone cut generous-size potato chunks.) Place potatoes in a large pot and cover with 1 inch of water. Add kosher salt to the water and bring to a boil, and then lower heat and set to a simmer for about 6 minutes, or just until the potatoes are fork tender, making sure not to undercook. Drain potatoes into a strainer and spray with cold water. Transfer potatoes to a large bowl and allow to cool for 15 minutes.

    Mix the remaining ingredients in a smaller bowl and then add to the potatoes. Place in the refrigerator for at least 1 hour. The potato salad needs time to meld the flavors together and should stay very cold until it is time to serve. When serving, Nana Malone would always sprinkle sweet paprika over the entire top. This can be doubled for a large gathering as we have often done.

Mujuddarah (Esau's Potage)

Jo Cameron • Edgecomb, Lincoln County

"I wasn't born in Maine but my family moved to Edgecomb in 1942, so I have always identified as a Mainer. I learned this (completely vegan!) recipe in Beirut, Lebanon, while abroad with my husband, Dr. Bruce Cameron. This dish is common throughout the Near East, all peoples, all religions. Let it be a warm welcome to many of Maine's immigrant friends!"

1 cup brown lentils
½ cup white rice
2 or more yellow onions

¼ cup or more olive oil
½ teaspoon or more toasted cumin seeds
Salt as wanted

Simmer lentils in saucepan until they can be crushed against the side of the pan. Add rice, along with enough water to cover. Simmer until both lentils and rice are soft and chewable.

Slice as many yellow onions as you want into "lunelles," that is, length-wise. In a frying pan, heat olive oil (at least ¼ cup, or more if desired), and fry onions until brown, letting some blacken and char. Add all but a handful of onions to the lentil and rice mixture, and mix thoroughly, along with toasted cumin seeds and salt, to taste.

Pour into serving dish and garnish with remaining onion slices. Drizzle with more olive oil, if you wish. This dish may be served hot or at room temperature. It's best at room temperature, maybe 1 or 2 days after preparing. This amount will feed a small army.

Tangy Lentil Burgers

Elizabeth Stanton • Portland, Cumberland County

"This vegan recipe was inspired by my visit to Ireland, where I had some wonderful lentil loaf at a restaurant. Since an entire lentil loaf is a lot for me to eat, the lentil burgers work well and I freeze them individually so I can enjoy many meals."

1 cup dry lentils, well rinsed
2½ cups water
½ teaspoon salt
1 tablespoon olive oil
½ medium onion, diced
1 carrot, diced
1 teaspoon pepper
1 tablespoon soy sauce (can use low-sodium)
¾ cup rolled oats

¾ cup breadcrumbs (seasoned or plain)
2 to 3 tablespoons ketchup
1 to 2 tablespoons finely chopped walnuts
1 tablespoon Sriracha sauce (or to taste)

Sauce:
¼ cup ketchup
2 tablespoons balsamic vinegar
½ teaspoon red pepper flakes

Boil lentils in the water with salt until lentils are soft and most of the water is gone, approximately 30 to 45 minutes.

Heat the olive oil in a frying pan. Cook the onions and carrots in oil until soft, 10 to 15 mins. Transfer mixture to a large bowl and combine with pepper, soy sauce, oats, breadcrumbs, ketchup, walnuts, and hot pepper sauce. When mixture has cooled slightly but is still warm, form into patties. This will make 8 to 10 patties. Place on aluminum foil sprayed with cooking spray or lightly oiled on cookie sheet.

In a separate bowl, combine ketchup, balsamic vinegar, and red pepper flakes, mixing to make a sauce. Spread on each burger.

Bake for approximately 20 to 30 minutes at 375 degrees.

Carrot Casserole

Doreen Duke • Rockport, Knox County

"My mother, Eleanor Hall, got this recipe from her local church and it became a mainstay at every family gathering. This recipe has been shared many times with friends, and many people have requested the dish to be brought for gatherings, especially at Thanksgiving."

2 pounds carrots
1 beaten egg
2 tablespoons parsley
½ cup butter
½ green pepper, diced
½ medium onion, diced
½ teaspoon salt
½ teaspoon pepper
2 tablespoons flour
2 tablespoons sugar
1 cup milk

Peel and cut up carrots. Place in a saucepan, cover with water, and boil, cooking until carrots are tender. Drain carrots, mash them and set aside. When slightly cooled, add beaten egg and parsley to carrots and stir.

Melt butter in a small pot and add green pepper and onion, and cook until a little soft. Add salt, pepper, flour, and sugar, and stir together to make a roux. Slowly add milk, and cook until thickened. Remove from heat and add to carrot mixture. Stir all together and put into casserole dish and bake at 350 degrees for 1 hour.

BEANS

Photo: Hunter family reunion picnic, 1958, near Augusta.
Notice the pot of beans on the picnic table!

Broder's Baked Beans

Brenda Broder • Oakfield, Aroostook County

"Our father owned a Red and White general store in Oakfield in the '70s. Every Friday evening before leaving the store, the beans were in water to soak overnight. Saturday morning when we arrived, the beans were started in the slow cooker. Around noon time, the beans would be ready to sell. I always hoped they didn't sell out so we could have some for our Saturday night dinner at home, but being the good businessman our father was, if he could sell them, he would. Memory tells me they were $1.25 a pint and $2.25 for a quart. They were good."

2 pounds dry beans (we prefer Jacobs Cattle or Soldier beans)
2 sweet onions, quartered
¾ cup brown sugar
¾ cup white sugar
1 tablespoon dry mustard
Black pepper to taste
1 pound salt pork or bacon
¼ cup molasses

Soak beans overnight (or for 8 hours, the beans can't really tell time) then par boil for ½ hour. Add to the pot all the remaining ingredients *except* the molasses. Cook for 3 hours or until soft, then add the molasses. Adding the molasses will slow the cooking process. Then have a rootin' tootin' good time, because beans will "talk behind your back."

The Way It Was: Church Suppers

Thomas W. Easton • Bridgton, Cumberland County

"Every Friday or Saturday night some one of the churches in town, or some other organization, would put on a public supper. Often these were based on baked beans, or on farm-cured ham in the spring. There would be beans of several kinds, prepared by the best cooks the organization could muster, and everyone tried them all. There would be salads, in winter largely cole slaw, but they varied at other times. Even cole slaw isn't routine among the sort of people I grew up with. Some shaved carrots into it, some had special salad dressings they concocted for the occasion, and sometimes no one ever found out what that interesting difference in Mrs. X's cole slaw really was. Old-time cooks had the patent office beat for protection; they simply never told. Chopped beechnuts were one additive to cole slaw that I haven't seen since. They were good! No such public supper ever ended without the main event, which wasn't the main course at all. Every cook in town had a special cake or pie recipe that was only used for these whingdings or for special family gatherings, like Thanksgiving dinner. The attempt to decide whether Mrs. A's pie, or Mrs. B's cake was up to standard, or whether that walnut cake was really better than this chocolate one with the coconut frosting, was really the main business of the evening. It often made stomach aches for the greedy young, and even made the soberer elders lose any intense interest in breakfast the next day. Nobody's regrets lasted long enough to influence their behavior at the next public supper."

Dad's Bean Hole Beans

Jayne Farrin • Presque Isle, Aroostook County

"This is my dad Lyman C. Farrin's recipe for 'bean hole beans.' He had a hole out in the backyard. When my parents had company or entertained, often Dad would prepare them. Mom did everything else, but Dad would get special recognition and praise because he was a man cooking. Dad doesn't mention soaking and parboiling, as that would have been done by my mom, who he called 'Mam,' but the beans would have been soaked and parboiled before placing them in the ground. I have great memories of him fussing with the fire."

6 cups yellow-eye beans
¾ cup molasses
1 tablespoon dry mustard
1 scant teaspoon salt

⅛ teaspoon pepper
1½ pounds salt pork or bacon
   (if salty, cut down on salt)

Dig hole approximately 3 feet in diameter and 18 inches deep. Build a good fire, adding a good grade of hardwood until the hole is half full of red coals.

Beans should be prepared as below and use an 8-cup steel pot with a cover having a lip hanging below the rim of the pot.

(Wash dry beans in cold water and drain. Place beans in a saucepan, and just barely cover with cold water. Bring to a boil and simmer on low heat for about 1 hour. Add remaining ingredients and stir gently. Pour into bean pot, cover with lid.)

Place pot in coals and cover it completely with coals to depth of 2 to 3 inches. Then cover hole and pot to a depth of 6 inches with dirt. Cook at least 12 hours.

Baked Yellow-Eye Beans

Martha Hadley • Fort Fairfield, Aroostook County

"Growing up on a farm in northern Maine meant being resourceful and managing a household on a strict budget. Baked beans were an inexpensive and healthy way to feed a large family. Every Saturday, my Mom would make a batch of homemade bread and a batch of baked yellow-eye beans for Saturday night supper. Often, there were beans leftover for Sunday brunch, either reheated or served cold on a piece of bread. When I grew up and moved to Ohio, I had trouble finding yellow-eye beans in the grocery store, so my Mom, who still lives in Fort Fairfield, started giving them to me for my birthday!"

2½ cups yellow-eye beans (about a ½ bag)
3 tablespoons molasses
4 tablespoons (½ stick) margarine
1 teaspoon dry mustard

1 teaspoon salt
3 tablespoons brown sugar
¼ cup chopped onion

Wash dry beans in cold water and drain. Place beans in a saucepan, and just barely cover with cold water. Bring to a boil and simmer on low heat for about 1 hour. Add remaining ingredients and stir gently. Pour into bean pot, and cover with foil. Bake at 300 degrees for 3 to 4 hours, checking periodically to make sure there's still liquid in the pot for the beans to cook in. Serve on Saturday night with red hot dogs, fried onions, and homemade bread.

Baked Beans à la Two Glorias

Vicki Doudera • Camden, Knox County

"For more than 20 years, a group of families in Camden and Rockport has celebrated Labor Day with an annual Lobster Bake on Rockport Harbor, complete with our own Labor Day Song, sung to the tune of "Eidelweiss." (The first verse goes, "Labor Day, Labor Day, this marks the end of the summer. Short and sweet, now complete, September will soon be discovered.") I always bring the baked beans. Sometimes I make them from scratch, but

when I don't have time, I use a quicker method from my mother, Gloria Guiduli. No matter how I make the beans, the trick is to bake and bring them in the Doudera Family Bean Pot, which was passed down to me years ago by my mother-in-law, Gloria Doudera. Yes, two great cooks both named Gloria! Hence the odd name for these delicious (and quick) beans!"

Tall can of B&M pork and beans
2 tablespoons molasses
2 tablespoons brown sugar
1 teaspoon mustard (I like Raye's)

4 tablespoons ketchup
Half a small onion, sliced
Several strips of raw bacon

Heat oven to 350 degrees. Combine beans, molasses, brown sugar, mustard, and ketchup, and place mixture in bean pot. Spread sliced onion and strips of bacon on top. Bake, uncovered, for about 1 hour, or until the top is set and bacon is crisp.

Mom's Saturday Night Baked Beans (from the original Ashby bean recipe)

Anne Ashby Theriault • Fort Fairfield, Aroostook County

"This bean recipe originated with my mother, Kay Ashby, using beans called Ashby beans, grown by my grandfather Fred D. Ashby on his farm in Caribou. When Ashby beans were not available, my mother chose Great Northern dry beans as a close substitute—not as small as pea beans, and not as large as yellow-eye. I have been very fortunate that my husband, Rosaire Theriault, is keeping the Saturday night beans alive in the family. He even uses Mom's bean pot out of an old G.E. stove that had what was called a deep well."

2 pounds dried Great Northern beans
1 onion, sliced or chopped
1 package or ¼ pound salt pork or bacon
½ cup brown sugar

⅓ cup molasses
2 teaspoons dry mustard
1 teaspoon ginger
1 stick butter

Sort and soak in large pot 2 pounds beans, covering overnight with cold water. Rinse in the morning and add fresh cold water to cover beans about 1 inch. Add all ingredients except for the butter (which is added after beans are cooked). Start beans in the oven at 350 degrees. After they start to boil, the temperature should be reduced to 325 degrees, as beans that boil too hard tend to pop their skins! Keep an eye on beans so they are always covered with water. You may need to add water during cooking, preferably boiling water. Beans should be fully cooked in 4 to 5 hours. Remove from oven and add the butter on top. If the beans were not as dark as you like, a teaspoon or so of Gravy Master can add color with no flavor change.

Lunchtime Log Drive

Brenda Bourgoine • Caribou, Aroostook County

"My family history is tied to lumbering, log drives, hunting and fishing along the St. John River in far Northern Maine. This photo is of a 'wanigan,' or 'wangan', a floating cook shack at the back of a log drive to feed the drivers. I remember, in the 1940s, that the wanigan tied up on the shore at our family homestead on the St. John River. The cooks were mostly men, their helper called a 'cookie.' Their woodburning cooking range was on board this flat-bottom boat. A good cook kept the river drivers happy, and they worked hard. Food was plain with little variety—no wonder cooking on a floating boat. I can't imagine cooking in such conditions. There is no written directions on making baked beans, which were served every meal, with bread or pancakes."

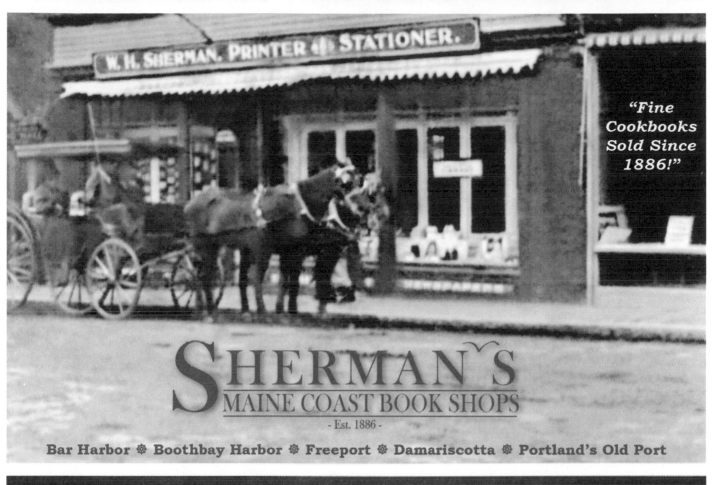

Marge and Brownie in Our Kitchens
Sandy Oliver

In Maine, two food writers, Marjorie Standish and Mildred "Brownie" Schrumpf, made themselves household names with their plentiful recipes, cooking advice and the reader exchanges with which they filled their weekly columns for dozens of years in the mid-1900s. In community cookbook fashion, both writers offered recipes from readers identified by name and portrayed food fads and favorites as Maine slid out from under the Depression and World Wars I and II.

Marjorie Holbrook Standish was born in 1908 and grew up near Brunswick, Maine, spending childhood summers at her grandparents' farm near New Meadow River, now part of the former Brunswick Naval Air Station. She attended Farmington State College, Normal School, as a Home Economics major, a common and at the time appropriate field for young women, graduating in 1931. Her career was teaching women how to use newly available electric stoves for Central Maine Power. She traveled around central Maine demonstrating stove use, no doubt collecting recipes as she went.

In 1948, she began writing a column for the Portland-based *Maine Sunday Telegram* that continued for 25 years and resulted in two compilation cookbooks, *Cooking Down East and Keep Cooking the Maine Way*. Marjorie's recipes caught on with Maine cooks, who clipped them from the newspapers and used them in their everyday cookery, enough so that their grandchildren report that "this recipe is an old family recipe," without knowing that Marge was the author.

Aside from her professional life, Marge involved herself in charity work, socializing with friends with her husband George, and enjoying a game of golf. She died in 1998.

Mildred Greeley Brown Schrumpf was born in 1903, grew up on a Readville farm, and attended Winthrop High School. She graduated from the University of Maine, having majored in Home Economics just as Marge Standish did. Also like Marge, Mildred worked with modern stoves, she as a tester for gas stoves on behalf of the Bangor Gas Company. Like Marge, she taught as assistant leader in statewide 4-H clubs and, eventually through the 1930s, as the Penobscot County 4-H club agent. Her job was to modernize 4-H home demonstrators in food preparation and preservation. From there, she worked teaching cooking in the University Extension Service, and she taught Home Economics at UMaine.

Mildred began her *Bangor Daily News* column in 1951, continuing for an unbelievable 43 years until 1994. She called it "Brownie's Kitchen." She, too, compiled recipes to author *Memories from Brownie's Kitchen*.

Brownie was always on the go and seems to have been tireless. Traveling all over on 4-H and Extension service business was her cup of tea. Teaching at UMaine, she came to know international instructors and students and started monthly international dinners featuring the foods of one country or another. She and her husband hosted potluck suppers at their home in Orono, and she was active in local politics, too. She died in 2001.

Both writers promoted Maine food and food products. Marge who lived in Gardiner and then in Augusta, was friendly with the Blaine House chef who adapted her recipes to Maine ingredients to help spread the word of Maine food. Brownie and her delegation promoted Maine food products at the annual Eastern States Exposition in West Springfield, Massachusetts, and she headed the chicken barbecues at Maine Broiler Festival Barbecues in the 1950s and '60s when Midcoast Maine was a major chicken producing area.

One feature of food and cookery in the 1900s was the increasing use of convenient pre-prepared foods in recipes, famously canned soups and JELL-O. Food producers, from canned fruit to chocolate to dates, from Dole to Marshmallow Fluff, operated test kitchens that developed ways to use their products in home cookery. Many of those products slipped into mainstream cooking, in recipes such as pineapple upside-down cake, countless date breads and cookies, Whoopie Pies made with Marshmallow Fluff, many, many JELL-O-based salads, and canned soup as a premade sauce for all kinds of casseroles.

Most home cooks preferred to use these products as if they were ingredients so that they added value to them by incorporating them in dishes. It was a way to participate in the process of cooking, "assisted scratch-cooking" if you will, still considered the honorable way of housekeeping in contrast to the cook who merely opened cans. The move toward whole, premade meals that the home cook warmed up and served was still a few decades in the future.

Both Marge and Brownie wrote about their childhood food memories and published traditional recipes from scratch for old-time Maine dishes. Both grew up when wood- or coal burning cookstoves dominated Maine kitchens. Both would recall hours in vegetable gardens and kitchen preserving the abundance. Both learned from scratch cooking before there was an alternative. Over time, both writers dedicated parts of their careers teaching other cooks how to adapt to modern cooking equipment, adopt up-to-date preserving techniques, and learn how to use the new products found in grocery stores by mid-century. By the 1950s, both incorporated in their recipes pre-prepared foods as ingredients, a common feature of many community cookbook recipes from the mid-1900s up to the present.

In twenty-first-century Maine, our computers and phones give us recipes. Meat loaf? One algorithm will toss up thousands of possibilities graded by strangers, promoted by bloggers half a continent away. Possibly the greatest thing Marge and Brownie did was to give Maine cooks weekly kitchen companionship via the newspaper. New ideas, friendly chat, and advice. The hardest part of cooking is trying to figure out what to make, and weekly these two food writers served up a collection of dinner and dessert recipes made with the ingredients Maine's home cooks likely kept in their pantries and fridges. Marge and Brownie's friendly voices in print were so very familiar, trustworthy, and welcome.

FISH & SHELLFISH

Photo: 'Pollock' is from *CAUGHT. time. place. fish.* by Antonia Small and Glen Libby (2016).
See Antonia's recipe for Corned Hake on page 121.

Baked Haddock with Nova Scotia Egg Sauce

Steve Peer • Lubec, Hancock County

"Living in Lubec in the 1980s, we would drive long distances for a fun night out. Sometimes for a little adventure we would travel six hours to Nova Scotia. Nothing was better than sampling the variety of local fish—haddock, cod, pollock, sole, and flounder—cooked in the many Bechamel-inspired sauces found in most small town restaurants in the Maritimes. As it turned out, we didn't need to leave Maine—the best fish of this style could be found in neighboring Jonesboro, at The White House Restaurant, prepared to perfection and served with fluffy, buttery mashed potatoes at the most unpretentious family-style eatery in Down East Maine."

1 pound haddock filets

Bechamel sauce:
3 tablespoons butter
3 tablespoons all-purpose flour
2 cups milk
½ teaspoon salt

½ teaspoon cracked black pepper
¼ teaspoon cayenne
½ teaspoon dried tarragon or
    2 teaspoons fresh
4 hard-boiled eggs
1 slice slightly dry bread, grated
½ teaspoon paprika

Preheat oven to 400 degrees. Butter an 8 x 8-inch baking dish. Cut fish filets into easy-to-serve portions and arrange in one layer in the pan. Place fish in the oven and bake for 25 minutes, or until the fish flakes easily with a fork.

While fish is baking, make the bechamel sauce by melting the butter in a medium-sized saucepan. Whisk in the flour and let cook for about 1 minute. Do not let it brown; this is a white sauce.

Gradually stir in the milk and whisk until thickened. Let cook for about 1 minute. Remove from the heat and stir in the salt, pepper, cayenne, and tarragon.

Peel and slice the eggs. Some folks do not include the egg yolk. Stir into the sauce, taking care not to break the slices up too much. Pour the egg sauce over the haddock filets in the baking dish.

Before serving, sprinkle the top with grated bread and paprika. You can add a little more salt and pepper if you wish. Makes 4 servings.

Beer-Steamed Mussels with Corn and Basil

Jake Austin • Gray, Cumberland County

"Growing up in Maine, the bounty of the sea is available year round and it's easy to take advantage. When Austin Street Brewery opened its doors in 2014, Will Fisher and I were both working full-time jobs while simultaneously operating the brewery. As you can imagine, there wasn't much time for meal prep. Enter Beer-Steamed Mussels: quick and delicious while incorporating a splash of the beer you're already sipping on."

2 pounds mussels in shells, beards removed, preferably Bang's Island
2 tablespoons olive oil
4 garlic cloves, minced
2 large shallots, chopped
2 ounces n'duja (optional)
¾ cup Austin Street's Pactolian Pils (or any lager)

2 ears corn, kernels cut off the cob
¼ cup heavy cream
Kosher salt and freshly ground black pepper, to taste
3 tablespoons fresh basil, chopped
Crusty bread, grilled, for serving

Rinse mussels under cold running water and scrub shells.

In a large saucepan pan with a tight-fitting lid, sauté olive oil, garlic, shallots and optional n'duja over medium-high heat until soft, 3 to 4 minutes.

Add the beer, mussels, and corn to the pot and immediately cover. Let mussels steam, stirring occasionally, for 5 to 10 minutes, until the shells open. Discard any mussels that don't open.

Add cream to the pan, and season with salt and pepper. Remove pan from stovetop and add the chopped basil. Serve with grilled crusty bread to soak up the juice.

Clam Cakes

Victor Trodella • Yarmouth, Cumberland County

"Clamming was a family tradition that I now enjoy with my friends on the southern Maine coast."

¼ cup flour
½ cup freshly chopped Italian parsley
½ teaspoon baking powder
½ teaspoon black pepper
½ teaspoon hot red pepper flakes
¼ teaspoon oregano
½ teaspoon salt

2 cups finely chopped sea clams
  (drain off all liquid)
1 finely chopped onion
2 eggs, beaten
¾ cup panko bread crumbs
2 tablespoons olive oil
Tartar sauce or Kewpie Japanese
  mayonnaise, for serving

Mix together flour, parsley, baking powder, black pepper, red pepper, oregano, and salt. Add clams and onions, and mix well. Add eggs, and mix, then add panko bread crumbs. Thoroughly combine.

Heat olive oil in a frying pan. Make clam mixture into ½-inch thick patties, and cook quickly over medium-low heat, turning once. Serve hot with tartar sauce or spiced Japanese mayonnaise

Salmon Souffle

circa 1880 • *St. Croix Recipe Book for Cooking*
Ladies of the Second Baptist Church • Calais, Washington County

The St. Croix River was a sacred space for the Passamaquody people, and the abundance of salmon an important food source. Today, Calais is home to the Atlantic Salmon Federation, which seeks to restore wild Atlantic Salmon populations. More of a savory pastry than a soufflé, this recipe turned leftovers into a tasty new dish for the next meal. —DL

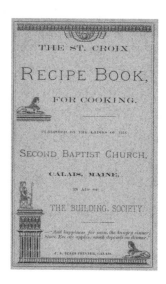

Remnants of cold salmon, a little butter gravy, a pinch of salt and pepper. Place this in a saucepan till hot. Have ready a dish with the sides lined with pastry. Place the salmon in layers with grated bread and bits of butter between the layers and grated bread over the top after pouring in the liquor in which it was stewed. Then cover with puff paste and bake in a quick oven.

Coconut Curry Lobster

Beto Guimaraes • South Portland, Cumberland County

"In northeastern Brazil, where I come from, we cook a lot of seafood in coconut sauce, which gave me the idea to try it with lobster. I began spending vacations with my partner's family in Friendship in 2007. I really only eat lobsters there and have developed a great relationship with Larry Wallace, where I buy my lobsters fresh off his boat. In 2017, we moved to South Portland. I still prefer fresh Friendship lobsters to all others."

2 tablespoons olive oil
2 medium onions, chopped
4 cloves garlic, minced
½-inch ginger, grated
Salt and pepper, to taste
14 ounce can diced tomatoes
14-ounce can coconut milk

2 tablespoons curry powder or
   1 tablespoon curry paste
Meat from about 4 lobsters,
   cooked and picked
1 bunch cilantro, chopped
2 lemons or limes
Red pepper flakes, for serving
Cooked rice, for serving

In a skillet, sauté onion and garlic in olive oil until golden and fragrant. Add ginger, salt, pepper and tomatoes, sauté for a bit, then add coconut milk, stir a few times, then add curry powder or paste. Simmer to reduce by about half. Add cooked lobster. Stir in chopped cilantro, reserving 2 tablespoons for garnish. Turn off heat, squeeze lemon or lime over the top, and sprinkle with remaining cilantro and red pepper flakes. Serve with rice. Makes 6 servings.

Broiled Eel Japanese Style

Sara Jenkins • Rockport, Knox County

"Maine eels, kabayaki style, are a favorite at Nina June Restaurant, where they're served over warm jasmine rice with a garnish of pickled radishes and cilantro, and sesame seeds sprinkled on top. First—the eels must be skinned, which is the only hard part of this otherwise easy dish. At the restaurant, the eels are decapitated and then packed in salt for a day to make skinning easier. To remove the skin, tug back a corner of the skin at the head end, then, using pliers or work gloves, pull the skin back the full length of the fish. Once you get started this is easy, like pulling off a pair of opera gloves. Cut the eel into approximately 3-inch lengths."

Two 1-pound eels, prepared as above

Unagi sauce:
¼ cup mirin (Japanese rice wine)

1½ tablespoons sake
4 tablespoons white miso paste
3 tablespoons maple syrup

Combine the mirin and sake in a small saucepan and bring to a simmer over low heat. Cook just long enough to throw off the alcohol, then whisk in the miso and stir to dissolve. Now turn the heat up to medium and add the syrup. Cook for 5 to 10 minutes, or until the unagi sauce is thickened, then set aside to cool. (This step can be done well in advance.)

When you're ready to cook the eels, set the broiler on high. Spread aluminum foil on a broiler pan and brush with a little oil. Add the eel pieces and brush each piece lightly with oil. Set under the broiler for about 5 to 7 minutes, then remove and brush with a good coating of the unagi sauce. Return to the broiler for another minute, until the sauce on the fish is bubbling and richly caramelized.

Remove and serve immediately as described above, or if you wish, set aside and serve later at room temperature.

Crabmeat-Stuffed Filet of Sole

Margaret Harris • Burlington, Penobscot County

"My mother first served a recipe similar to this at her family's cottage at Hancock Point, back in the 1970s. It was quite a hit. I've taken a few liberties with her recipe, as she wasn't fond of scallions or mushrooms. She died in 2015 at the age of 98."

½ cup plus 1 tablespoon butter, divided
2 scallions, chopped
½ sleeve Ritz crackers, crushed
1 pound crabmeat, cooked and picked

6 medium sole filets
2 teaspoons lemon juice, divided
4 ounces fresh mushrooms,
    cleaned and sliced

Preheat oven to 375 degrees.

In a sauté pan set over medium heat, melt ½ cup butter, then add chopped scallions. When scallions are tender, add crushed crackers and mix well.

In medium bowl, combine cracker mixture and crabmeat. Mix well. Divide stuffing into 6 portions.

Place 1 portion of stuffing in each filet, then roll up and fasten with a toothpick, and place on non-stick cookie sheet. Brush 1 teaspoon of lemon juice over the filets. Bake for 20 to 25 minutes.

While fish is baking, melt remaining tablespoon of butter in a sauté pan, and add mushrooms, cooking gently until tender. To serve, spoon mushrooms over plated fish and sprinkle with remaining lemon juice.

Sylvia's Secret Lobster Newburg

John Wilson • Jonesport, Washington County

"Mom, Sylvia Wilson, used to cook this on special occasions. We always believed she slaved for hours—little did we know. I am not sure if it came from her side of the family or my dad, Levi Wilson's, side."

6 tablespoons butter
3 tablespoons flour
1 teaspoon salt
⅛ teaspoon nutmeg
Dash paprika
3 egg yolks

2 cups light cream
1 cup milk
1 pound cooked lobster meat, picked from
    shells and roughly chopped
3 tablespoons sherry

Heat butter in a large skillet and stir in flour, salt, nutmeg, and paprika, mixing until blended.

In a medium bowl, beat egg yolks slightly and stir in cream and milk. Stir egg mixture into flour mixture and cook, stirring constantly, until mixture thickens. Stir in lobster and sherry, and cook until heated.

Congolese Makayabu (Salt Fish)

Angelique Bitshiluala • Portland, Cumberland County

Angelique moved to Portland from the Democratic Republic of Congo. She works in food service at Maine Medical Center and volunteers with the organization In Her Presence, a Maine-based nonprofit that brings together immigrant women from across communities and generations. Makayabu is traditionally served with boiled amaranth leaves and fried plantains. While some of the flavors of home have been hard to find, in Portland, salt fish (cod), plantains, and amaranth leaves are available at Moriah Grocery on Cumberland Avenue. Maggi seasoning is available in many grocery stores; if you can't find it, substitute equal parts soy sauce and Worcestershire sauce.

1 pound salt cod

1 eggplant

Vegetable oil, for frying

Salt, to taste

3 bell peppers, preferably mixed colors, sliced lengthwise

2 large onions, sliced in rings

2 cloves garlic, minced

One bunch chives, snipped or torn into pieces

½ teaspoon Maggi seasoning, or to taste

In a medium-sized bowl, soak salt cod in cold water. Refrigerate overnight while soaking. (This rehydrates the fish and removes much of the salt.) Rinse, and pat dry.

Slice off the eggplant stem and slice lengthwise in half, then slice each half crosswise into thirds. Peel eggplant, then continue to cut into triangular chunks. Place chopped pieces into a bowl of cold water and set aside.

In a large frying pan, heat ½ inch of oil. Add the rehydrated salt cod and fry until browned, 5 minutes each side. Salt to taste and continue to cook until golden brown. Remove pan from heat, then take out fish with a slotted spoon and place in a big bowl.

In a new pan set over medium heat, warm 1 tablespoon of oil and add peppers and onions. Stir, adding a few shakes of salt. Add some eggplant pieces, and pour in a small amount of water if vegetables begin to stick. Stir in garlic, chives, and Maggi seasoning. Spoon vegetables over fish before serving with amaranth leaves and fried plantains.

Nana Johnson's Fried Lobster

Brett Johnson • Bailey Island, Cumberland County

"Eileen Shea Johnson was my 'Nana,' wife to Capt, Lawrence E. Johnson, the namesake of our family home on Bailey Island. In the 1950s, Nana owned Rock Ovens restaurant in Harpswell, and this recipe was one of her signature dishes. In 1955, a group of Bowdoin professors who were regulars awarded her with a 'diploma' for a Doctorate of Culinary Arts. My sister Cathy has the original diploma, and a newspaper clipping with this recipe was found inside the back of the frame. Nana always used reconstituted powdered milk in the batter, but you can substitute fresh."

1 egg
1 cup milk (fresh or mixed from powdered)
½ tablespoon baking powder
⅛ teaspoon salt

About 2 cups sifted flour
(enough to make a heavy batter)
2 pounds cooked lobster claws and tails, cut
into large chunks
Vegetable shortening or oil, for frying

In a medium-sized bowl, beat together the egg and the milk. Sift together the dry ingredients, and add them to the bowl, beating thoroughly "like salad dressing." Pat dry the lobster pieces, and dip them in the batter. Heat oil to 350 degrees in a fryer or deep skillet, and fry the lobster pieces until golden brown. Take care to keep the temperature at 350 degrees, or the lobster will become overcooked. Note: The same batter can be used to make onion rings, which go nicely with fried lobster!

Lobster on the Rocks on Eagle Island in Sunset, at sunset.
See LaCombe family recipe for Dynamites on page 142.

Maine Sea Scallop, Mushroom, and Potato Gratin

Chris Hart • Augusta, Kennebec County

"Being the Chef at the Blaine House has been an incredible experience! Previously I worked in the large-scale hotel industry where production was the main focus. Now I get to source local ingredients myself and be hands-on with the cooking. We even have our own gardens of vegetables, herbs, and flowers where we pick everything fresh. It is an environment that chefs dream of! Though I get a lot of the credit around here, I couldn't do what I do without our fabulous team at the Blaine House. Everyone works together to make the Governor proud to hold events here. I have had the pleasure of working for two administrations thus far in my career and hope to be here for many more to come."

4 medium gold potatoes, peeled and diced

2 tablespoons canola oil

2 pounds Maine sea scallops, muscles removed

Salt and black pepper, to taste

4 ounces bacon, chopped

3 shallots, minced

8 ounces oyster mushrooms, sliced

4 sprigs thyme, picked and minced

¼ cup cognac

1 stick butter

¼ cup flour

1 cup lobster stock

1½ cups heavy cream

3 tablespoons parsley, chopped

4 ounces Gruyere cheese, grated

2 cups bread crumbs (see Note)

Note: To make homemade breadcrumbs, grind 6 slices of bread, mix with 2 tablespoons melted butter, salt, pepper, minced garlic, and chopped parsley, to taste, and bake in a 375-degree oven until golden.

Place diced potatoes in a large, heavy bottomed pot, and cover with cold water. Set over medium-high heat, and bring to a boil. Cook for 5 to 10 minutes, until potatoes are not quite tender. Drain and immerse in cold water to stop cooking. Set aside.

Heat a large sauté pan over medium heat with canola oil until hot. Season scallops with salt and pepper, and sauté until caramelized, about 1 minute. Flip scallops and sauté other side quickly, about 30 seconds, then remove to a platter and set aside.

To the same pan, add chopped bacon and cook until crispy. Add shallots and cook for 1 minute. Stir in mushrooms and thyme, and cook for 3 to 4 minutes, until all the water cooks off. Pour in cognac to deglaze the pan, then cook off all the liquid. (Be careful, it may ignite for a second!) Stir in the butter, then add the flour, and mix to make a roux, cooking for 2 to 3 minutes. Continuing to stir, slowly pour in the lobster stock, bring to boil, and add heavy cream. Stir until sauce is smooth, then add parsley.

Preheat oven to 400 degrees. Arrange scallops and reserved potatoes in a casserole dish or individual gratin dishes. Cover with sauce, then top with Gruyere cheese and bread crumbs. Bake for about 15 minutes, until bubbling and golden brown.

Salt Cod

Michael Ball • Swanville, Waldo County

"Georgianna Fleischman, a noted cook on North Haven Island, shared this recipe with me in the mid-1960s. Babe, as she insisted she be called, got it from a seaman from Nova Scotia who asked her to make it while she was providing his room and board when he was serving as a relief crewman on the North Haven ferry. I've enjoyed making salt cod every now and then since 1967, and am grateful to George."

1 pound salt cod	1 pound salt pork
Several onions	Several potatoes
Apple cider vinegar	Butter (optional)
Sugar, to taste	Pepper (optional)

The day before you intend to serve: Remove the loose salt from the cod and put it to soak in a large volume of water. Refrigerate. Change the water when it becomes salty.

Slice the onions. Immerse them in vinegar in a small bowl, and add sugar to the marinade.

To prepare: Dice the salt pork into small cubes and rend over medium heat until golden brown. Drain, reserving the oil.

Peel (or not) the potatoes, and cut to a size suitable for fork mashing. Boil until tender, then drain and mash with a fork.

Fill a saucepan with cold water, add the soaked cod, and bring to a simmer. Cook until fish flakes.

To serve: Place the potatoes on a plate. Moisten with butter or reserved pork oil. Cover the potatoes with a layer of cod. Cover the cod with a layer of marinated onion slices. Top with a sprinkling of the crisp salt pork cubes. Serve with a side of creamed corn (canned or homemade). Accompany with extra vinegar marinade, butter, reserved pork fat, salt, and pepper.

Lobster Mac and Cheese

Helena Strang • Topsham, Sagadahoc County

"When I was growing up we rarely ate lobster because it seemed so expensive, though looking back it was cheap compared to now. Even today it still feels like a treat to get it. I put a *lot* of lobster into this dish, buying the already picked lobster at our local seafood store, but you can certainly use less. When I want to bring a dish to a party that will wow everyone, this is what I bring."

16 ounces cavatappi pasta

8 ounces fontina cheese, shredded

4 ounces sharp white cheddar cheese, shredded

6 tablespoons unsalted butter, divided

4 slices white sandwich bread

¼ cup flour

4 cups milk

8 ounces mascarpone cheese

3 tablespoons brandy or cognac

¼ teaspoon cayenne pepper

¼ teaspoon freshly grated nutmeg

Salt and freshly ground black pepper, to taste

32 ounces cooked lobster meat, cut into 1-inch chunks (meat from approximately five 1¼ pound lobsters)

3 tablespoons chives, minced

2 scallions, sliced (optional)

Preheat oven to 375 degrees. Bring a large pan of salted water to a boil over high heat. Add pasta and cook, stirring occasionally, cutting cooking time on package in half. Drain pasta and set aside.

Combine shredded cheeses in a bowl, and toss well to combine. Set aside.

Melt 2 tablespoons butter in a pan over low heat. Remove crusts from bread and discard. Tear remaining bread into tiny bits, and place in a small bowl. Add melted butter, and toss to coat breadcrumbs evenly. Set aside.

In a large saucepan or stock pot, melt remaining butter over medium heat. Add flour and cook, whisking constantly, until flour mixture is smooth and just starting to darken. Slowly whisk in milk and simmer, whisking frequently, until sauce has thickened, about 10 minutes. Remove pan from heat, and

stir in 2½ cups of the shredded cheese mixture, the mascarpone, and the brandy. Add cayenne and nutmeg. Stir until cheese is melted and incorporated, and adjust salt and pepper, as needed.

Add half of the lobster to the cheese mixture, then stir in cooked pasta. Add half of the chives, and half of the scallions, if using. Stir well to combine. Transfer mixture to a 9 x 13-inch baking dish. Sprinkle with fresh breadcrumbs and the remaining shredded cheese. Bake until golden brown and bubbly, about 30 minutes. Sprinkle remaining lobster over the top during the last 15 minutes of cooking time. Let cool for a few minutes and sprinkle with remaining chives and scallions before serving.

Lobster Crab Etouffee

Billy Doukas • Portland, Cumberland County

"In their migration through the Maritimes and into Maine, the Acadians brought with them this dish known as etouffee, meaning 'smothered,' which is usually combined with shrimp or crawfish. Our family makes a Maine variety with lobster. Although it has many ingredients this is a simple recipe to follow and is a perfect offering for a group of friends and family celebration." Billy Doukas was the winner of Maine Public's Third Annual Create It Maine Recipe Contest in 2019.

Lobster Stock:
1 gallon water
10 lobster bodies
1 large fish tail, preferably halibut
4 ounces anchovy oil

1 pound plus 6 ounces butter
4 ounces olive oil
1 large bunch celery, chopped
4 large sweet onions, coarsely chopped
4 tablespoons finely minced garlic
4 large peppers, coarsely chopped: 2 green,
    1 yellow, 1 red
⅓ cup flour, for roux
1 teaspoon black pepper
1 teaspoon cayenne pepper

1 teaspoon Aleppo pepper or
    red pepper flakes
2 teaspoons cumin
Salt, to taste
16 ounces whole peeled tomatoes
5 to 6 cups of Lobster Stock
Meat from three 1¼-pound lobsters, picked
    and coarsely chopped
1 pound crab meat
4 ounces heavy cream
4 ounces lemon juice
1 large bunch fresh parsley, finely chopped,
    for serving
1 bunch scallions, thinly sliced, for serving
Chopped chives, for serving

Prepare the Lobster Stock by boiling water, lobster bodies, fish tail, and anchovy oil, covered, for several hours. Cool and strain through a cheesecloth set into a fine mesh sieve, then set aside. This stock recipe makes more than is needed for this recipe, and can be frozen for future use.

In a heavy 6-quart pot, melt 4 ounces butter with olive oil over low heat, and add celery, onions, garlic, and chopped peppers. Stir and cook until semi-soft over low to medium heat.

In a separate small saucepan, melt 6 ounces butter on low heat, and gradually add flour, stirring, until you get a medium clay thickness of roux. Add the roux gradually to the vegetable mix, stirring over low heat. Continue to cook until vegetables are glazed and tender, stirring consistently, then add ½ teaspoon each of black pepper, cayenne, and Aleppo pepper, and 1 teaspoon of cumin. Continue cooking over low heat for 30 minutes. Add 1 cup of Lobster Stock to the vegetable mixture while stirring.

Place the whole peeled tomatoes in a bowl and cut coarsely with a knife before adding to the vegetable mixture. Add more stock, as needed, until the mixture reaches a gravy-like consistency. Add the remaining spices, tasting until you reach your desired level of heat and flavor.

In a medium saucepan, melt 6 ounces butter on low heat, and add lobster meat, seasoning lightly with salt and pepper. Cook for 2 to 3 minutes, raising the heat to medium, and then add to the vegetable mixture. In the same saucepan, melt 6 more ounces of butter and stir in the crabmeat. Add to the vegetables and lobster. Stir in the cream, cover, and simmer for another ½ hour or longer, if possible. The crabmeat will blend into the gravy-like dish, but enhance the flavor. Taste, adding lemon juice, if desired. Serve over rice or crusty grilled bread, topped generously with fresh herbs.

Gluten-Free Scallop and Lobster Mac 'n Cheese

Marnie Reed Crowell • Sunset, Hancock County

"When I was asked by fisherman Marsden Brewer to help with a recipe collection and web site, together we discovered that certain foods such as kelp, cheeses, and the combination of lobster and scallops resulted in outstanding umami/glutamate enhancing effects."

2 eggs, whisked
Two 12-ounce cans evaporated milk
12-ounce box gluten-free
    macaroni noodles
½ cup (1 stick) butter, melted
2 cups shredded mild/sharp cheddar
    cheese mix

2 cups shredded Velveeta cheese
1 heaping cup shredded Parmesan cheese,
    plus 2 tablespoons for sprinkling
2 mid-sized whole farmed scallops,
    steam shucked and gutted
Claw and tail meat from 4 lobsters, cooked
    and coarsely chopped

Preheat oven to 400 degrees. In a large bowl, combine whisked eggs and evaporated milk, and mix together until fully combined.

In a large pot, boil pasta according to package direction. When pasta is *al dente*, not mushy, drain the water and return to the pot. Pour melted butter over the pasta and stir until all the pasta is covered with the butter. Add the milk and egg mixture. Gradually add the cheddar cheese, Velveeta, and 1 cup of Parmesan to the pot and stir over medium heat until cheese is melted. Stir in the scallops and lobster meat.

Spray a 9 x 13-inch baking dish with cooking spray. Pour the macaroni and cheese, scallops, and chopped lobster bits into the baking dish. Sprinkle reserved Parmesan on the top and bake for 20 to 25 minutes. Makes 8 generous servings (freezes well)

Fried Brook Trout

1913 • *Houlton Cook Book*
Ladies of the Unitarian Society • Houlton, Aroostook County

Early fishing camp recipes are hard to come by in cookbooks. This rustic recipe for a large landing of trout is also an unusual find in an early community cookbook, as it is sourced from a man. Dr. F.F. Innis was a well-known figure in The County and "a thorough sportman and gentleman" according to some guidebooks of the area. He considered himself a fish culturist, and helped stock the rivers and lakes of the area. Dr. Innis had passed in 1906, but the inclusion of this recipe here shows the fond regard in which Houlton residents held him. —DL

Fry out 6 slices salt pork. Clean trout and wipe dry, roll in flour and lay in hot fat; salt and pepper to taste. Fry over a hot fire 10 minutes, then turn and fry 10 minutes, then turn and fry 10 minutes more. Turn off the fat. Put in ½ pound butter and fry 5 minutes, turn and fry 5 minutes more (be careful not to let the butter burn). The trout will be a beautiful brown. Butter will brown trout better than pork fat and also imparts a delicious flavor. —Submitted by Dr. F.F. Innis

Mom's Wicked Awesome Crab Cakes

Angela Lundquist • Kenduskeag, Penobscot County

"Most of our cherished family memories have taken place outside. We love camping in the summer at Hermit Island or Abol Bridge Campground. We love hiking the trails in Baxter State Park. We love Popham and Ogunquit beaches, but our favorite destination will always be Acadia National Park. We've developed a collection of family recipes that can be made in an iron skillet and cooked over an open fire. This is one of those recipes that is best enjoyed near a campfire or the beach in the great Maine outdoors!"

Nonstick olive oil spray, for pan
1 tablespoon clarified bacon grease
½ pound Stonington fresh wild caught
   crab meat
1 sleeve Ritz crackers, crushed

2 eggs
2 tablespoons fresh chives, finely chopped
1 tablespoon citrus seafood rub
Salt and pepper, to taste
Juice from one fresh lemon

Prepare a skillet with non-stick olive oil cooking spray. Preheat pan to medium/medium high. Add the clarified bacon grease and coat the bottom of the pan. In a bowl, hand mix the crab meat, cracker crumbs, eggs, chives, and seafood rub seasoning. Form into patties about ¾ inch thick. This recipe will make four large crab cakes. Place crab cakes into the hot skillet and sprinkle with salt and pepper, then sprinkle on the fresh lemon juice. Cook until each side is golden brown, about 3 to 4 minutes per side. Serve warm.

Corned Hake and Mashed Potatoes

Antonia Small • Port Clyde, Knox County

Sponsored by
Maine Food
for Thought
Tours

"This recipe comes via Mel Cushman, wife of Captain Randy Cushman of the fishing vessel *Ella Christine* of Port Clyde. When I began photographing the ground fishermen of Port Clyde in 2008, I soon met Randy, who was anxious to know if I'd had corned hake yet. I confessed I hadn't. Soon after I went to pick up my fish share from Port Clyde Fresh Catch and Glen Libby handed me hake. 'You don't happen to have a recipe for corned hake, do you Glen?' I inquired. He pulled out a recent newsletter that include this recipe. If the combination of flavors sounds perplexing, I encourage you to try it; it's become a household favorite of ours. Returning guests often inquire about whether there might be hake on the menu."

1 onion, sliced
1 cup vinegar
1 to 2 pounds hake
1 to 2 pounds potatoes

Melted butter
Salt pork (or bacon)
Salt and pepper, to taste

Place onion slices in vinegar in a bowl and cover. Let marinate for at least 2 to 4 hours (longer is better).

Place hake in a pot and salt generously. Refrigerate for 2 to 4 hours, covered with a lid so it will "corn." Take hake out of refrigerator and rinse thoroughly, cover with cold water and boil until flaky.

While hake is cooking, boil potatoes and mash them, seasoning to taste. Dice salt pork or bacon and fry until crispy.

Drain hake and serve over mashed potatoes, topped with melted butter, salt pork or bacon, and pickled onions. Baked winter squash and homemade biscuits are the perfect accompaniments to this!

Bluefish and Empanadas

Juanita Cuellar Nichols • Freeport, Cumberland County

"The bluefish were swarming in the mid 1970s when I first came to Maine and were often on the menu for the family cookouts down at the shore. We feasted on fresh summer foods as we watched the tide change. I will always remember the first time I tasted the smoky flavor of the bluefish and my surprise at how good it tasted and how happy I felt to be part of a new family and a new place.

My husband grew up in Maine in an old hipped-roof colonial in Edgecomb that was surrounded by fields, woods, and the beautiful sounds and rhythms of the Sheepscot River. My first visit to Maine, which would become my home, was to this magical place where I would marvel at the birds soaring over the trees and the miles of mudflats that were like patterns on a blanket. Here, I learned to use my fingers to pull off the skin of a clam before dipping it into hot butter and to roll out pie dough and fill it with the sweetest blueberries I had ever tasted. Here I learned to anticipate the foods of the season and the pride of growing your own tomato. And it was here in Maine that I also first experienced the joy of sitting at the shore dining on the freshly caught grilled fish wrapped in chicken wire that my husband's brother prepared, surrounded by family and the gentle sounds of the salt water from the river falling over the rocks as the tide came in.

My family was from Colombia and immigrated to New York when I was five years old. In our new country, we could still enjoy our typical dishes. All year round we could find the avocado, plantains, and cilantro we needed at the Safeway. My father made empanadas, and my mother stewed lentils with cumin and oregano and made yellow rice with turmeric. In the city, we also ate apples in the spring, strawberries in the winter and frozen fish on Friday nights. And like our neighbors, we ate hamburgers and hot dogs in the summer and roast turkey stuffed with white bread in the fall. And while eating Colombian dishes was always special, it wasn't long before our weekly menus included spaghetti with meat sauce, coq au vin, baked ham, macaroni and cheese and Mrs. Smith's apple pie.

My husband and I raised our three daughters in Maine, spending many summer days at family cookouts, and in the winter, during the holidays, enjoying the traditional dishes from Colombia that we looked forward to all year long. We still gather outside in the summer for birthday celebrations in July with strawberry shortcake, and in August, with blueberry pie. And on Christmas Eve, all three daughters, now with their own families living in Maine, work together in the kitchen to make the empanadas, rolling out the cornmeal dough, filling the little circles with the meat and potato filling, and frying them in hot oil until they are golden and crispy. A little taste of Colombia on a dark winter night in Maine—what a treat."

See Juanita's **Empanadas Colombianas** recipe on page 156.

New England Portuguese Clam Boil

Linda Perry • Topsham, Sagadahoc County

"Growing up in Southern Massachusetts with Portuguese heritage, one of my favorite summer meals was the New England Portuguese Clam Boil. It brings back memories of wonderful family gatherings and many 4th of July meals. When I moved to Maine and mentioned it, no one knew what I was talking about. I told a friend that I was putting the recipe in my column in *The Cryer*. She said what most of my other new Maine friends have said, 'You mean a Clam Bake, right?' Confirmation that I needed to share this easy and very flavorful recipe! I usually reserve some broth and add extra clams, potatoes, onions, and linguica sausage to make a delicious clam chowder the next day. The amounts for this recipe are completely dependent on how many people you're serving! Adjust amounts so that each person gets some of everything they want."

Soft shell steamer clams, approximately
   1 to 1½ pounds per person
Potatoes, cut in half or large chunks
Onions, cut in quarters
Hot dogs

Chourico or linguica sausage,
   cut into 4-inch pieces
Pork breakfast sausage, crumbled
Corn on the cob, shucked and cut
   crosswise in half

In a large bowl, soak clams for several hours in ice water sprinkled with cornmeal. This will clean them. While they're soaking, prepare the rest of your ingredients.

Place potatoes and onions in a very large pot and cover with water. Simmer for about 20 minutes, until potatoes are almost tender. Add the remaining ingredients, cover, and simmer another 15 minutes until the hot dogs split and the clams are open. Discard any clams that don't open.

Ladle out the clams, vegetables, and sausage and serve with melted butter and some of the clam broth. Don't forget to save some of the broth for tomorrow's chowder!

New Year's Eve Cioppino

Louis Fontaine • Sidney, Kennebec County

"I've been making this soup for New Year's Eve for over 20 years, and it has never failed to please a table surrounded by family and friends. You can use any seafood in the soup, but the secret to a delicious flavor is to combine at least one mollusk with one crustacean. I usually use a combination of lobster in the shell, shrimp or crabmeat, scallops and mussels. Accompany with sourdough bread and plenty of napkins. This dish is messy and takes a long time to eat but your hands are busier than your mouth, so there's plenty of time for conversation."

Cooked lobster, in the shell
  (1 for every two people)
2 tablespoons olive oil
2 onions
1 clove garlic
3 cups crushed tomatoes
2 cups V-8 juice
1 cup dry white wine

1 teaspoon dried basil
½ teaspoon dried oregano
½ teaspoon dried rosemary
1 pound chopped spinach
1 pound raw shrimp
1 pound scallops
2 pounds mussels
Salt and pepper, to taste

Dismember cooked lobsters and crack shells for easy eating. Remove tail meat and slice into 1-inch pieces and set aside.

In a large pot or Dutch oven, warm the olive oil over medium heat. Chop the onions, add to the pot, and sauté. Crush the garlic clove and add to the onions. When onions are soft, add the tomatoes, V-8 juice, and wine. Add the spices and bring to a boil. Lower heat so the soup is boiling gently and cook for 15 minutes. Add the spinach, shrimp, and scallops, and boil gently for 10 minutes. Taste and adjust seasonings, adding salt and pepper, if desired.

Add lobster claws, knuckles, legs and tail pieces. Add the mussels. Soup is done when the mussels open.

Seafood Pie by Marilynn Ames

Judith Ames Legendre • South Portland, Cumberland County

"My mother, Marilynn Ames, worked on the *Women's Society of Christian Service Cookbook 1970* with her friends from the United Methodist Church of Auburn, Helen Boulay, Theo Parker, Rita Dean and Mae McFadden. My mother and father, Byron Ames, typed the recipes on a typewriter in our kitchen. Most of the people that contributed to this cookbook have passed on, including my parents. I honestly don't remember my mother making this pie; my father probably did. He was a better cook. I have made the pie numerous times over the years, it is always yummy and I still have the cookbook!"

½ cup mayonnaise
2 tablespoons flour
2 eggs, beaten
½ cup dry white wine
1 cup fresh crab meat

1 cup cleaned raw shrimp
½ cup shredded Swiss cheese
⅓ cup sliced green onion
Unbaked pastry shell

Combine mayonnaise, flour, eggs, and wine. Mix until well blended. Stir in crab meat, shrimp, cheese, and onion. Pour into pastry shell. Bake at 350 for 45 to 60 minutes, until done. Makes 6 servings.

Marinated Fried Smelts

Krista Kern Desjarlais • New Gloucester, Cumberland County

"I grew up eating this recipe and the pickled version below for lunch with my mother. It's a recipe that she prepared in Sweden, but it's applicable here as we have smelt, too! My father loved the warm fried version with potatoes, but he was never a fan of the pickled, so she and I ate them with buttered dark bread and hard boiled eggs. It's a food memory I'll cherish forever. Now that they have lived in Maine for almost twenty years, this recipe has evolved to use local smelts and herbs my mom freezes from her garden over the winter, like dill and parsley and tarragon, as a frugal way to preserve the green soft herbs after a long winter, and to eat with freshly caught smelt in the early spring before the ground can be planted again."

2 pounds smelts

Salt and pepper, to taste

4 tablespoons flour

Oil for frying

Clean the smelts. Cut off the fins. Wash and dry well. Sprinkle with salt and pepper. Dip the fish in flour. Fry on both sides in hot oil until golden brown. Let cool on rack to keep them crisp. Serve with fried potatoes and pumpernickel bread.

Marinated Fish

1 cup water

6 bay leaves

8 peppercorns

1 teaspoon salt

1 carrot, thinly sliced

1 cup sliced onion

1 cup vinegar

Up to 3 pounds fried smelt

Bring the water to a boil. Add the spices, carrots, and onions. Simmer until carrots are soft and onions are transparent. Add the vinegar. Cool. When it is lukewarm, pour the marinade over the fried fish. Chill overnight before serving.

Lobster a'la Newburg

Carol Walsh • Windham, Cumberland County

"A cousin of my father's, whose name was Sunie Day Clifford, had a homestead on Clifford Road in North Edgecomb. She was born in the 1880s and never married. She contributed this recipe to the 1903 North Edgecomb cookbook, sponsored by the Ladies of the Congregational Society. Back then lobster was so cheap, not recognized as a delicacy, but hearty for this recipe. An elder cousin of mine, who knew I loved to cook, gave me the cookbook, which is in very delicate condition. We also have a family picture where Sunie Day Clifford is holding me while we celebrate my 1st birthday in 1957."

¼ cup butter
2 pounds cooked lobster meat, picked
½ teaspoon salt
Four grains cayenne

1 tablespoon sherry
1 tablespoon brandy
⅓ cup cream
2 egg yolks, slightly beaten

Melt butter. Add lobster cut in small pieces and cook three minutes. Add seasoning and wine, and cook one minute. Then add cream and beaten egg yolks. Stir until thickened.

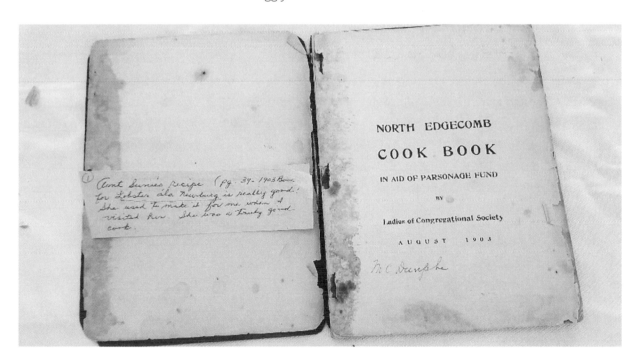

Shrimp Wiggle from the 1940s

Lisa Millimet • Camden, Knox County

"This recipe is from my grandmother Lulu Augusta Gray Gingras's recipe box; brown with age, the index cards now sepia, its recipes retro, to say the least—many of them centered on seafood, reflecting her connection to the great Gulf of Maine in Massachusetts and here. She did not come from Maine, but she had a strong connection here, visiting a friend in Damariscotta every year, driving up in her Nash Rambler with the seat that turned into a bed. She was New England through and through, served salmon and peas on the fourth of July and Finnan Haddie that reflected her Scottish heritage, whether we wanted it or not. And she loved Maine. She was the first woman in her home town to get her license, notoriously doing so to chase down my devastatingly handsome and French grandfather. I'm thankful she was so successful!

Driving around Maine and Massachusetts in the beginning of the 20th century was certainly a pioneering move, as was her relationship to the typewriter, which enabled her, with only an 8th grade education, to support her family after her father's death, an inroad to her long and committed work life. Some of the recipes are typed, but mostly they are written in her disciplined and Victorian script, which, annually, she would bribe me to practice with a $5 bill. I still have one. Born in 1886, she was always dressed beautifully, an ever-present blue costume jewelry pin on her blouse or jacket, always with gloves and a netted hat, and a hanky that smelled of flowers in the purse with the snapping clasp I can still hear. She was the rock and center of our family, guiding her daughters and then grandsons to expertise in music—one of them became a professional musician—and she made me the grandmother I am today. It was all because of her, my Nana, who always said it was her brothers who got the looks but she got the spunk and the unwavering focus on family, never missing a beat even after her husband's death. She continues to speak to me from these recipes, ones I will lovingly hand down to my grandchildren."

1 tablespoon butter
1 onion, minced fine
½ can tomato soup

½ cup milk
One can small Gulf shrimp

Melt butter in a small saucepan and sauté the onions. When onion is cooked, add remaining ingredients. Stir all together, heat well, and serve on crackers or pieces of toast.

Leah's Fried Rice with Lobster

Laura McCandlish • Brunswick, Cumberland County

"In the midst of lobster recipe testing, my Chinese friend Leah (Ya) Zuo brought her fried rice to a dinner party. Leah is a professor of Chinese History and Asian Studies who hails from Wuhan, China and lives here in Brunswick. As I dallied in the kitchen, my husband brilliantly suggested topping her rice with sautéed lobster. Thus, a great dish was born."

2 large eggs, beaten

1 teaspoon cornstarch, dissolved into 2 tablespoons water

4 tablespoons grape-seed or peanut oil

1 medium onion, diced

1 cup carrots, cubed and parboiled for 5 minutes

1 cup corn, freshly cut from cob, drained from can or defrosted

1 cup peas, defrosted or freshly shelled

1 tablespoon garlic, minced

1 tablespoon ginger, minced

4 cups cooked jasmine rice, cooled

Ground cumin or Moroccan seasoning blend, to taste

Minced Chinese pickled vegetable (available at Asian market) or kimchee, to taste (optional)

¼ cup minced scallions, green parts only

¼ cup cilantro, chopped

2 tablespoons butter

½ pound shelled lobster meat, chopped

½ teaspoon fish sauce

1 tablespoon soy sauce

A quarter lemon or lime

2 tablespoons Thai basil, chopped

Beat eggs with cornstarch-water solution. Add 1 tablespoon oil to wok or skillet and turn heat to high, covering hot surface with oil. Add egg and cook, folding over into an omelet, until done. Transfer with a spatula to a plate and cut into bite-size pieces.

Put a second tablespoon of oil in wok and return heat to high. Add onion and sauté about 10 minutes, until softened and beginning to brown. Add parboiled carrots, corn, and peas to skillet and stir-fry with onions until hot, about 1 or 2 minutes. Transfer cooked vegetables to a bowl.

Put remaining oil in skillet, followed by garlic and ginger. Stir-fry briefly, then add the rice, bit by bit, breaking up any clumps.

Return vegetables and egg pieces to skillet and stir to integrate. Season with Moroccan spices or cumin, and if available, minced Chinese preserved vegetable (mustard plant stem) or kimchee to taste. Add salt and pepper if necessary. Remove from heat and stir in scallions and cilantro.

In a separate pan, melt butter and add shelled lobster meat, heating until fully cooked. Season with fish sauce, soy sauce, a spritz of lemon or lime, and Thai basil. Incorporate with fried rice and serve. Makes 6 servings.

Photo: Sister Frances Carr was born in Lewiston in 1927. She was placed among the Shakers at the age of 10 years and as a young adult became the head cook of the community.

New England Boiled Dinner

Ann Sloatman • South Portland, Cumberland County

"The New England Boiled Dinner is a classic and a favorite of my mother, Beverly Merchant Sloatman. At 91 she is still enjoying it! Our family's version first appeared in the cookbook *Maine Coastal Cooking,* which was printed by my grandfather Sidney L. Cullen, of the *Courier Gazette,* with cover artwork created by my grandmother, Flora Gray Cullen. It's a collection of very old Maine recipes reprinted in 1963 and 1979 with some updates. The Courier Gazette also published *Maine's Jubilee Cookbook* for Maine's Sesquicentennial. This was used extensively by our family and had many local favorite recipes from the Rockland area."

4 pounds corned beef brisket
6 medium beets, peeled and trimmed
1 yellow turnip, peeled and trimmed
6 medium carrots, peeled

6 medium potatoes, peeled
(or not, as desired)
1 small cabbage, quartered
6 medium parsnips, peeled
6 onions, peeled (optional)

Cover meat with cold water, bring to a boil, then lower the heat and allow meat to simmer gently for 3 hours or until tender. In the meantime, boil beets separately, to serve with the corned beef.

About 1 hour before the meat is done, skim it free of excess fat, add turnips, carrots, potatoes, and quartered cabbage. Continue cooking and add parsnips during the last 20 minutes of cooking. Continue cooking until all is tender. Onions may be added to the vegetables, if you desire.

Serve sliced meat on a platter, with vegetables. Pass chili sauce, mustard, mustard pickles, horseradish, and vinegar.

Maine Party Chicken

Jane C. Legard • Sebasco Estates, Sagadahoc County

"This chicken recipe is rightly named. Could anything be easier? We got this recipe from my husband's mother. Her friend who lived three cottages down on Water Cove tried this as a new recipe for a group of friends. Nana couldn't believe she would dare to try something new when having people for dinner. Then when dinner was served she was both surprised and delighted. The recipe was a big hit! Now we live on Water Cove and the two of us have become a four-generation family of 16 and still growing. We celebrate every holiday together and have a summer family gathering at the Lake House, with those who like camping bringing a tent. We all share in the menu planning and in the cooking, and everyone loves to have Maine Party Chicken on the menu. This recipe is easy to multiply. If you are serving men, they are sure to be back for seconds—better make that 6 chicken breasts!"

4 large whole boned chicken breasts

8 slices bacon

1 package or small jar dried beef

1 can cream of mushroom soup, undiluted

½ pint sour cream

Divide each chicken breast in half, giving you 8 servings. Wrap each half with a piece of bacon. Cover the bottom of a buttered shallow 9 x 13-inch baking pan with thin slices dried beef. Arrange chicken breasts on dried beef. Mix soup and sour cream together. Spoon over all. Cover pan, refrigerate 24 hours.

Bring to room temperature while preheating oven to 275 degrees. Bake uncovered for 3 hours. This long, slow cooking is fine when guests are expected.

Lunchtime Gloop

Stephen King • Bangor, Penobscot County

In addition to his bestselling books, author Stephen King is also renowned for the following recipe: "My kids love this. I only make it when my wife, Tabby, isn't home. She won't eat it, in fact doesn't even like to look at it."

- 2 cans Franco American Spaghetti
  (without meatballs)
- 1 pound cheap, greasy hamburger

Brown hamburg in large skillet. Add Franco American Spaghetti and cook until heated through. Do not drain hamburg, or it won't be properly greasy. Burn on pan if you want—that will only improve the flavor. Serve with buttered Wonder Bread.

Grandma Nemitz's Turkey Stuffing

Bill Nemitz • Buxton, Cumberland County

Journalist Bill Nemitz has written his award-winning column for the *Portland Press Herald* since 1995. Though he grew up in Massachusetts, Bill and his wife raised their five children in Maine.

- Turkey's liver, giblets, gizzard, neck,
  and heart
- 1 pound pork cutlets
- 1 large white onion
- 3 stalks celery
- 1 teaspoon each salt and pepper

- 1 teaspoon each dried parsley,
  rosemary, and thyme
- 2 eggs
- 1½ loaves stuffing bread, torn into pieces
  and left out so it gets stale

In a large pot, cover giblets, gizzard, neck, and heart with water. Bring to a boil, then simmer 1 hour. Remove innards from broth and pick meat off bones. Set meat aside, and be sure to save the broth.

While broth is simmering, sauté turkey liver and pork cutlets, then put aside.

Combine all meat, along with the onion, celery, and seasonings, and run through a meat grinder. Beat eggs and mix into ground meat.

Add meat mixture ("wet stuff"), a handful at a time, to bread. Use reserved broth to moisten, as needed.

Stuff turkey. Bake leftover stuffing in separate casserole pan.

Grandmother Hamden's Chicken Pie

Jessie Crockett Estêvão • Dixfield, Oxford County

"This recipe comes from my great grandmother Ethel Hamden Crockett, whose family was from the Dixfield area and lived as farmers and lumberjacks. The photo is from a different branch of our family: The seated woman Elva Duplisea Nadeau, is one of many strong and determined women in our family tree. Elva wanted to become a teacher, but her father arranged for her to marry the man in the photo, William Nadeau. She spent her wedding day crying because she didn't want to leave high school at age 16 to get married. The story has a happy ending, however. After the three children Francis, Geneva, and Laurence (the baby on her lap and my grandfather) were born, she left William. While testing the pool of men for a suitable partner she worked at Bath Iron Works as a welder during World War II before enlisting as a WAC to become a nurse. She eventually married a wonderful man named Gordon. When I knew her, she never walked when she could run, and she never spoke when she could sing."

Cook chicken, first seasoning with salt and placing 2 or 3 stalks of celery and an onion inside. Cool and cut in rather small pieces, meat only, no skin or giblets. One chicken should make 1½ quart casserole-size pie.

Boil down broth to make a flavorful stock. If done the day before and refrigerated, it will be a jelly; when ready to put pie together heat broth and use hot.

Break Boston Commons crackers into rather large pieces. Place layer in casserole, top with layer of chicken pieces. Dot with butter, and sprinkle with salt unless broth is quite salty. Pour in part of broth, hot, and add a bit of cream. Repeat layers of crackers and chicken, pour in rest of broth, or just enough so it shows between meat pieces. It should stand awhile for crackers to soak or it may be too dry. If liquid is too low after soaking, add more cream and a bit of water.

Extra shortening added to your regular biscuit recipe will make a good short crust. Mixing with cream instead of milk helps too.

Roll biscuit dough quite thin, make large hole in center of crust. Bake 45 minutes at 400 degrees. If it seems to be getting too brown, place a piece of brown paper on top for part of baking time. Lift small piece of crust from center to test for doneness.

Hushweh (Chicken and Rice)

Dr. Eric Hooglund • Waterville, Kennebec County

"Hushweh is a traditional Lebanese stuffing served at Sunday dinner after Mass. It was primarily stuffed into roasting chickens, but over the years it has become a popular side and main dish. It can stretch a long way to feed a big crowd. The chicken stock, cinnamon, and allspice gives this dish its distinctive Lebanese flavor and the meat makes it a special dish for family gatherings. The recipe can be adapted based on budget with less or more meat, depending. This recipe came from Waterville and was published in the *St. Joseph Maronite Catholic Church Traditional Lebanese Cookbook, 75th Anniversary Edition*, revised and edited by Dame Marie Fefa Deeb and the St. Joseph Rosary Sodality in September 2015. The cookbook was first published in the late 1970s to commemorate the 50th Anniversary of the Sodality. Many of its recipes can be sampled during St. Joseph's Public Church Suppers and at its annual 'Hafli' Lebanese Festival.

Many don't realize that by 1910, the Waterville Lebanese community was the largest Arabic-speaking community in the State of Maine, as well as one of the largest in the United States. They came to the U.S. between 1880-1920, when Lebanon was part of the Turkish Ottoman Empire, during the phase of U.S. open immigration. The immigrants established St. Joseph's Parish in 1924; however, the present Church building—on Front and Appleton Street along the Kennebec River in Waterville—was completed in 1951. As of 2020, it's the only Maronite Catholic Church in the State of Maine."

1 pound ground beef or lamb
¼ cup Mediterranean pine nuts
Cinnamon and allspice, to taste
Salt and pepper, to taste

1 cup long or medium grain white rice
1 cup water
1 cup chicken broth
2 to 3 cups cooked chicken, slices or pieces

Brown ground meat, pine nuts, and seasonings in a large saucepan. Wash and drain rice. Add rice to meat mixture. Do not stir, but use a spatula to lift rice to mix and coat. When rice reaches a "dry" appearance, add water and broth. Bring to boil, cover and reduce heat to low, and cook until rice is done. Add cooked chicken. Mound on a platter and serve with Lebanese bread and salad.

Braised Lamb Shoulder

Sam Hayward • Bowdoinham, Sagadahoc County

Award-winning chef and co-owner of Portland's acclaimed Fore Street restaurant, Sam Hayward was an early pioneer of the farm-to-table restaurant movement in Maine. A tireless advocate for Maine agriculture and local ingredients, Hayward has maintained a three-decade relationship with Lee Straw of Straw Farm in Newcastle, and Straw's island-raised lamb has become a signature dish on the Fore Street menu. A version of this recipe appeared in the *New York Times* in 2004, in an article celebrating Hayward's approach to braising local lamb, written by Nancy Harmon Jenkins. In 2008, Hayward wrote further about island lamb for the magazine *The Art of Eating*.

1 boned lamb shoulder, 3½-4½ pounds, trimmed	1 medium carrot, coarsely chopped
3 tablespoons coarse sea salt	1 medium yellow onion or 2 large shallots, trimmed and chopped
Zest of 1 lemon, removed in strips	1 celery stalk, coarsely chopped
¼ cup chopped flat-leaf parsley	1 cup dry red wine
4 garlic cloves, peeled	2 cups beef or chicken stock
1½ tablespoons black peppercorns	Salt and freshly ground black pepper
1 to 2 tablespoons extra virgin olive oil	3 to 4 small white turnips (optional)

Rub lamb thoroughly with salt. Set aside. Mince together lemon zest, parsley, and 2 garlic cloves. Grind peppercorns in coarsest setting of grinder. Mix peppercorns and minced mixture, and rub over lamb. Place lamb in covered container and refrigerate overnight.

Preheat oven to 350 degrees. Discard any liquid from container holding lamb. Coarsely chop remaining garlic cloves.

Place large Dutch oven or heavy roasting pan over medium-high heat. Add oil, then brown lamb on all sides. Transfer lamb to a plate. Add carrot, onion, celery, and chopped garlic to the pan, and reduce heat to medium-low. Sauté until the vegetables are tender, then return lamb to the pan. Add wine and stock, and bring to a bare simmer.

Cover pan loosely with foil and put in oven. After 15 minutes, reduce heat to 250 degrees. Braise until lamb falls apart easily when a fork is inserted and gently twisted, 3 to 5 hours, depending on the age of the lamb and the size of the shoulder. Check pan occasionally during cooking, adding hot water if the pan begins to dry.

When meat is done, transfer to a platter and cover with foil. Strain cooking liquid, and set aside to let fat rise. Skim off the fat, and reserve, if desired, for later use. Reheat skimmed gravy and season to taste with salt and pepper. Slice lamb and serve with gravy. If desired, add small white turnips, peeled and cut into chunks, to the pan for the final 25 minutes of cooking, and serve alongside. Makes 6 servings.

Thai Fiddlehead Stir Fry

Laurie Reynolds • Freeport, Cumberland County

"When I was growing up in Fryeburg in the 1970s, I spent a lot of time in the kitchen of my neighbor, Sally Walker. Raised in Thailand in a Chinese family, Sally moved to the United States when she married Frederick Frye Walker, whose family founded Fryeburg. When she arrived in Maine, Sally only knew how to cook Asian food, so my mom gave her lessons in American dishes, while Sally shared recipes for Thai stir fries. This one, made with seasonal fiddleheads, was one of my favorites."

½ pound beef sirloin, frozen
¼ cup soy sauce
1 tablespoon minced ginger
1 tablespoon minced garlic
½ teaspoon salt
½ teaspoon pepper
Flour, for dredging
4 to 6 slices bacon

1 cup onion, thinly sliced
1 cup fiddleheads, trimmed and blanched
1 cup string beans, trimmed
1 cup chopped bok choy
1 cup sliced celery
1 cup thinly sliced carrots
1 to 2 tablespoons oyster sauce

Take beef out of freezer and begin to thaw. When meat is barely thawed, slice thinly into strips. In a medium bowl, mix together soy sauce, ginger, garlic, salt, and pepper. Add beef and marinate for 1 hour. Before cooking, dredge each slice of beef in flour.

Place bacon slices in a wok set over high heat, and cook until crispy. Remove bacon from wok and drain on paper towel. When cool enough to handle, crumble bacon into a small bowl.

Bring bacon fat to a shimmer in the wok, and fry onion in the fat. Add the beef and stir fry. Remove meat, then stir fry vegetables in the fat. When vegetables are tender, add oyster sauce, starting with 1 tablespoon and adding more sauce to taste. Return cooked beef to the mixture and serve with rice.

Sicard Family Tourtiere

Michele Pfannenstiel • Cumberland, Cumberland County

"My mom does not have fond memories of my Memere's cooking, but this recipe is apparently one of the few things Memere made well. We eat this on New Year's day as a family. There have been variations made based on food preferences (for homemade versus store-bought pastry, grinding the meat ourselves first) and food allergies. It has been modified a bit from the vague directions handed down to account for actual measurements and temperatures. It makes plenty for a large family with leftovers for breakfast before everyone gets their day going on January 2nd."

1½ pounds white potatoes, peeled and cubed
4 tablespoons butter, lard, or tallow
1 large onion, chopped
1 pound ground pork
1½ pounds ground beef
1 slice stale bread

1 tablespoon cinnamon
1 tablespoon allspice
½ tablespoon clove
½ tablespoon salt
Pepper, to taste

Pastry for 2 double-crust pies

Steam, boil, or microwave potatoes until cooked and soft.

Melt fat in a large skillet, making sure to have the cover nearby. Add onions, and sauté until translucent. Add pork to the skillet, and cook until fat starts to render and the pork starts to cook through. Add beef and mix thoroughly. Cook on low until meat reaches 165 degrees. Crumble bread into mixture, then add cinnamon, allspice, cloves, salt, and pepper. Thoroughly mix, then cover and let simmer on low for 30 minutes.

Preheat oven to 425 degrees. Remove meat mixture from heat and mash in cooked potatoes. Place meat and potato mixture into prepared bottom crusts. Smooth out mixture and cover with top crusts. Place in oven for 5 minutes, then reduce temperature to 325 degrees, and cook for 45 minutes or until crust is golden. Serve hot with cranberry sauce for New Year's brunch!

Chicken Cuniglio Style ("Mock Rabbit")

Elizabeth DeWolfe • Alfred, York County

"My paternal grandfather, William Louis Ferrigno, was born on Hurricane Island in 1903, the son of Italian immigrants working in the stone-carving industry. As the industry collapsed, his family moved south, settling in Rhode Island. My grandfather and grandmother, Susie Nigrelli Ferrigno, honeymooned in Old Orchard Beach in the 1920s. My parents brought us to Maine lakes for vacations in the early 1970s and when I married in 1987, my husband and I settled in Maine, first in Auburn, then Saco, and finally Alfred. This recipe weaves together the heritage of Italian immigrants who found work in Maine and Italian-Americans whose history continued to intersect with this state. I have cooked this for years. My first cooking lessons came from  my Nana Ferrigno. As a young girl, I sat in a nook by my Nana's stove and watched her cook. I never saw her look at a recipe. After she passed, I ended up with her handwritten recipes. They very much reflect cooking by sight and taste rather than precise measurement. My favorite part is her commentary. On this recipe for Chicken Cuniglio Style, Nana notes on a piece of masking tape: 'This is the one I use. It's perfect.' Yes, it is."

5 pounds chicken, cut into pieces
1 bottle Spanish green olives, pits removed
½ box raisins
½ cup capers
4 cloves garlic
2 tablespoons olive oil

¼ cup wine vinegar
Four 8-ounce cans tomato sauce + 1 can water (or two 15-ounce cans tomato sauce with ½ can water)
1 rounded tablespoon sugar

Wash and pat dry chicken; set aside.

Prepare Spanish olives, removing pits. Rinse olives to remove extra salt, cut in half. Rinse raisins 2 or 3 times. Rinse capers 2 or 3 times. Slice garlic cloves.

In a large Dutch oven or heavy pan, brown chicken in a little oil until slightly golden, then remove chicken and set aside. Remove some of the oil (about 1 tablespoon) and put it in a saucepan.

Add to the large pan the cans of tomato sauce and the water. Add 1 rounded tablespoon of sugar and let this simmer for ½ hour. Add chicken pieces. Cook about 20 minutes.

In the meantime, in the saucepan fry the garlic in the reserved oil from the chicken until golden. Add the olives, raisins, and capers. Stir about 5 minutes. Add the wine vinegar; mix well. Cook 5 more minutes. Pour all these "goodies" over the chicken and continue to cook about 20 minutes, checking for doneness.

Delicious over rice or pasta. This tastes even better on day two, and the recipe freezes really well. Recipe can be halved.

Dynamites

June LaCombe • Pownal, Cumberland County

"My father Vaughn A. LaCombe's first job after graduating from the University of Maine in Orono with a master's degree in Educational Administration was as the principal of Patten Academy. He thought Patten, on the edge of the North Woods, was a great place for an avid fisherman. Living there in 1955 in a rented farmhouse in the midst of potato fields was an adventure for all of us. My father's mother, Edna Hapworth LaCombe, who we called 'Grammie,' sent this recipe to my mother when we lived in Patten on the Happy Corner Road. Grammie's husband, Victor, sold Dynamites at local fairs during the Depression. There comes a time in the fall when I crave this hot spicy meal. We often serve them at our family gatherings—we even served it at my sister's wedding—and it became part of the title of our family cookbook called 'Dynamites and Lobster on the Rocks.' Dynamites are good made with either lamb or beef.

My grandmother's recipe started: 'This cool weather reminds me of Dynamites, so I will give you the recipe you asked for, will give it to you as it was given to me. No exact amounts....'"

Meatballs:
Hamburg (ground beef or lamb)
Onion
Garlic
Salt, pepper
Italian cheese (grated Parmesan
    or Romano)
Breadcrumbs
Eggs
Rosemary leaves

Pepper Sauce:
2 pounds sweet peppers
2 bunches celery

1 pound onions
1 teaspoon red pepper flakes
Salt
½ cup olive oil
Water (just enough to cook it)

Red Sauce:
1 can tomato paste
Salt and pepper
Red pepper, to taste
Water

Grated Italian cheese

Brown meatballs in butter or olive oil and add to cooked vegetables to simmer. Fill steamed Italian rolls (or hotdog rolls) with meatballs and vegetable mixture. Top with hot sauce and grated cheese.

Acadian Chicken Stew

Matt Pelletier • Eagle Lake, Aroostook County

"This comes from my grandmother, Exelia (Saucier) Pelletier. She grew up in Eagle Lake and Soldier Pond. After World War II she and my grandfather, Raoul Pelletier, moved to Connecticut. When my parents married they moved to Maine, and whenever we went to visit Grandma and Grandpa, this meal, with ployes, was always on the table. It tastes like a hug from my grandparents."

8 pieces chicken, combination thighs and legs, bone in

2 medium onions, sliced

4 potatoes, peeled and quartered

2 to 4 carrots, peeled and cut into rounds (optional)

2 to 4 stalks celery, chopped (optional)

Salt and pepper, to taste

2 tablespoons summer savory (or more, to taste)

2 cups flour

2 teaspoons baking powder

Pinch salt

1½ cups milk (enough to make thick dough)

Gravy Master seasoning, to taste

Preheat oven to 350 degrees. Grease the sides and bottom of a Dutch oven. Place half of the cut chicken pieces on bottom of Dutch oven. Layer with half of the cut onions and potatoes, and half of the optional carrots and celery, if using. Salt and pepper to taste. Sprinkle liberally with summer savory.

Make a simple biscuit dough. Combine flour, baking powder and salt. Add milk to make a thick dough, starting with 1 cup and adding more, if necessary. Mix lightly, and do not over mix or the biscuits will be hard. Divide dough in half, reserving one half. Drop dollops of the dough onto the other ingredients in the Dutch oven.

Add another layer of all ingredients, finishing with the last layer of biscuit dough. Add enough water, seasoned with Gravy Master, to just cover the contents of the pot.

Cover pot and place in the oven for at least 2 hours. Check the doneness of the potatoes to see when it is ready. Bake with the cover off for the last 15 minutes for added browning.

Macoranadi

Spiros Droggitis • Biddeford, York County

"My father, Charlie Droggitis, and his brother, Archie, not wanting to go into their father's shoe shine/shoe repair business, started Charles' Cafe in Biddeford in 1935, where they served sandwiches and beer to Biddeford's mill workers and other patrons. After Uncle Archie brought back a 35-foot mahogany bar purchased at an auction in Boston, the restaurant became The Wonder Bar Steak House, a premier restaurant in southern Maine. Uncles Alex and Jimmy later joined the family business, which the four Droggitis brothers operated until closing in 1981 and selling in March 1982.

There were few opportunities for my mother, brother, sister, and I to sit down at the dinner table for a family dinner with our father, since he was typically at The Wonder Bar serving dinners to others. However, Sunday afternoons for either a late lunch after church or an early dinner before Dad had to go back to work offered such an opportunity. One of the dishes our Mother made was Macoranadi, a simple pasta dish with beef short ribs in a tomato/cinnamon sauce. I'm not sure if this is a Greek dish, or one influenced by my mother's father, who was a Greek immigrant to this country but of Italian descent. My wife Ottilie and I continued the tradition of Sunday family dinners with our five children. Macoranadi was one of our go-to meals."

2 pounds beef short ribs	8-ounce can tomato sauce
3 large onions	1 cinnamon stick
6-ounce can tomato paste	1 pound ziti

Cover short ribs with water. Bring to a boil. While meat is cooking, cut onions. Place in a large pot with tomato paste, tomato sauce, and cinnamon stick. Bring to a boil and simmer for 1 to 2 hours. Cook ziti. Take beef out of water, place in ziti with sauce, and let set for 15 minutes before serving.

Maine Spuds Going Dutch! (Boerenkoolstamppot)

Henny van der Scheer • New Gloucester, Cumberland County

"I grew up on a farm in the Netherlands, moved to the USA in 1992, and have been living in Maine since 2006. On our farm in the Netherlands, we grew potatoes and sugar beets. The potato harvesting season was very similar to what it was here in Maine. In the fall we would have a break from school to help out with harvesting. Potatoes have always been a big staple in the Dutch kitchen. The main course of my childhood was potatoes, meat, and some sort of vegetable. I grew up with 'Boerenkoolstamppot,' and my American husband and I make this this quintessential Dutch winter dish at least once a month. It is exceptionally good with home-grown Maine potatoes and kale from the garden!"

3 pounds potatoes	1 pound smoked sausage or kielbasa
1 pound curly kale	½ cup milk
1 teaspoon salt	2 tablespoons butter
1 large white onion	3 tablespoons sweet chili sauce
1 large red pepper	Pinch ground pepper

Peel and halve potatoes. Clean, trim, and cut kale into small pieces. Add the potatoes, kale, and a pinch of salt and just enough water to cover all in a large pot. Cover and boil gently for about 25 minutes, until potatoes are fully cooked.

Dice onion and red pepper. Slice sausage. Sauté onion and pepper in a large skillet for about 10 minutes. Add sausage and sauté for another 5 minutes.

Drain the potatoes and kale. Add milk and butter and mash with a potato masher or mixer. Add sweet chili sauce. Add in onion-pepper-sausage mixture. Add salt and pepper to taste and serve.

French Cretons

Chad Conley • Portland, Cumberland County

"I made this with my grandmother, Irene Dodge, around 2007, and it's a cherished family food memory. Irene was born to a French-speaking family in Lille, Maine. This recipe was passed down from her family and shared every year around the holidays. She'd make a container for everyone in the family to take home. On the recipe card, where it lists number of servings, she just wrote 'large.'"

5 pounds pork shoulder
2½ pounds beef chuck roast
15 soda crackers, crushed
2½ medium onions, chopped
½ teaspoon pepper

1½ teaspoons salt
½ teaspoon sugar
1 teaspoon ground cinnamon
½ teaspoon ground cloves

In a large pot, cook pork shoulder and chuck roast together in water for 1 to 1½ hours. Cool, strip meat and fat from bone, and put meat through a meat grinder. Add crushed soda crackers and onion, then strain juices and remove excess fat. Mix in a pan altogether, with enough juices to make a smooth thickness (like thick frosting). Add pepper and salt and cook for 30 minutes, stirring often. Then add sugar, cinnamon and clove, adding more to taste, if desired. Serve on toast.

Grammie Ham (Smothered Smoked Picnic Shoulder)

Lauren Webster • Peaks Island, Cumberland County

"This recipe comes from the farm country of Oxford and Franklin Counties. My grandmother had eight children and helped run a dairy farm. This modified pulled pork is a family tradition—it's not the prettiest dish, but it's an amazingly tasty one!"

Smoked picnic shoulder ham
Yellow mustard
Brown sugar
Whole milk

Submerge the picnic shoulder ham in water and boil steadily for 2 to 3 hours. Slice off excess fat and rind.

Place boiled ham in a large baking dish with a cover, smother in yellow mustard, "bread" (sprinkle) with brown sugar, and submerge as much as allowable in whole milk—make sure to place a foil lined cookie sheet underneath in case it boils over! Cook at 350 degrees for 4 to 6 hours, until the meat falls off the bones.

Remove ham from pot and place on a serving platter. Strain curd from cooking liquid to make the brown sugar-mustard sauce into gravy. Thicken with flour, if needed.

Note: Smothered ham can also be made in a crock pot. Follow instructions above, but cook on low setting for 8 to 10 hours.

Jinny's Filet Mignon Salad

Heather Paquette • Kennebunk, York County

"My grandmother Virginia Gearan owned The Glass Menagerie in Kennebunk in the 1980s. She had wonderful appetizers at the restaurant, and she was even featured in *Yankee Magazine*. Looking through her recipes, my mother and I found her secret steak salad recipe—it's to die for!"

Dressing:
1 egg
3 tablespoons champagne vinegar
4 teaspoons Dijon mustard
1 teaspoon salt
2 teaspoons lemon juice
1 teaspoon Worcestershire sauce
Dash Tabasco
⅓ cup olive oil

Herb mix:
½ pound mushrooms, sliced
½ cup scallions, sliced (white part only)

14-ounce can
    hearts of
    palm, drained and sliced
2 tablespoons fresh chives, chopped
2 tablespoons fresh parsley, chopped
2 tablespoons fresh dill, chopped

2 pounds filet mignon, seasoned
    with Lawry's salt, cooked rare,
    sliced into thin strips, and chilled
Red leaf lettuce, for each plate
Marinated small tomatoes

Mix all dressing ingredients except olive oil, and place in the pitcher of a blender. Slowly (drop by drop) add olive oil. Blend until emulsified.

Combine all ingredients for the herb mix. Add herb mix to chilled filet and toss. Add dressing and mix together. Arrange red leaf lettuce on a serving plate. Place filet salad in center and surround with marinated small tomatoes.

No. 10
DANA STREET

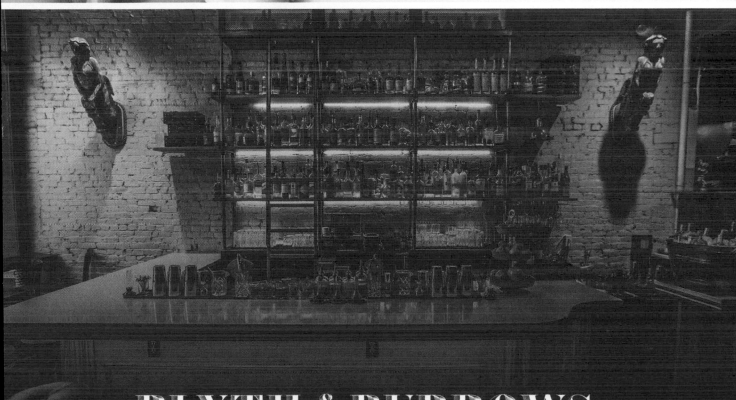

BLYTH & BURROWS
EXCHANGE STREET

Iraqi Kofta with Eggplant and Rice

Nahlah Alsafar • Portland, Cumberland County

Nahlah Alsafar is from Iraq and has been living in America since September 2016. She worked as an elementary school lunch aide before taking classes to earn her GED. Nahlah loves to cook for her family.

1 onion, diced
1 clove garlic, minced
1 pound ground beef
Salt, to taste
1 to 2 tablespoons flour
Arabic 7 spice, to taste
Oil, for frying

1 to 2 eggplants
14-ounce can crushed tomatoes
2 tablespoons tomato paste
1 small bunch parsley, chopped
1 cup broken vermicelli noodles
2 tablespoons oil
2 cups white rice

Finely chop the onions and garlic. In a medium-sized bowl, combine onions, garlic, meat, salt, flour, and Arabic 7 spice. Using your hands, mix together, then shape into ovals. Heat 2 tablespoons oil in a skillet, and fry meat mixture, rolling with a spoon to ensure even browning. Add more oil, if necessary.

Slice eggplants in half, crosswise, then cut each half into slices ½-inch thick. Toss with salt, then pat dry. In a separate frying plan, heat 2 tablespoons oil over high heat. Fry eggplants on both sides until they are lightly golden, then drain on a paper towel.

In a small pot, combine crushed tomatoes with tomato paste, then add salt and enough water to make a loose sauce. Warm sauce mixture over medium heat.

Preheat oven to 400 degrees. Pour half of sauce into a pyrex baking dish, coating the bottom of the dish. Wrap each meat patty, or kofta, in a cooked eggplant slice and tuck into the cooking dish. Pour remaining sauce over the kofta and eggplant. Top with chopped parsley. Bake for 10 minutes.

While kofta are baking, sauté vermicelli in oil in a large pot. When vermicelli starts to brown, add rice and a generous amount of salt, stirring mixture to coat. Pour in 3½ cups water and simmer until rice and vermicelli are tender.

Serve kofta hot, with rice and vermicelli.

Lithuanian Kielbasa

Cynthia Snow • Manchester, Kennebec County

"My Lithuanian grandmother, Bernice Placzankis Baylis, was a consummate cook of many Lithuanian dishes. Ma and Grandpa owned a yellow triple-decker on Bradley Street in Lewiston. Ma's kitchen always seemed filled with sun and savory aromas. Even though they were in town, Ma had a small vegetable garden in the back of the building and she canned dill pickles. An unquestionable family favorite dish was Lithuanian Kielbasa, and it was made for every holiday. My mother, who was not Lithuanian, wanted to learn how to make the sausage, so she had to sit in Ma's kitchen to write down the recipe as Ma cooked, asking questions on ingredient amounts. She  was inevitably answered with, 'A little of this, a little of that.' Over the years, my mother became a real expert sausage maker and replaced the counter mounted hand crank model with an efficient electric one. She taught two of my sisters how to make it, so the tradition has been passed on."

1 tablespoon salt
6 pounds pork butt, stew sized cubes,
    trimmed but not completely
4 onions, chopped

4 to 5 cloves garlic, minced
1 teaspoon allspice
Approximately 6 sausage casings

Note: A meat grinder with a sausage attachment is needed to make the sausage.

Sprinkle salt over the pork butt. Mix all ingredients together.

Knot end of casing and slide onto sausage attachment of grinder. Leave some slack, so casing does not burst. Have a needle handy to pierce any air bubbles that appear as you stuff sausages. Run prepared ingredients through sausage grinder, and stuff into casing.

Freeze sausage if not using right away, or you can boil in a large pot of water. Simmer for about 45 minutes until sausage reaches an internal temperature of 165 degrees.

Ayuh Paella

Ellen Barnes • Camden, Knox County

"For twenty-five years I was the cook/owner of a Maine Windjammer, along with my husband, Captain Ken Barnes. Most of these sailing vessels are pure sail, that is without inboard engines, and most use a wood stove to feed upwards of thirty people three wonderful locally sourced, totally home-cooked meals per day, while cruising in one of the most pristine sailing areas in the world. The *Schooner Stephen Taber* is one of the two vessels in the fleet approaching their 150th year of service. Our son Noah is now the captain/owner along with his wife Jane and their young son Oscar. This is one of my favorite meals to make onboard."

2 boneless chicken breasts, cut into pieces	1 pound Maine shrimp, peeled
¼ cup olive oil	1 pound Maine scallops
2 tablespoons paprika	1 green pepper, cut into strips
4 teaspoons coarse salt	1 cup peas (frozen are fine)
⅓ pound cubed pork loin	1 cup peeled, seeded, chopped tomatoes
¼ pound chourizo sausage, cut into 1-inch pieces	1 dozen fresh Maine mussels, in shell
⅓ cup diced onion	8 to 10 cups fish/lobster or chicken broth
⅓ cup minced garlic	4 cups long-grain rice
½ pound cooked lobster meat, cut into bite-sized pieces	½ cup brandy
	1 teaspoon saffron
	1 lemon

Coat chicken with some oil (saving some for browning meats), paprika, and salt and let sit covered in the refrigerator for at least 2 hours.

When ready to prepare, heat remaining olive oil in a pan and cook chicken until browned. Add cubed pork and sprinkle with salt and pepper and cook until browned.

Add chourizo and cook for about 2 minutes. Add onion and garlic and cook for about 3 minutes more Add lobster, shrimp, scallops, and green peppers and cook again for a short time.

Add peas, tomatoes, mussels, and 3 cups of broth. Sprinkle rice over whole pan and add 4 cups of broth and the brandy. Grind the saffron and combine with the remaining broth and pour over the rice. Season with black pepper. Reduce heat and cook until almost all of the liquid is absorbed and the rice is al dente. This should take about 15 to 20 minutes. Add stock a little at a time as needed.

Arrange artfully on a bib platter. Squeeze the lemon over the paella before serving. Enjoy with a good full-bodied red wine! Makes 6 to 8 servings.

Formerly Ed's Chicken

Craig Sipe • Orr's Island, Cumberland County

"My brother-in-law, Ed, from North Carolina whipped this dish up on the spur one night over 25 years ago and immediately forgot it. But I made mental notes and have served this chicken for years to great reviews. One time, Ed was up for a visit, and I made the chicken for him. He loved it and asked me for the recipe. He was surprised to learn that it was his recipe—though not anymore! We both came up with the name of the recipe: Formerly Ed's Chicken."

Marinade:
¼ to ½ cup ranch dressing
1 tablespoon Worcestershire sauce
¾ teaspoon minced garlic

¼ cup soy sauce
A couple dashes of liquid smoke

2 pounds boneless chicken breasts

Mix marinade ingredients. Pound chicken flat and pierce with a tenderizer. Place chicken in a plastic bag with the marinade. Refrigerate overnight.

Grill over medium-high heat for 6 minutes per side, or until done. Grilling time will vary depending size/thickness of chicken breasts. Serve immediately.

Grandmere's Savory Canadian Meat Stuffing

Robyn Norton • Berwick, York County

"I was born and raised in Maine, the greatest state in the Union. We are a proud mix of French Canadian and Native American. My grandmother Inez Cantin passed recipes down from her mother, to my mother, to me. I've traveled many times, but I always come back home to Maine."

1 pound lean ground beef or pork
1 large white onion, chopped
4 stalks celery, chopped fine
1 tablespoon salt
1 teaspoon ground black pepper
1 tablespoon garlic powder
1 tablespoon onion powder
2 tablespoons poultry or Bell's seasoning
1 teaspoon rosemary

1 teaspoon ground cloves
1 teaspoon ground cinnamon
½ teaspoon ground allspice
1 cup rice
1 cup seasoned bread crumbs
2 cups turkey broth, plus more as necessary
1 sleeve crushed Saltines
1 cup turkey drippings, plus more as necessary

Put all ingredients in large pan, except Saltines and turkey drippings. Cook on medium heat until meat is well cooked, approximately 1 hour, stirring occasionally. Add more broth, then the Saltines. Continue to stir occasionally so mixture will not stick to bottom of pan. Add another cup of broth and cook until absorbed. Cover pan with tinfoil and refrigerate overnight to develop more flavor.

About 1 hour before serving, add 1 cup of turkey drippings. Simmer for 30 to 40 minutes. Add more drippings, as necessary, and adjust seasonings to taste.

Picadillo

Jose Azel • Lovell, Oxford County

"After leaving Cuba at the age of seven, most of my adult life as a National Geographic photographer was spent in different locations, from New Jersey and Pittsburg to New York City and Miami. In 1987, my wife Anna and I bought a house in Western Maine and I have called it home ever since. Three children and 32 years later, here we are, still loving it. One thing we have always done as a family is sit down to supper together. The Cuban classic picadillo has always been one of the family favorites: a meat and a bean dish served together, in whatever proportions the person eating them likes, over white or brown rice."

1 large yellow onion
1 large green bell pepper
2 tablespoons olive oil
1 large can black beans
   (or two regular-size cans)
1 tablespoon oregano
3 or 4 bay leaves
Salt and pepper, to taste

1½ pounds ground meat
1 tablespoon cumin
1 packet Goya Sazon (optional)
2 tablespoons tomato paste
1 cup raisins
1 small jar Spanish olives,
   approximately 1 cup
Cooked rice, for serving

Dice the onion and the green pepper and split evenly in half.

In a saucepan, sauté half the onion and half the green pepper in 1 tablespoon oil. Add the black beans, oregano, and bay leaves. Salt and pepper to taste. Simmer on low while you cook the ground meat.

Place the other half of the onion and pepper in a skillet, and sauté in the remaining tablespoon of oil until the vegetables are softened and onions are translucent. Add the ground meat to the skillet, and stir in the cumin and Sazon and salt and pepper, and cook for a few minutes until the juices of the meat begin emerge. Add the tomato paste and stir until thoroughly incorporated into the meat, adding a little bit of water, if necessary. Finally, add the raisins and olives. When the raisins are plump, simmer for a few minutes more.

Serve beans and meat with rice, allowing each person to assemble their own bowl.

Empanadas Colombianas

Juanita Cuellar Nichols • Freeport, Cumberland County

"My family immigrated to New York City from Colombia when I was five, but we brought the flavors of home with us. As a child, I remember my father rolled balls of dough into discs and stuffed them with spicy meat for empanadas. Raising my daughters in Maine, I taught them to do the same."

3 cups precooked yellow cornmeal
  (we use Masarepa)
2 teaspoons salt
1 tablespoon Goya Sazon with saffron
2 tablespoons vegetable oil
4 cups diced potatoes
Enough chicken stock to cook the potatoes
2 tablespoons olive oil
½ cup chopped onions

½ cup chopped scallions
2 cups chopped tomato
2 large cloves of garlic
4 tablespoons chopped red pepper
4 tablespoons chopped fresh cilantro
Black pepper, to taste
1 pound ground beef
Vegetable oil, for frying
Aji (see next page)

In a bowl, mix the cornmeal, 1 teaspoon salt, and Sazon together. Add the oil and enough water to form a stiff dough, and form into a ball. Knead for a few minutes and then put the ball in plastic wrap and let it rest for about 20 minutes.

Cook the potatoes in chicken stock until they are tender. Drain and mash gently.

In a large skillet, heat olive oil and add onion. Cook at a moderate temperature for about 5 minutes and then add the scallions, tomatoes, garlic, pepper, cilantro, remaining salt, and pepper, to taste. Cook for 10 to 15 minutes. Add the beef and cook for another 15 minutes.

Combine the potatoes and meat mixture in a bowl and mix together.

Break the dough into little pieces (about 1½ to 2 tablespoons each) and form each piece into a ball. Put the balls between two pieces of plastic wrap and roll to make a circle. Put about 1 tablespoon of filling in each circle. Using the plastic wrap sheet on the bottom, fold the dough to cover the filling and form a half circle. Seal the edges with your fingers.

Fill a frying pan with vegetable oil and heat until a drop of water sizzles in the oil. Place several empanadas in the oil and fry until golden brown. Do not crowd them. Drain on paper towels. Serve empanadas hot with the aji and a squeeze of fresh lime. Makes about 40 empanadas.

Aji

1 onion, chopped
2 fresh tomatoes, chopped
1 bunch fresh cilantro, roughly chopped

1 or 2 limes cut in small wedges
Hot sauce (if desired)
Salt and pepper, to taste

Combine onions, tomatoes, and cilantro in a bowl. Add ¼ cup water, and a splash of hot sauce, if desired. Season with salt and pepper.

Roasted Chicken

Representative Chellie Pingree • North Haven, Knox County

"Growing up listening to my mother talk about being raised on a family farm, I learned to value 'real food.' My mother learned how to process a chicken and feed a farm crew by the age of 10, and many years later, I was proud to put those lessons to work on my own family farm. I am sharing this recipe to highlight not only a delicious meal option but to encourage you to think about the place where your ingredients are coming from—who grew these birds, who processed them, and who will you share this meal with? From candlelight dinner to community supper, I hope this recipe fills you up with the goodness that Maine farms have to offer."

1 large Maine apple (preferably a
    heritage variety), cored
1 large onion
2 stalks celery
1 head garlic

Several fresh sprigs thyme, from the garden
Salt and pepper, to taste
3½- to 5-pound broiler (roasting chicken),
    locally grown, pasture raised, and organic
2 to 3 sprigs fresh rosemary, from the garden

Preheat oven to 325 degrees.

Chop apple, onion, celery, and several cloves of garlic, and mix together in a bowl with thyme and salt and pepper. Stuff the broiler with the mixture from the bowl, and, making small cuts in the breasts, insert the sprigs of fresh rosemary and remaining cloves of garlic into the meat.

Place broiler breast-side down in the roasting pan (preferably on a rack to prevent bird from touching the bottom of the pan). Roast for 15 minutes per pound, then take temperature with a meat thermometer. When internal temperature reaches 160 degrees, remove chicken from oven and let rest until the internal temperature reaches 165 degrees.

Red Hot Mumbai Spicy Lamb Chili Dog

Cherie Scott • Boothbay Harbor, Lincoln County

Cherie Scott, host of "Mumbai to Maine," was born and raised in India and has lived with her family in Maine since 2008.

"It was a weeknight, around 7 p.m. when I received a text from my husband. He was home with the kids and sent me a picture of my son eating a Red Snapper hot dog (my son's go-to dog) and buttered corn. The second picture he sent confused me for a second. It was a Red Hot on a bun with what looked like chili spooned all over it. My husband was making dinner for our son, Justus, and decided to make himself a hot dog too. He looked at my spicy Mumbai lamb chili and in a moment of inspiration, put them both together.

'I thought, I'll just spoon the chili all over the dog and make it a spicy chili dog,' Guy texted. 'It was duh-li-icious! I had to make myself another one!' I never would have thought to combine those two together to make a 'Mumbai to Maine' dinner-on-the-fly!"

6 tablespoons sunflower oil, vegetable oil or unsalted butter

4 small white onions, finely chopped

6 cloves garlic pressed into a paste

4 teaspoons ginger paste

2 serrano green chilis, diced with seeds

1½ pounds ground lamb

4 teaspoons garam masala

1 tablespoon red hot cayenne powder or, for a milder version, use Kashmiri Chili powder

1 teaspoon cumin

1 teaspoon coriander

1 teaspoon turmeric

32-ounce can tomato puree, no spices added (check the label)

1 tablespoon lemon juice

1 bay leaf

½ cup freshly chopped cilantro

Salt and freshly ground pepper to taste

6 Red Hots

6 New England Split Buns

6 tablespoons salted butter, melted, at room temperature

½ cup freshly chopped cilantro

½ cup diced red onion

½ cup plain, full fat Greek yogurt

To prepare the chili: Heat the oil or butter in a wide non-stick pan or Dutch oven on medium heat for a minute. Throw in the chopped onions. Sauté them for 10 minutes until golden brown.

Add the garlic and ginger pastes and the green chili, cooking for 3 minutes while stirring frequently. Now turn up the heat slightly and add in the ground lamb, stirring well for 1 minute, breaking up the lamb. Add in the powdered spices and combine well, continuing to stir for 30 seconds. Pour in the tomato puree and stir well, combining the sauce with the spiced lamb mixture. Finally, add in the lemon juice and the bay leaf. Give the pot one good final stir. Bring to a low boil and then turn the heat down to a simmer and cover the pot with a lid.

Cook on gentle heat/simmer for 20 minutes. Turn off the heat, stir again, add in the chopped fresh cilantro. Season with salt and freshly ground pepper to taste. Note: This is a thicker-style chili that tastes even better the following day especially on top of the Red Hot dog.

To prepare the Red Hots: Heat a cast-iron pan or griddle on medium heat for a minute. Pour 4 tablespoons of melted butter on the griddle. Lay the split buns on the griddle, cooking each side for 35 seconds until slightly toasted and golden brown. Place buns on a plate.

With a knife, make diagonal slits in each dog, ½-inch apart. Keeping the heat at medium, pour the remaining 2 tablespoons of melted butter on the griddle. Lay the 6 Red Hot dogs on the melted butter and let them cook for 1 minute on each side.

To assemble: Place each warm buttered Red Hot dog on a toasted buttered bun. With a large serving spoon, scoop up a heaping of Mumbai lamb chili and carefully spread it across the hot dog. Sprinkle with fresh cilantro, diced red onion and a dollop of plain full fat Greek yogurt.

Ben's Routin' Tootin' Puerto Rican Solution

Ben Diaz • Westbrook, Cumberland County

"Born in Puerto Rico, at a young age my family moved to NYC, then Boston and I eventually moved to Maine as a young man. I was introduced to deer hunting by a seasoned Maine hunter from Gray named Richard MacDonald and spent many years hunting with him and his sons. Years later, my church youth group was putting together a cookbook and my wife Penny said I should submit my 'recipe' for venison marinade. I'd never written it down—it was always just a little of this and that—but I came up with this recipe. Friends near and far say it's used a lot and loved. I guess after 50+ years here, I now consider myself a Mainer!"

¼ cup soy sauce	¼ cup balsamic vinegar
1 tablespoon olive oil	2 tablespoons minced garlic
2 teaspoons dried sweet basil	2 teaspoons dried oregano
1 teaspoon paprika	1 teaspoon chili powder

Combine all ingredients and use as a marinade for just about anything: venison, chicken, or beef. Best if marinated overnight! If liquid gets absorbed, add a little more soy sauce and balsamic vinegar. For those daring souls, add some jalapeño sauce!

Rogan Josh Curry

John Karonis • Freeport, Cumberland County

"Growing up in Cushing in a Greek household, we enjoyed lots of seafood and lots of lamb. After high school I moved away and ended up working in the UK for a several years. We fell in love with Indian food there and all the fragrant spices Indian cuisines utilize. This dish, Rogan Josh, became a staple in our family (my kids call it "Rogan *John*"). We've since moved back to Maine and have enjoyed this meal on countless winter nights, it's a real go-to when we're craving flavorful comfort food. While the traditional Kashmiri dish is made with lamb, we often use chicken breasts. Make sure you let it simmer for an hour to develop the flavors. Also ensure you make enough sauce… it's great over rice and with naan."

3 tablespoons ghee or unsalted butter

2¼ pounds chicken breasts or lamb, cut into 2-inch pieces

3 tablespoons SKORDO Rogan Josh Curry Powder

2 to 4 crushed cloves garlic, chopped finely

8 to 10 ounces yellow onion, sliced thin

1 large (28-ounce) can chopped or whole tomatoes in juice

1 tablespoon tomato puree

1¼ teaspoons salt

3 ounces heavy cream

2 teaspoons SKORDO Garam Masala

2 tablespoons picked cilantro leaves

Melt 2 tablespoons ghee or butter over medium heat and lightly brown the meat in 2 to 3 batches. Remove each batch with a slotted spoon and set aside.

Lower heat and add curry powder and garlic. Stir and fry for 30 seconds. Adjust heat to medium and add the meat along with juices. Stir and fry for 3 to 4 minutes, add onions, fry for an additional 5 to 6 minutes stirring frequently.

Add tomatoes and tomato puree, stir, and cook for 2 to 3 minutes. Add 4 ounces warm water and salt, bring to boil, cover and simmer, partially covered, for 1 hour. Stir in heavy cream and remove from heat.

In a small saucepan, melt the remaining ghee over low heat. Add the garam masala to the melted ghee and stir briefly until fragrant. Add the mixture to the meat, stirring to combine. Before serving, stir in cilantro leaves. We typically serve this with basmati rice and naan. Makes 4 to 6 servings.

String Beans with Lamb and Cracked Wheat Pilaf

Andrea Martin • Portland, Cumberland County

Acclaimed actress and comedian Andrea Martin grew up in an Armenian family in Portland. "This recipe is in honor of my mom, Sybil Martin. The dish is my mom's traditional Armenian dinner for a cozy Sunday night meal. Make the stew the day before so that the flavors have a chance to marry."

1½ pounds lamb, cut into cubes
Butter, for frying
2 onions
14-ounce can whole tomatoes

1 teaspoon dried oregano (or more, to taste)
Salt and pepper, to taste
1½ pounds string beans
Cracked Wheat Pilaf (recipe below)

In a large skillet, sauté and brown lamb in butter. In the same pan, slice onions and sauté with meat for 2 to 3 minutes. Add can of whole tomatoes, and use a spoon to crush tomatoes against the side of the pan. Add oregano, salt, and pepper. Lower heat and let simmer until meat is done. In 30 minutes, test for doneness with a fork. If water is evaporating, add more water.

Raise heat to high and bring to vigorous boil, add string beans, then simmer for 15 minutes or until beans are done. Serve with pilaf and tossed salad. Eat, laugh, hug your loved ones, and enjoy.

Cracked Wheat Pilaf

½ cup very fine egg noodles
1¼ sticks butter
1½ cups coarse cracked wheat

3 cups chicken broth
Handful of pine nuts

Brown noodles in butter.

While noodles are browning, wash cracked wheat in strainer with hot water until water runs clear from bottom.

Add cracked wheat to butter and egg noodles, and toss around. Add broth and pine nuts, and bring to a boil. Lower heat to a simmer, cover and cook for 25 minutes on low.

Chicken Croquettes

Phoebe Schilla • Waterville, Kennebec County

"Maine never leaves you. Twenty-five years after leaving Maine certain things—the gift of the snowday, the red hot dogs, brown bread in a can, and going 'upta' camp are still a part of my DNA. I've lived in California for over twenty years now as a private chef and caterer. My clients have no time to cook, no time to connect over food. 'Too busy' is a curse of modern times.

I was brought up in a very different way. My people liked to eat, and a few of them did like to cook, but we were not foodies or culinary artists. The birth of my foodie self ties in directly to my grandparents, Lydia and Joe (who I called Memere and Pepere), and neither one of them cooked. Lydia and Joe were married for 63 years and lived in Winslow the duration, venturing out in 100 miles in any given direction but no further. Joe worked at Scott paper mill and Lydia's claim to fame was being the original Marden's old lady. Lydia was most emphatically not a cook. I would see her in the kitchen three times a year: Thanksgiving, to put the turkey in the oven; Christmas Eve, to make the tortiere pie; and Easter Sunday, making a ham.

Memere and Pepere ate out three times a day, at local diners and family-owned restaurants. Early on, they taught me the value of driving around for a good meal and knowing who had the best fried clams or clam chowder. Through them, long before the food network existed, I knew that Perry's Nut House had the best and most decadent penuche fudge. Toby's in Saco and Red's Eats in Wiscasset had the best batter fried clams and clearmeat lobster rolls. Flo's in York had the best hotdogs, with mayo, 'flo' sauce, and celery salt, no less. We frequented many a small diner—Pepere would take me out for lunch on Saturdays, just the two of us. I learned the joys of bread pudding in parfait glasses with softly whipped cream, and coconut cream pie, which is still one of my all time favorites. Breakfast on weekends for many years meant cinnamon rolls from the Red Hearth restaurant in Waterville, split in half and fried in butter before we dropped Memere off at work. A cinnamon roll fried in butter remains one of my guilty pleasures and one that I have passed on to my children.

The food that we shared was simple and seasonal. We stopped at roadside stands for fresh corn and Memere's favorite tiny pickling cucumbers on the way to garage sales and antique shows. We would pick wild raspberries by the roadside and blackberries, too! Memere and Pepere always had a secret spot. Maine shrimp season was eagerly anticipated, and we would get tiny shrimp in 5- and 10-pound batches. Standing next to my Pepere, I would help him pinch the heads off the shrimp and prepare some to cook and some to freeze. Wearing a flannel shirt and suspenders, he would hum slightly as we worked. He taught me to cook them in heavily salted water, like sea water. Summertime brought briny soft shell clams and hardshell lobster with sweet flesh at Young's lobster pound in Belfast. When ice fishing season hit, we would get smelts from friends who went smelting, gut them, dip them in seasoned flour, and slide them into a cast-iron skillet burbling with melted butter until they were golden brown and crunchy on the edges. When the snow melted in the spring, we would tap maple trees and tie empty milk jugs around the tap to collect the sap. We would boil the sap into rich, dark maple syrup. Some would go for pancakes and some would get further treatment and become maple taffy, swirled over crushed ice or fresh snow from that last late spring snowfall.

Mary's Restaurant in South China was a favorite place to eat on Friday night. We would pile in the car and pick up Memere from Marden's and head out. My mom and I would frequently get the chicken croquettes, which is one of my all-time favorite comfort foods. Although I make it with chicken, it really is the ultimate post-Thanksgiving recipe. I have recreated the recipe and embellished it slightly, but every time I taste it I am transported to my childhood."

Chicken Croquettes

4 tablespoons butter
¼ cup finely minced shallot
2 teaspoons finely chopped garlic
6 tablespoons flour
1 cup chicken stock
2 cups finely chopped roast chicken
(leftover rotisserie chicken is
perfect here)

3 tablespoons chopped fresh parsley
1 teaspoon chopped fresh tarragon or a
pinch of dried
Salt and pepper, to taste
½ cup flour for dredging
1 egg, beaten with 1 tablespoon water
1½ cups panko-style breadcrumbs
1 quart oil for deep frying

Melt butter in a medium saucepan over moderate heat. Add shallots and gently sauté until they are translucent. Add garlic and continue to cook for 30 seconds or so, until it is fragrant. Add flour to the shallot mixture, and whisk to combine. Pour in the chicken stock in 2 or 3 stages, whisking well after each addition to ensure there are no lumps. Remove saucepan from heat and add the chopped roast chicken and fresh herbs. Season to taste with salt and pepper. Transfer the chicken mixture to a bowl, cover with plastic wrap and place in the fridge to chill for an hour.

After an hour, shape the chilled chicken mixture into 4 parts. They should look like slightly flattened logs.

Take 3 small bowls out: One for flour, one for egg wash, and one for panko. Roll the croquettes one at a time into the flour, then egg, then panko, making sure to coat them evenly at each step. Chill the coated croquettes in the fridge for at least 1 hour (overnight is fine).

When you're ready to fry the croquettes: Heat the oil in a wide, deep, saucepan until it registers 355 degrees on an instant thermometer. Slide the croquettes into the oil 2 at a time. Allow to cook until nicely browned, about 2 minutes per side. Remove the croquettes from the oil and drain on paper towels or on a rack. Croquettes are most delicious when eaten immediately, but you may also keep them warm in a 325-degree oven until ready to serve.

PASTA & PIZZA

Photo: Jessie Perkins and Rachel Kelly in the Buck's Harbor Market kitchen.
See recipe for Butch's Steel Pan Greek Pizza on page 168.

Nana Q's Mac & Cheese

Steven Quattrucci • Portland, Cumberland County

"This is an adaptation of a family recipe created by my Nana Q, Assunta 'Tessi' Quattrucci. Nana Q and Grampy Q (Gaetano Quattrucci) were Italian immigrants who settled in the India Street neighborhood of Portland in the 1920s. Guy and Tessi raised nine children and ran a popular restaurant and bar on India Street called the Balboa Cafe in the 1930s and 1940s. Feeding nine hungry kids during the Depression was no easy feat, and this Italian mac & cheese is the kind of simple, affordable meal Nana lovingly prepared for the family. She and Grampy Q always served the kids first, eating only after everyone had been served."

2 pounds dried pasta
6 cups homemade red sauce
1½ pounds ricotta
1½ cups grated Pecorino, divided
½ pound provolone, torn into ½-inch pieces
    (Nana Q used scraps from the ends)

1 teaspoon salt
1 teaspoon finely ground black pepper
1 cup fine bread crumbs
2 tablespoons finely chopped Italian parsley

Cook the dried pasta in salted water, following package instructions. Drain, and combine cooked pasta with red sauce, ricotta, 1 cup Pecorino, provolone, and salt and pepper.

Preheat oven to 375 degrees. Butter a casserole dish and sprinkle with bread crumbs and reserved ½ cup Pecorino. Pour in the pasta mixture and bake for 30 to 45 minutes (depending on the size and shape of the casserole dish). When ready, provolone should be melted and top should be nicely golden brown.

Before serving, top with chopped Italian parsley. Serve with some extra homemade red sauce and Pecorino or Parmesan for the table.

Jared and Izzy's Wedding Macaroni and Cheese

Representative Jared Golden • Lewiston, Androscoggin County

"This recipe was one of my favorite meals growing up. My wife Izzy and I liked it so much we decided we had to have it at our wedding reception and my mom used the recipe to cook for all 150 of our guests."

2 tablespoons butter
1 cup cottage cheese (not lowfat)
2 cups milk (not skim)
1 teaspoon dry mustard
Pinch cayenne
Pinch nutmeg

½ teaspoon salt
¼ teaspoon pepper
1 pound sharp or extra-sharp grated
   cheddar cheese
½ pound uncooked elbow pasta

Heat oven to 375 degrees. Use 1 tablespoon of butter to grease a 9-inch round or square baking pan.

In a blender, puree cottage cheese, milk, mustard, cayenne, nutmeg, salt, and pepper together. Reserve ¼ cup grated cheese for topping. Combine remaining grated cheese, milk mixture, and *uncooked* pasta. Pour into buttered pan, cover with foil, and bake 30 minutes.

Uncover pan, stir gently, sprinkle with reserved cheese and dot with remaining butter. Bake uncovered 30 minutes until browned. Makes 6 to 8 servings.

Butch's Steel Pan Greek Pizza

Julia Bailin • Brooksville, Hancock County

"For more than 30 years, my family has been lucky enough to have a little camp in Brooksville. Made famous by Robert McCloskey's *One Morning in Maine*, Brooksville is objectively The Most Wonderful Place in the Whole Wide World.

On Monday nights in August, we'd head down the road to the Buck's Harbor Market for a special treat, handmade pizza and FLASH! in the Pans steel drum street dancing. This weekly summer staple, co-founded by Carl Chase and Butch Czerwinski, was part of the larger magic created by the Blue Hill Peninsula's community pan phenomenon. Butch owned the Buck's Harbor Market and played in the band. He also made the pizza. The street was blocked off, swollen with joyfully uninhibited dancers of all ages. We'd sit on the wide front steps of The Market, eat the most delicious Greek pizza right out of the box, fight over the last slices, and then get up and dance through the sunset into dark.

After our freshman year in college, my best friend Jessie Perkins and I both got jobs at The Market: I had the early shift, helping Butch at the busy breakfast counter serving local fisherman, builders, and summer handymen. Then I'd bake several dozen cookies, and at lunchtime I'd slice up Sheila Moir's show-stopping Francese bread, still hot from the oven and burning my fingers, to make deli sandwiches for the summer kids taking sailing lessons at the Buck's Harbor Yacht Club down the street. In the afternoon, Jessie's shift would start at Cafe Out Back, the restaurant behind the market. She was the pizza girl, making pies for eat-in or takeout. And Butch himself, creator of the beloved Greek pizza from my childhood, trained my very own best friend how to make it the way I had always known it. I've tried dozens of other Greek pizzas, but nothing ever compares to this one.

Nearly 20 years have passed since that hot, wonderful summer, and The Market has changed ownership a few times. The most important thing is that it still stays open year-round for the tiny, generations-deep community who remains in the winter, which now includes my own parents, providing a critical lifeline of camaraderie, food staples, and hot coffee every day. The Monday night steel pan street dances have moved to Blue Hill, bigger than ever, and still making that intoxicating calypso sound. If you've heard it before, you know sitting down is not an option. And while I am wistful for the old Buck's Harbor Market of my youth I will always have Butch's Steel Pan Greek Pizza, and now, so do you. As Jessie might say with dry, witty confidence: 'You're welcome.'"

1 ball white pizza dough
   (store-bought is just fine)
A little bit of cornmeal
2 or 3 cloves finely chopped fresh garlic
4 or 5 large red tomatoes, very thinly sliced
1 bag of shredded pizza cheese: 50/50
   mozzarella and provolone (If you can't
   find the mix, buy one of each and
   mix it yourself)
15-ounce can or jar of marinated artichoke
   hearts, broken up by hand (see Note)

1-ish cup pitted, hand-crushed kalamata
   olives (using regular black olives is
   punishable by law)
1 to 2 cups crumbled feta cheese
Dried basil, to taste
Parmesan cheese
   (the kind you shake out of a jar)
Bonus points: olive oil infused with
   roasted garlic

Note: We would use artichoke hearts that came quartered and packed in water then marinate them ourselves in cheap Italian salad dressing—buying them pre-marinated in a jar lends a different kind of flavor. This may in fact be the key to making it taste as much like Butch's as possible, however, you may have to take what you can get for artichoke hearts unless Sysco delivers to your house.

Preheat your oven as hot as you can get it, up to 600 degrees if you can!

On a large sheet pan, sprinkle the cornmeal and spread evenly. Ensure all your toppings are ready to go, as you will want to work quickly when it is toppings time.

If your dough is refrigerated, take it out and bring to room temperature. Gently stretch dough to just a little bigger than the size of your sheet pan. Don't rush, or you will create holes. If it is proving difficult, lay it down on a flat surface (but NOT your cornmeal-covered sheet pan!) and rest it for a few minutes and then proceed again. Once you have the size and shape right, lay it on top of the cornmeal-dusted pan.

Now it's time to work quickly: Smear the chopped fresh garlic all over the crust. Place the thinly sliced tomatoes all over crust, with edges touching each other but not overlapping for good coverage. Sprinkle the shredded mozzarella/provolone cheese mix over the whole thing with a light hand. Use less than you think you need—there is more cheese coming. Then scatter the hand-crushed marinated artichoke hearts so there are some in each bite. Add kalamata olives to your liking. Then top with crumbled feta, but not too much because you already put mozzarella and provolone on. ("Too much cheese on a pizza is a common rookie mistake," according to Butch.)

Sprinkle dry basil and Parmesan over the whole thing before it goes in the oven. Now bake it as hot as you can get it. At the store, we used to do it for 8 mins in a 600-degree oven. This is the part that definitely is impossible to do at home, so crank it up and then closely watch your pizza, it won't take long. When it comes out, brush the crust with garlic-infused olive oil.

Mom's Homemade Manicotti

Ronica Richardson • Oxford, Oxford County

"My mom made everything from scratch. This meal she taught me when I was little and I still continue to make for special occasions."

Noodles
6 eggs
1½ cups flour
¼ teaspoon salt

Sauce
⅓ cup olive oil
2 large onions, chopped
1 garlic clove, crushed
1 large can tomato sauce
1 large can tomato puree
6-ounce can tomato paste

Salt, to taste
Sugar, to taste
Italian seasoning, to taste

Filling
1 pound cottage cheese
1 pound mozzarella, shredded
¼ cup grated Parmesan
2 eggs
1 teaspoon Italian seasoning
Salt and pepper, to taste

To make the noodles: Combine eggs, flour, 1½ cups water, and salt. Beat with a mixer until smooth. Let stand ½ hour.

Place a non-stick frying pan over medium to low heat. Pour 2 tablespoons batter in the pan. Rotate quickly by hand to make the round shape. Remove with plastic spatula, and place onto waxed paper. Watch the noodles closely—they'll be done when they dry out on top.

To make the sauce: In a medium saucepan, heat olive oil. Add onions and garlic. Cook until fragrant, then add tomato sauce, tomato puree, tomato paste, salt, sugar, and spices. Simmer 40 to 45 minutes.

To make the filling and assemble: Mix together cottage cheese, mozzarella, Parmesan cheese, 2 eggs, seasoning, salt, and pepper.

Preheat oven to 350 degrees. Take a noodle and put a little filling on it and roll. Place in a greased pan, repeat until you have used all the noodles, and cover noodles with sauce. Bake for 45 minutes. Let sit for 10 minutes before serving.

Noodle Pudding (Luchen Kugel)

1951 • *100 Selected Recipes*
Levine Chapter B'nai Brith/Waterville Chapter Hadassah • Waterville, Kennebec County

This traditional Jewish dish with Central European roots is a sweet-savory casserole, often used to celebrate the end of Shabbat, the Jewish sabbath. Like all popular dishes at the heart of a community, exact proportions of the ingredients are much debated. The recipe can be found in the earliest known Jewish cookbook of Maine. —*DL*

1 box wide noodles
2 eggs
½ teaspoon salt
⅛ tablespoon pepper
2 tablespoons butter

½ teaspoon cinnamon
3 tablespoons sugar
½ pint sour cream
¼ pound cream cheese

Put noodles in pan of salted boiling water, cook hard until noodles are soft. Put in colander and pour over cold water, drain thoroughly, then put into buttered baking pan and add well beaten eggs, salt, pepper, cinnamon, sugar, cream, and cheese. Mix well, sprinkle top with dots of butter in moderate oven until top browns. Serves 6 to 8 people.

Baker family Passover seder in Auburn, circa 1960, where Luchen Kugel was most definitely not served.

Ending Hunger in Maine by 2030

By Jim Hanna

Maine people are resilient, as we have to be, facing harsh and changeable conditions on land and sea. There was a time when we, collectively, addressed far more of our local food needs than we do today. The modern food system provides much for us, bringing fresh and packaged foods great distances, distributed through supermarkets, before they arrive on our tables. Still, people struggle to feed their families for reasons common 400 years ago, 200 years ago, and today. Bad luck, poor health, unexpected expenses, and a tough winter are among the obstacles of getting enough good food to thrive and be healthy.

Food gathers us. We organize around sources of food, seeking simple ways to nourish ourselves. Maine curates its brand identity as "the way life should be," a phrase grounded in a back-to-nature movement articulated in Scott and Helen Nearings' book *Living the Good Life*. But before the Europeans' arrival, the people indigenous to this land also spoke of their "good life." Each Wabanaki tribe had a word or phrase that expressed the collective wellness of a thriving community. Always at the center was food.

When Wabanaki people met French explorers in 1604, they helped those early settlers to survive the winter at St. Croix. The Wabanaki greeted them with an ethic of sharing and gratitude for what the land and sea provided. The new immigrants, instead of learning the natural cycles of this new place, began to compete with the people living here and impose their priorities and values. Eventually, they displaced them from their homes, interrupted their relationships to the earth, and disrupted their self-sufficiency. An ideology of superiority remains the foundation of inequality and maintains food insecurity today.

What should be obvious but needs to be repeated is that food insecurity results from inadequate income for a family to meet its food needs. Additionally, we have become disconnected from our food, no longer relying on our immediate environment to cultivate, forage, hunt, or fish for the main sources of our diet. We have forgotten how to appreciate our food. We don't know where it comes from. We don't know how to make it delicious and nourishing. We ignore the marginalizing effect when families do not have enough good food or the knowledge to prepare it.

The honest stories told about who is poor and why reveal the causes and provide a framework for solutions. We must review historical moments when our communities made choices that privileged those already empowered to be more powerful, while stripping others of basic necessities. Economic and racial justice are inseparable. Any plan to end hunger must reference intentional policy choices in our past that resulted in disparate outcomes for targeted groups. The resulting economic inequality impacts not just people of color but is the foundation supporting the poverty that afflicts everyone who can't put nourishing food on their table. This poverty is a cost to and a burden on us all.

Over 30 years ago, a serious discussion began that if we are to solve the problem of hunger, we need to measure our progress toward that end. In the mid-1990s, the U.S. government adopted the term "food insecurity" to assess and explain poverty-related food deprivation. The U.S. Department of Agriculture defines food security as "access by all people at all times to enough food for an active, healthy life." Each year, through the Census Bureau, the USDA conducts a survey to assess the extent to which U.S. households struggle to get adequate food.

In September 2019, the USDA released its 24th annual report on Household Food Security in the United States. An estimated 11.1 percent of American households were food insecure; that is, they lacked enough food for all household members. Maine had an overall food insecurity prevalence of 13.6 percent, and more concerning is the approximately 33,500 Maine households (5.9%) experiencing very low food security (VLFS), significantly above the national average on both counts. In this survey, only Alabama, Arkansas, Kansas, Louisiana, Mississippi, and Oklahoma have a higher prevalence of VLFS than Maine.

Does this mean our food system is broken? My bias is that the place our food system needs most healing is where it prevents people from accessing healthy food. Beginning with access, our food system must be woven back together and made whole.

One answer lies in our local food resources. Local food supports nutritious diets, stimulates regional economies, sustains healthy environments, and creates strong social connections. This means that increasing local production, processing, and access can alleviate hunger through a variety of strategies while building a resilient and equitable food system. Local food is an important tool to build food-secure communities. Knowing the farmer who grows your food is one of the most meaningful things you can do to strengthen your community.

Maine has a unique and historic opportunity to rally together and address the complex social problems of hunger and food insecurity. On May 21, 2019, Governor Janet Mills signed LD 1159: Resolve to End Hunger in Maine by 2030. No other state has made a similar commitment, and this bill underscores our "Dirigo" motto and spirit: Maine leads. With support from the Department of Agriculture, Conservation and Forestry, an advisory team presented its initial report to the legislature on March 3, 2020, outlining the comprehensive strategy required to build food and economic security with Maine families.

In keeping with the spirit of a cookbook, I have included *A Menu To End Hunger*. Together. Together we can develop solutions that will make food and economic insecurity a thing of the past.

A MENU TO END HUNGER

ACT
- **Buy local:** Knowing your farmer strengthens our food system
- **Love your food and your neighbor:** Preparing healthful food nourishes you, your family, and community and prevents food waste

ADVOCATE
- **Tell your story:** Sharing our struggles is courageous, inspires empathy, and reveals our collective failure to ensure everyone can achieve their potential
- **Know who is hungry and why:** Reclaim your humanity from complicity in a system that makes people poor

GIVE
- **Money:** Support efforts to address the root causes of hunger and poverty
- **Time:** Join with others who are building food security because none of us can solve hunger alone

Jim Hanna is the executive director of the Cumberland County Food Security Council and has been a Community Supported Agriculture member of Willow Pond Farm in Sabattus since 1991. He has worked intentionally to strengthen Maine's food system for almost 30 years. His children and grandchildren are blessed to be growing in Maine.

COOKIES & BARS

Photo: Sylvia Pease with Grammy Minnie Trueworthy on her farm in Porter.
See Grammy's Molasses Cookies recipe on page 180.

Nana Louise's Molasses Cookies

Cynthia Scholar-Kellis • Cape Elizabeth, Cumberland County

"Nana Louise was my mother, and grandmother to my daughters Elizabeth Buckwalter and Leigh Kellis. My daughters and I are co-owners of The Holy Donut. These cookies were a childhood favorite of my girls—I have the recipe card in her writing and I still make them today."

1 cup sugar, plus more for rolling
¼ cup molasses
¾ cup shortening
1 egg
1 teaspoon vanilla
2 cups flour

3 teaspoons baking soda
½ teaspoon ginger
½ teaspoon cinnamon
½ teaspoon salt

Mix sugar, molasses, shortening, egg, and vanilla. Add dry ingredients and mix well. Shape into 1-inch balls and roll in sugar. Bake in 350-degree oven for 10 minutes.

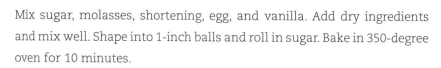

Cat Tongues (Langues de Chat)

Phyllis Siebert • Eastport, Washington County

"I was the Blaine House chef from 1972 to 1996, serving under Governors Curtis, Longley, Brennan, McKernan, and King. This recipe is a favorite that I used at the Blaine House for receptions such as inaugural open houses for coffee, tea, and sweets. There was just one of these cookies left after all guests had left after the Longley inaugural reception. The guests stood in line down State Street, in the bitter cold to enjoy our refreshments. I remember that Mrs. Longley was the first First Lady to wear the Maine Tourmaline necklace. Polly Curtis had worked with the Maine Jewelers Association to create it but it was not finished in time for her to wear it. I recorded this recipe in my book, *Recipes & Reminiscences – A Blaine House Cookbook*."

1 cup sugar
1 cup butter
2 large egg whites

1 teaspoon vanilla
2 cups flour (white, almond, or coconut)

Preheat oven to 400 degrees. Combine all ingredients in the bowl of a stand mixer and beat batter well until it resembles thick whipped cream. Fit a pastry bag with a half-moon tip. Grease well a cookie sheet or line it with parchment paper. Pipe dough in pencil thin strips leaving half an inch between each. Bake for 5 minutes until the edges are slightly tinged with brown. Remove from oven, cool on the pan for 5 minutes, and remove to a cooling rack with a spatula. This recipe makes a lot of delicate, yummy cookies!

Russian Tea Cakes

Mary Dempsey • Lewiston, Androscoggin County

"Every December, my mother Amanda Dempsey would make these tea cakes. My siblings Alicia and Patrick and I grew to expect them. After Mom passed, my sister and I continue to make the recipe in her honor. Simple cakes, messy cakes, but delicious with a cup of tea. You can change the taste a bit by using different nuts, or leave them out entirely if there's a nut allergy—it's a wonderful cookie however you choose."

1 cup butter
½ cup powdered sugar
1 teaspoon vanilla
2¼ cups all-purpose flour

¾ cup finely chopped nuts
    (although Mom just cut them into small
    pieces so you would know you had a nut)
¼ teaspoon salt
More (unmeasured) powdered sugar to roll
    the cookie in

Preheat oven to 400 degrees.

Mix butter, ½ cup powdered sugar, and vanilla in a large bowl. Stir in flour, nuts, and salt until dough holds together.

Shape dough into 1-inch balls. Place about 1 inch apart on an ungreased cookie sheet (the dough doesn't spread). Bake 10 to 12 minutes or until set but not brown. Like shortbread, they don't brown; they're done when firm to the touch. Remove from the cookie sheet. Cool slightly on wire rack.

Roll warm cookies in powdered sugar; cool on wire rack. Roll in powdered sugar again before serving.

Grandma Shreder's Molasses Cookies

Rita Buckley • Rockport, Knox County

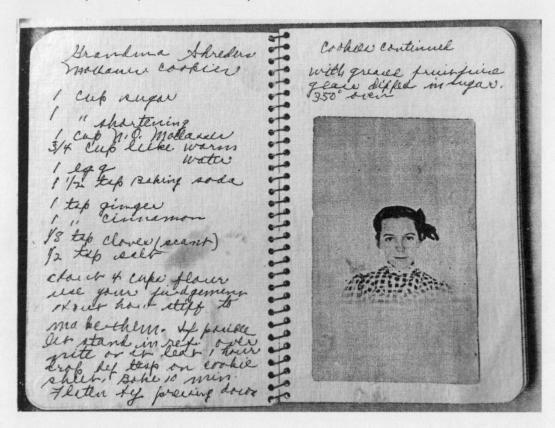

"My grandmother, Alice Lucy Seil, lived seven houses down the street from us when I was growing up. She lived to be 100 years old. Her cookie jar was never empty. Whenever we ran away from home—which was always to Grandma's—or just visited her, we were treated with molasses cookies. This molasses cookie recipe was her mother's, my great-grandmother Shreder. One time my grandmother accidentally used salt instead of sugar to press the cookies down. Rather than destroy the cookies she tried to hide the offense with chocolate frosting—it didn't work, but oh how we loved these cookies. When she passed, attendees at her funeral received the recipe, written in her own hand, with a beautiful picture of her at age 18. Eating these cookies brings back nostalgic memories of childhood times spent playing outdoors in a simpler age where everything was cherished and nothing was wasted."

Bangor Brownies

circa 1910 • *A Book of Selected Recipes*
Ladies Aid of the M.E. Church • Naples, Cumberland County

Hattie Harmon's ancestors were amongst the earliest settlers of Naples—present before it was incorporated as a town—but her Bangor Brownie recipe was very new. Some think the brownie was the creation of a Maine housewife, but whatever the source, this is one of the earlier appearances of a perennial American favorite. —DL

Two squares chocolate (melted), one cup sugar, one-half cup butter, one cup flour, two eggs, one-half teaspoon baking powder, three-fourths cup chopped nuts (not too fine). Pour into a pan, three-fourths of an inch thick. —*Submitted by Hattie Harmon*

Date Nut Bars

Katherine Crosson • Cape Elizabeth, Cumberland County

"Our Grammy, Mary Harriet Crozier, was born in Portland in 1889, taught public school, raised five children and was an extraordinary grandmother to thirteen. Known for her fabulous baking skills, she could effortlessly host holiday dinners, birthday parties, and backyard cookouts for the entire family. For 94 years, faith and family always came first. While she measured, sifted, and mixed, she engaged us—always interested in our lives, patient, instructive, and loving. In her kitchen, treats were always nestled between layers of crisp waxed paper in her red-and-black cookie tin. Our entire family holds special memories of times spent with her, usually around a plate of cookies and a tall glass of milk."

2 egg yolks	2 egg whites
½ cup butter	½ cup brown sugar
1½ cups flour	1 teaspoon vanilla
1 teaspoon baking powder	¼ cup milk (if needed)
1 cup chopped cut dates	

Preheat oven to 300 degrees. Cream egg yolks and butter. Sift flour and baking powder. Fold into the egg and butter mixture. Add chopped dates. Spread mixture in a 9 x 9-inch square pan.

Beat egg whites, brown sugar, and vanilla until stiff (add milk by tablespoons if not stiff enough). Spread egg white mixture over the batter in the pan. Bake for 45 minutes and cool in pan before cutting into bars.

Grammy's Molasses Cookies

Sylvia Pease • Hiram, Oxford County

"I have many fond memories of Grammy Minnie Trueworthy. The True-worthy grandchildren looked forward to visiting her farm kitchen, where she always had a glass jar filled with soft molasses cookies sitting on the shelf. Minnie was born in 1888. Her mother died when she was 18 months old. At age 2 she moved in with relatives on Kennard Hill in Porter. She worked her way through Kents Hill Seminary studying Latin, Geometry, and the classics. After graduating from Kents Hill in 1910, she returned to Porter, where she met and married my grandfather, Harry Trueworthy. Minnie and Harry bought a farm on the Brownfield Road, where she began her life as a farmer's wife. Her days were filled with cooking, quilting, caning chairs, gardening, raising chickens, and caring for their two children. She was an active member of the Riverside Meth-

odist Church, the Parsonsfield-Porter Historical Society, and the Oxford County Extension. Minnie never learned to drive so she depended on family and friends for rides to community events. She was a staunch Democrat and for many years worked as a Ballot Clerk for the Town of Porter. Harry and Minnie sold milk, vegetables, eggs, strawberries, raspberries, chickens, ice, hay, and wood to the locals. In 1925, Minnie bought a knitting machine and she sold stockings for $1.00 a pair. Within a few months she had paid for the yarn and the machine. She and Harry smoked and pickled meat for the locals. They charged 3 cents a pound. They kept daily journals filled with records of their expenses and profits. In the summer months they sold dairy products, vegetables, and meat to Camp Hiawatha, the neighboring girls' camp. Harry died in 1952 as a result of getting stepped on by a steer. Minnie remained on the farm and passed away in 1967.

My father Lloyd and mother Isabel raised five Trueworthy children on the farm adjacent to Minnie and Harry. Everyone worked on the farm. Like my grandfather, we grew vegetables and had a barn full of cattle. We sold milk to the Elm Row Diary. I'm grateful for those farm days. My family never took a vacation. We never owned a new car, and we wore hand-me-down clothes. We heated our house with wood, and we didn't have indoor plumbing. We took our Sunday night bath in Mama's wash tub in front of the old wood stove. As my brothers and I look back on those farm days, we have many fond memories, including swimming in Trafton Pond, making ice cream, sliding on the hill, and Mama's cooking."

1 cup molasses
½ cup shortening
¼ cup brown sugar
1 egg
2½ cups flour

2 teaspoons baking soda
¼ teaspoon salt
1 teaspoon ginger
1½ teaspoons cinnamon

Combine molasses, shortening, sugar, egg, and ¼ cup hot water. Mix in dry ingredients until well combined. Let the dough stand in the refrigerator until cold. If dough is too soft, add more flour. Roll out on floured board to ¼ inch thick. Cut into desired shapes. Bake at 350 degrees for 8 to 10 minutes.

Raspberry Almond Bars

Debra Wallace • Cumberland, Cumberland County

"My mother-in-law, Greta Wallace, was born and raised in Westbrook of immigrant parents from Denmark. Greta, a proud Dane and a spritely 91 year old today, has attended the same Lutheran church in Westbrook since she was an infant. She submitted this recipe to the church's cookbook, A *Taste of Trinity*. What makes the recipe extra special is it was always made using Greta's homemade raspberry jam of freshly picked berries from her garden. Those raspberry bushes continue to produce delectable fruit to this day!"

1 cup all-purpose flour
¾ cup quick-cooking oats
½ cup granulated sugar
½ cup butter or margarine, at room
   temperature

½ teaspoon almond extract
½ cup red raspberry preserves
⅓ cup sliced almonds

Heat oven to 350 degrees. Line an 8- or 9-inch square baking pan with foil. Lightly grease foil.

Mix flour, oats and sugar in a large bowl. Add butter and cut in with pastry blender or 2 knives until mixture resembles coarse crumbs. Stir in extract until blended.

Reserve about 1 cup oat mixture. Press remainder evenly over bottom of pan, adding more mixture if needed to cover. Spread preserves over top to about ½-inch from edges.

Mix almonds with reserved oat mixture. Sprinkle evenly over preserves, then press down gently. (Some preserves will show through.)

Bake 25 to 30 minutes or until edges are golden. Cool in pan on rack.

Lift foil by ends to cutting board. Cut in bars.

Grandma's Apricot Squares

Sharon Bresler • Gray, Cumberland County

"This recipe originates with my grandmother, whose cooking traditions came from her Eastern European Jewish immigrant family. She was the first generation of her family born in the U.S., and as a child, she was the interpreter and navigator of city life for her grandmother, who spoke no English. All three of my grandmother's sons volunteered to fight during World War II. Her oldest, my father's older brother, was killed in action in Europe. After my grandmother died, I learned that when the War Department sent her the invitation to become a Gold Star Mother, she rejected it. In her letter of explanation, she wrote that the restriction on Gold Stars—that the fallen soldier had to have been a native born American—was unacceptable. She clearly saw that sacrifice is sacrifice, and where the soldier was born was not as important as why he died. I wish I'd known about that letter while she was alive."

1 ½ pounds dried California apricots
1 to 1 ½ cups sugar
1 cup butter
2 cups brown sugar
2 eggs

2 teaspoons vanilla
3 cups flour
3 cups quick oats
2 teaspoons baking soda
Pinch of salt

Preheat oven to 350 degrees. Butter and flour a 9 x 13-inch pan.

Pour hot water over the apricots; let stand for 5 minutes. Drain, then put apricots, 1 ½ cups cold water, and 1 cup sugar in a pan and cook over low heat until smooth. Add more water if mixture gets too stiff to stir, and more sugar to taste. They should retain some tartness. Set aside.

Cream butter and brown sugar together. Stir in eggs. Add vanilla. Mix together dry ingredients. Add to creamed ingredients and mix thoroughly to make a very stiff dough.

Press dough into prepared pan. Smooth apricots on top. Bake for 20 to 30 minutes. Cut into 1-inch squares while in the pan, and let cool before serving.

Fudgy Organic Chocolate Nib Brownies

Donna and Kate McAleer • Rockland, Knox County

"Our family roots in Maine go back generations, spending vacations and holidays in Spruce Head and Rockland, and eventually moving to the Mid Coast permanently. The attraction of Maine was the unbeatable combination of quality of life and the innovative food movement. We launched Bixby & Co. in 2011, and the company proudly wears the label 'Made in Maine!' When we expanded into 'Bean-to-Bar' chocolate making in 2017, we became Maine's first and only such producer. Making our chocolate begins with sourcing organic, ethically grown and harvested beans from various countries (many of which we've visited and met the farmers), such as Haiti, Dominican Republic, Belize and Guatemala. We also buy as many of our ingredients from Maine as possible. Making chocolate from scratch offers limitless opportunity for creativity and collaborations. This special brownie recipe is just one example—made from Bean to Bar chocolate and nibs! We hope you enjoy!"

- ½ cup (1 stick) organic unsalted butter
- 9 ounces organic 70% Bixby Bittersweet Bean to Bar Baking Chips
- 1⅓ cups organic dark brown sugar, firmly packed
- 4 organic eggs, at room temperature
- ½ teaspoon sea salt
- ⅔ cup organic cane sugar
- 1 tablespoon organic vanilla extract
- 1¼ cups organic all-purpose flour, leveled
- ½ cup organic Bixby Bean to Bar Cocoa Nibs

Preheat oven to 350 degrees. Line a 9 x 13 x 2-inch baking pan with parchment paper and rub with butter.

Place the stick of butter in a small saucepan on medium heat. After butter melts a few minutes, remove from heat and add the baking chips, stirring until the chocolate melts and the mixture becomes smooth.

Using a mixer, place brown sugar in the bowl and beat in the 4 eggs, one at a time. Add the sea salt, cane sugar and vanilla extract and beat until smooth.

Use a rubber spatula to mix the butter and chocolate mixture in by hand. Mix in the flour by hand, and then stir in half of the chocolate nibs (¼ cup). Pour into baking pan and sprinkle the balance of the nibs over the top of the batter. Bake for 25 minutes, until brownies are firm. Cool brownies on a rack. Keep the brownies tightly covered when storing.

Jam Jams

Carolyn Kelley • Caribou, Aroostook County

"My mom put these cookies together like a sandwich with her favorite jelly, date or fig filling. The recipe came from her mother's cookbook. Mom loved to cook and we loved waking on Saturday mornings with her making donuts for us along with all the beans, bread and potato salad and the fixings for Saturday night supper. She lived to be 101 and still did the cooking for herself and others. When I make them, I like a lemon frosting between the cookies."

1 cup shortening
1 cup brown sugar
1 egg
½ cup molasses
2 teaspoons baking soda
4 tablespoons hot water

1 teaspoon salt
1 teaspoon vanilla
1 teaspoon ginger
2 ½ cups flour (more, if needed)
Jelly, jam or frosting, to fill

Cream shortening and brown sugar, then add egg and molasses. Dissolve baking soda in water and add to mixture, along with rest of ingredients. Chill dough overnight. Flour a clean countertop and roll out thin. Bake in 375 degree oven for 8 to 10 minutes. When cool, fill with jelly, jam, or frosting.

Hermits

1906 • *Every-Day Cook Book*
Ladies of Freedom • Freedom, Waldo County

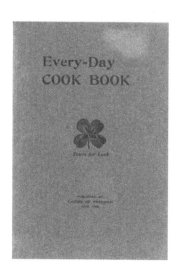

Hermits are a spice drop cookie popular in early America but with flavor roots deep in the European middle ages (the mixture of raisin, cinnamon, and clove is a classic medieval combination). Beyond the flavor, the cookie was a favorite because it stored well for a long periods of time. —DL

3 eggs, 1 ½ cups sugar, ½ cup of butter and lard mixed, ¼ cup water, 1 teaspoon cream tartar, ½ teaspoon soda, 1 cup chopped raisins, 1 spoonful each of cinnamon and cloves, flour enough to stir stiff enough to drop from a spoon.

President George H. W. Bush's Lemon Bars: For Lemon Lovers of America!!

Vesta Rand • Yarmouth, Cumberland County

In 1984, Vesta Rand's 4th grade class at Central Intermediate School in Auburn solicited recipes from the governors of all fifty states to put together a cookbook called *Governors' Gourmet Recipes*. They reached out to other notable politicians, as well, and this recipe was submitted by then-Vice President George H. W. Bush, with the note, "This is a favorite of ours—I borrowed the recipe from my dear friend Antoinette Hatfield, wife of (Oregon) Senator Mark O. Hatfield."

Crust:
1 cup margarine
2 cups powdered sugar
2 cups flour

Lemon filling:
4 teaspoons lemon juice

Rind of 2 lemons
4 eggs, well beaten
2 cups sugar
1 teaspoon baking powder
4 tablespoons flour
1 cup shredded coconut (optional)

Mix together crust ingredients and spread out (batter is stiff) in a greased jelly roll pan. Bake 15 minutes at 350 degrees, until pale tan or paler. Cool.

Mix together lemon filling ingredients, including shredded coconut, if desired. Pour over crust and bake at 350 degrees for 25 minutes.

Mike's Famous Damariscove Oatmeal, Raisin and Chocolate Chip Cookies

Michael Pander • Boothbay, Lincoln County

"My wife and I are volunteer 'relief caretakers' on the Boothbay Region Land Trust's Damariscove Island, covering for some of the days off of the paid caretakers. I make a double batch of these cookies each time we go, both for ourselves and for visitors. They're always a hit. The island is several miles off Boothbay/Southport and transportation may be postponed due to fog or heavy seas. We are confident that we could survive quite comfortably if these cookies were the only food we had left."

¾ cup butter, softened/kind of melted
1½ cups brown sugar
2 eggs
1½ teaspoons vanilla extract or paste
1¼ cups all-purpose flour
1 teaspoon baking soda

1 heaping teaspoon ground cinnamon
½ teaspoon salt
2¾ cups old fashioned rolled oats
1 cup raisins
1 cup semi-sweet chocolate chips

Preheat oven to 375 degrees.

In a large bowl, cream together butter and brown sugar. Beat in eggs and vanilla until fluffy. In a separate medium bowl, stir together flour, baking soda, cinnamon, and salt. Gradually beat the dry ingredients into the butter mixture. Stir in oats, raisins, and chocolate chips. (This takes a strong wooden spoon, or you can just use your hands.) Blend thoroughly.

Drop blobs of dough about 1 ½-inches round onto an ungreased baking pan, smooshing them down just a little. Leave space for cookies to expand during baking. This recipe will make about 2 cookie sheets-full.

Bake 8 to 10 minutes. Let cool slightly on the sheets, then remove to racks to cool completely.

Note: It's easy to over-bake these cookies as they don't **look** done, even when they *are* done. They are done when they are still quite soft on top. If they stay in the oven until crisp, they will be too hard.

PIES & CRISPS

Photo: Maggie Metzler eating wild Maine blueberries in Winterport.
See Jake Metzler's recipe for Worcester Family Blueberry Buckle on the next page.

Cranberry Raisin Pie

Faye Luppi • Poland, Androscoggin County

"This recipe was passed down from my great-grandmother Elizabeth (Lizzie) Abbott, who lived up on the hill in North Paris. The recipe card was written by her daughter-in-law, my grandmother Aubine Abbott. Every Thanksgiving and Christmas, I make this pie for my family. It's hard to find the seeded raisins now; the jumbo seedless raisins work almost as well. My son makes the pie crust without the lard (which was likely part of the original recipe) for vegetarian family members. We especially enjoy the pie for breakfast the morning following our holiday family dinners."

½ package seeded raisins or jumbo black seedless raisins (roughly 10 ounces)

2 cups cranberries, cut in half

1 cup sugar

Oleo "size of walnut" (or 2 tablespoons butter)

½ teaspoon vanilla

Shake cinnamon

Little salt

1 tablespoon cornstarch, mixed with a little cold water

Pastry for double crust pie

Cook together raisins, cranberries, and 1 cup hot water. Add sugar, oleo or butter, vanilla, cinnamon, and a dash of salt. Thicken with 2 "dessert spoons" of cornstarch (about 1 tablespoon), mixed with a little water. Put filling in unbaked pie crust, and put on a lattice-work top crust. Bake 20 minutes at 450 degrees.

Worcester Family Blueberry Buckle

Jake Metzler • Winterport, Waldo County

"Growing up, we all looked forward to those first blueberries ripening so the first buckle of the year could be baked by my grandmother. Each August was marked by raking blueberries on family lands Downeast, and a fresh buckle was always a welcome reward following a hard day's work. As good as it is, a buckle never lasts long!"

Bottom:

2½ cups flour

1 cup sugar

1 teaspoon salt

3 teaspoons baking powder

⅓ cup soft shortening

2 eggs

1 cup milk

3 cups wild Maine blueberries—
   fresh or Wyman's frozen

Top:

¾ cup sugar

½ cup flour

1 teaspoon cinnamon

¼ cup soft butter

Preheat oven to 350 degrees.

Mix all "Bottom" ingredients except blueberries until well combined, then fold in blueberries. Place batter in greased 13 x 9-inch pan (aluminum preferred).

In a separate bowl, combine "Top" ingredients into a mixture (it should be crumbly), and sprinkle in pan over the batter. Bake for about 50 minutes.

Louise Guyol Owen's Lemon Meringue Pie

Caitlin Hunter • Appleton, Knox County

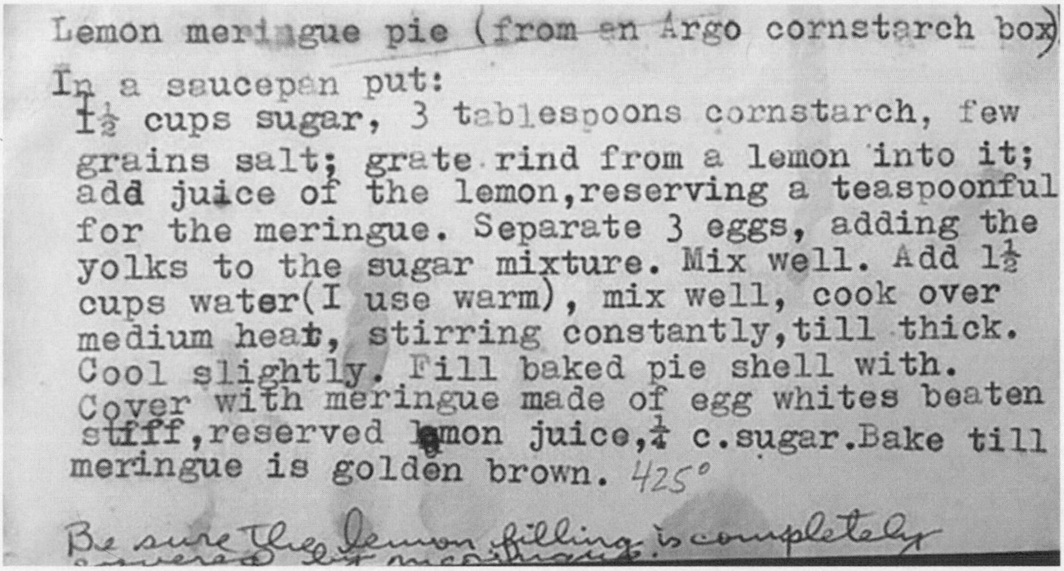

Lemon meringue pie (from an Argo cornstarch box)
In a saucepan put:
1½ cups sugar, 3 tablespoons cornstarch, few grains salt; grate rind from a lemon into it; add juice of the lemon, reserving a teaspoonful for the meringue. Separate 3 eggs, adding the yolks to the sugar mixture. Mix well. Add 1½ cups water(I use warm), mix well, cook over medium heat, stirring constantly, till thick. Cool slightly. Fill baked pie shell with. Cover with meringue made of egg whites beaten stiff, reserved lemon juice, ¼ c. sugar. Bake till meringue is golden brown. 425°

Be sure the lemon filling is completely
covered if meringue

"My grandmother, Louise Guyol Owen passed along this recipe when I was a young bride in 1978. She typed everything, and I am proud to still own her typewriter. Whenever she made this pie, she made sure to point out the 'golden tears' that form on the meringue."

Innkeeper's Pie

Katie Murphy • North Yarmouth, Cumberland County

"This pie was served at The Pocket Watch Shop in North Yarmouth. Valda Verrier operated this unusual gift shop and tea room in a rural town where there was nothing like it for miles around. The Shop was located in the Verriers' beautiful 1906 house that originally stood two miles away from the North Yarmouth Congregational Church. In 1962, the Verriers had the house put on a flatbed truck and moved to a new location on New Gloucester Road. The Pocket Watch Shop operated until the early 1970s. It's a private home today. This recipe was preserved by the North Yarmouth Historical Society. The pie often shows up at community potluck suppers."

Pastry for single crust pie
1½ squares unsweetened baking chocolate
½ cup warm water
⅔ cup plus ¾ cup sugar, divided
½ cup butter
2 teaspoons vanilla, divided

1 cup flour
1 teaspoon baking powder
½ teaspoon salt
½ cup milk
1 egg
½ cup chopped toasted nuts

Line a 9-inch pie plate with crust, making a high, fluted edge. Set aside. Preheat oven to 350 degrees.

Combine chocolate and water in a saucepan set over medium heat. Stir until chocolate is melted. Add ⅔ cup sugar and bring to a boil, stirring constantly. Remove from heat and stir in ¼ cup butter and 1½ teaspoons vanilla. Set aside.

Sift together flour, baking powder, ¾ cup sugar, and salt. Cream remaining ¼ cup butter. Gradually add milk and remaining ½ teaspoon vanilla. Add the sifted ingredients and beat for 1 minute at medium speed. Add egg, and beat for another minute more, until smooth.

Pour batter into pie crust. Stir sauce and pour carefully over batter. Sprinkle top with chopped nuts. Bake 50 to 60 minutes or until a toothpick comes out clean. Cool, and serve with whipped cream.

Lemon Sponge Pie

Peggy O'Connor • Belfast, Waldo County

"My grandmother, Lura Barter Bell, from Barter's Island, and then Boothbay Harbor, and my mother, Barbara Bell Sturtevant, from Boothbay Harbor, and later Bath, were the only people I knew who made this pie, which has a light, cakey top. I would tell people of it, and no one was familiar with it. I loved it so much that as a child I remember asking for it on my birthday, instead of a cake. Many years later, I remember stopping in to Moody's Diner, and there, on the menu, was lemon sponge pie. It was good, but not quite as good as my Mom's or Nana's. When I next stopped at Moody's, the pie was not on the menu, and I haven't seen it since. I'm so glad to have had this recipe in our family."

Pastry for single crust pie
1 cup sugar
1 tablespoon butter
3 tablespoons flour, leveled

2 eggs
1 cup milk
3 tablespoons fresh lemon juice

Preheat oven to 400 degrees.

Line a 9-inch pie plate with crust.

Cream together sugar and butter; add flour. Separate eggs, and beat whites stiff. Beat yolks separately, then add half cup milk to yolks and stir. Add yolk mixture to sugar mixture, then add rest of milk. Add lemon juice, then stiffly beaten whites, and stir gently together. Pour into uncooked pie crust. Cook for 40 to 50 minutes. If top of pie or crust starts to darken before pie is done, drape aluminum foil over the pie and return to oven.

Blue Ribbon Blueberry Pie

Diane Mann • Lubec, Washington County

"I won a blue ribbon for this recipe at the annual Blueberry Festival in Machias."

Single pie crust, fully baked and cooled
12 ounces wild Maine blueberries, fresh or
   Wyman's frozen
1 cup sugar
3 tablespoons cornstarch

¼ teaspoon salt
1 tablespoon butter
½ teaspoon cinnamon
3 cups fresh wild Maine blueberries
Whipped cream, for serving

Start by baking a single pie crust and letting it cool.

Place 12 ounces of blueberries in a saucepan with ½ cup water, sugar, cornstarch, salt, butter, and cinnamon. Bring mixture to a boil, and cook until thickened. Remove from heat and let cool.

Place uncooked fresh blueberries in baked pie shell. Pour the cooled cooked blueberry mixture over the top of the the fresh blueberries.

Top with whipped cream.

New England Pumpkin Pie

1886 • *Three Hundred and Fifty Tried and Tested Formulas*
Ladies of the Second Congregational Church • Biddeford, York County

Recipes such as this, using ingredients that reflected the world of the native peoples and of early settlers, were part of recognition of a national cuisine that started with the nation's Centennial of 1876. Note that the recipe is simply a formula for the filling, giving neither instructions for a crust nor baking time. —DL

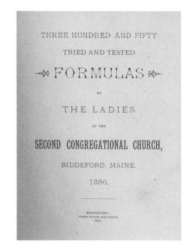

Peel and cut your pumpkin into small pieces and put into a kettle with very little water; cook from six to eight hours, stirring frequently to prevent burning. When done, rub through a colander. One pint of pumpkin, two quarts of rich milk, four eggs, two cupfulls of sugar, or more, one scant teaspoonful of ginger and four of cinnamon.

Wyman's®

Moxie Pie

Ali Waks Adams • Brunswick, Cumberland County

"I moved to Maine in the spring of 2014. That first year was all about getting to know our new home, and on a whim I decided to enter a recipe in the Moxie Festival's Recipe Contest. I took the inspiration for this pie from Shoo Fly Pie, a Pennsylvania standby (we'd moved from Philadelphia), and tried to 'Maine it up.' Turns out I did pretty well, because I won the contest!"

Moxie Syrup:
1 liter Moxie

Cornmeal-Lard Pie Crust:
1 cup all-purpose flour
⅓ cup coarse ground cornmeal
1 teaspoon sea salt
¼ cup chilled leaf lard,
    cut in ½-inch pieces
¼ cup chilled butter, cut in ½-inch pieces
¼ cup ice water

Crumb Topping:
1¼ cups all-purpose flour
½ cup packed dark brown sugar
½ teaspoon Maldon
    salt flakes
½ teaspoon nutmeg
½ teaspoon ground ginger
½ teaspoon allspice
½ cup chilled unsalted butter, cubed

Filling:
½ cup Moxie Syrup, plus more for drizzling
½ cup molasses
¾ cup boiling water
½ teaspoon baking soda
1 teaspoon Angostura bitters
½ teaspoon ground cloves

To make the Moxie syrup: Pour the Moxie into a large heavy-bottom saucepan over medium high heat. Cook for about 45 minutes to 1 hour, stirring occasionally until it becomes a thick syrup and coats the back of a spoon. You will have a bit more than you need for this recipe (pour the extra over ice cream, use it in a milkshake, put it in a cocktail, or brush it on meat like you would a barbecue sauce). Set aside ½ cup of syrup for the pie filling. The syrup can be made a few days ahead and stored in the refrigerator; bring it back to room temperature before using it.

To make the crust: Whir the flour, cornmeal, and salt in the bowl of food processor to combine. Add the lard and butter. Pulse about 10 times, until the mixture resembles coarse cornmeal; it's OK if a few lumps remain. With the processor running, slowly pour in the ice water, stopping when the dough starts to form a cohesive mass; you may not need all the water.

Dump the dough out of the processor bowl onto a sheet of plastic. Form it into a disk and chill for at least 1 hour, or overnight.

Roll out the dough into a circle about 12 inches in diameter and about ¼-inch thick. Lay gently in a deep-dish 9-inch pie pan and flute the edges decoratively. The pie crust can be made and shaped at least 1 day ahead. If made 2 to 3 days ahead, store it in the freezer.

To make the crumb topping: Whisk together the flour, sugar, salt, and spices. Work in the butter with your fingers until thoroughly combined. The crumb topping can be made a day ahead and refrigerated until needed.

To assemble the pie: Preheat the oven to 450 degrees.

Whisk together the Moxie syrup, molasses, water, baking soda, bitters, and cloves. Pour the filling into the prepared pie shell. Top evenly with the crumb topping. Bake for 15 minutes.

Lower the oven temperature to 350 degrees. Bake the pie another 20 minutes. When the pie is done, it will jiggle slightly but not slosh about.

Cool for 20 to 30 minutes, or until you can't stand it anymore and have to eat it! Serve with unsweet-ened whipped cream and drizzle with the Moxie syrup.

Marsha, The Almost Perfect Woman's Rhubarb Crisp

The humble Farmer • St. George, Knox County

Beloved writer and humorist, Robert Skoglund, AKA The humble Farmer, has delighted Mainers with stories and essays on his radio show, and as a contributor to the *Maine Sunday Telegram*. He and his wife, Marsha, the Almost Perfect Woman, also operate a bed and breakfast in St. George. "One day at 175 pounds, I quit eating sweets. No pie, cake, cookies, muffins, crisps or ice cream for 9 years brought me down to a comfortable 140 pounds. There came a day when I decided that 9 years of no sweets was enough. To break my fast, the Almost Perfect Woman made me a rhubarb  pie. I ate a piece. And I ate a second piece. When I reached for a third, Marsha said that three was too many. I pointed out that three pieces of pie in 9 years is only one every three years. And one piece of pie every three years is really not all that much."

Set out 300 rhubarb plants in well manured, loamy soil. When rhubarb ripens, pick about 9 stalks and cut into one-inch pieces. Drop in a 9-inch square pan or pie plate until ¾ full.

Sprinkle a couple tablespoons of sugar and a small box of strawberry jello over the fruit.
In a small bowl, melt 1 stick butter or margarine. Add to bowl 1 cup flour, 1 cup sugar, 1 egg. (Optional: ¼ – ½ cup chopped walnuts.) Mix all together and pour over fruit. Bake at 350 degrees for 45 minutes or until crust is golden brown.

Although we do not want it to be advertised, any other fruit or berries with favorite spices can be substituted for rhubarb.

Rhubarb Custard Pie

Jane Cleaves McKenna • Bowdoinham, Sagadahoc County

"Growing up, rhubarb was the first fruit in early spring, so my mother would make this pie, since no strawberries were available. When I owned my first home in Bowdoinham, I knew a rhubarb patch was a priority. I was working at L.L.Bean at the time, and mentioned this to a long-time Bean employee, Justin Williams. I was in my late 20s, and Justin over 70, but he totally understood and asked me to come over to his house after work. Justin lived behind the original showroom, near the Jameson Tavern. When I arri-

ved, he had dug up several rhubarb plants from behind the house. I also got detailed instructions on how to plant them. Today, two moves later, I have dug up these rhubarb plants each time, moving them into new gardens. I usually make more than six pies in the spring, each time remembering my old friend Justin and our family traditions of the first fruit pie of the year."

1 generous tablespoon butter	1 generous tablespoon flour
1¼ cups white sugar	2½ to 3 cups finely chopped rhubarb
3 large fresh eggs	Pastry for a double-crust pie

Preheat oven to 425 degrees.

Cream butter and sugar first. Add eggs and then flour. Beat well until batter is smooth and creamy. Add the chopped rhubarb to the batter.

Line a 9-inch pie tin with one pie crust, and pour the batter and rhubarb into it. Make an X-crossed open weave top using the other pie crust, and lay it on top.

Bake for 15 minutes, then reduce oven temperature to 375 degress for 30 to 40 minutes more, until top is browned. Allow to cool before serving.

Venison Mincemeat

Paula Moore • Orono, Penobscot County

"This recipe comes from an old cookbook, *All Maine Cooking,* by Ruth Wiggin and Loana Shibles, that came with my husband when I married him. We make this every year that he gets a deer. I always make mincemeat squares so my husband, Don, can more easily carry them on a hunt."

6 cups ground venison liberally moistened
with stock
12 to 14 cups chopped or coarsely ground
Baldwin apples
3 cups ground beef suet
3 ground oranges, 1 with skin
1 package ground seeded raisins
1 package seedless raisins
1 package golden raisins
1 pint canned citron (including liquid),
or four 4-ounce packages dried
1 package currants

1 jar grape jelly
1 jar red jelly (chokecherry,
crabapple, or currant)
1 pint molasses
1 pint sweet cider
2 cups sugar
5 teaspoons salt
3 teaspoons cinnamon
2 teaspoons powdered cloves
2 teaspoons nutmeg
2 cups water

Cook piece of venison (neck meat is fine) in salted water until very tender. Cool in liquid.

Mix all ingredients well and cook slowly, uncovered, in a very large heavy kettle (pressure canner is ideal) about 3 hours or until rich-looking. Stir occasionally to prevent sticking. Taste during cooking for sweetness and seasoning. Makes 7 or 8 quarts.

Westport Island Upside-Down Apple Pie

Susan Goodwillie Stedman • Westport Island, Lincoln County

"When a variation of this pie won the pie contest at a local farm years ago, the recipe was featured in the local paper. I added the cranberries and have served it to loud 'huzzahs' from family and friends ever since. Whenever dessert is needed at a party or potluck, I'm asked to bring it."

5 tablespoons butter
1 cup light brown sugar
½ cup pecan halves
2 pie crusts
3 crisp apples

1 or 2 handfuls fresh cranberries
1 tablespoon sugar
1 teaspoon cinnamon
Vanilla ice cream, for serving

Preheat oven to 375 degrees. Melt 3 tablespoons butter. Mix with brown sugar. Spread across bottom of 9-inch deep pie plate. Press pecan halves on brown sugar mixture flat sides up.

Fit one pie crust over sugar/pecans. Fill crust with peeled, sliced apples and cranberries. Sprinkle generously with sugar and cinnamon. Dot with remaining butter. Arrange second pie crust over apples, sealing edges.

Bake for 43 minutes. Let cool. Use dinner knife to loosen edges and a spatula to loosen under pie, then turn out upside down onto a large serving plate. Scrape any leftover brown sugar/pecan mixture onto top of pie. If making ahead, re-warm before serving with vanilla ice cream.

Stars and Stripes Pie

Jim Stott • York, York County

Jim Stott, co-founder of Stonewall Kitchen was inspired to make jam by memories of his grandmother Pearl's delicious blueberry pie. "I wanted to create the smell of her freshly baked pie filled with tasty, ripe blueberries. And we did just that. Every time I open our Wild Maine Blueberry Jam, I think of my grandmother."

Pastry dough for a 9-inch double-crust pie
(homemade or favorite store-bought)
1 egg, beaten
1 tablespoon milk

Blueberry Filling:
1 pint fresh wild Maine blueberries
2 tablespoons granulated sugar
3 teaspoons cornstarch

¼ cup Stonewall
Kitchen Wild Maine Blueberry Jam

Strawberry Filling:
2 pounds fresh strawberries, de-stemmed
and roughly chopped
¼ cup granulated sugar
3 tablespoons cornstarch
½ cup Stonewall Kitchen Strawberry Jam

Preheat oven to 400 degrees.

On a flat, lightly floured workspace, roll out ¾ of the pastry dough into a 12- to 14-inch circle (or slightly larger than the pie plate you are using). Gently fold the dough in half and place into the pie plate. Allow the edges to hang over the sides and trim so that the overhang is the same length around the pie. Gently fold the overhang under and crimp the edges.

Roll out the remaining pastry dough to be about ¼-inch thick. Using a small and medium star-shaped cookie cutter, cut out 15 to 20 stars. Re-roll the remaining dough if needed, and cut out 5 strips that are 1 inch wide and long enough to cross the pie.

In a small bowl, gently toss the blueberries with the sugar and cornstarch until the blueberries are coated, then mix in the Wild Maine Blueberry Jam. In a large bowl, repeat with the strawberry filling ingredients.

Starting with the blueberries, carefully scoop them into the top left section of the pie. While spooning them in, use a spatula to form a triangle so the blueberries are just filling in that section. Once the blueberries have all been placed, carefully spoon the strawberries into the remaining part of the pie.

Gently lay the strips of pastry across the strawberry section of the pie to create the flag's stripes. Trim the edges as needed and tuck the ends under the pie crust. Place the stars on top of the blueberries.

In a small bowl, whisk together the egg and the milk. Using a pastry brush, gently brush the egg wash over the stripes, stars, and the edge of the pie crust.

Bake at 400 degrees on the middle rack of the oven for 20 minutes. Reduce the oven temperature to 350 degrees and bake for an additional 40 to 50 minutes, until the crust has browned and the filling has been bubbling for at least 5 minutes. Remove from oven and allow to cool before cutting and serving.

STONEWALL KITCHEN

The Berry Best of Maine

STONEWALLKITCHEN.COM

CAKES

Photo: Nancy Finnemore and Mattie (Gould) Finnemore at Nancy's Bridal Shower & Tea
in Limestone. The Finnemore family recipe for Stinky Foot Cranberry Apple Jelly is on page 40.

Margery Tucker's Chocolate Roll with Chocolate Sauce

Donna Johnson • Buxton, York County

"Margery Tucker was one of 13 children of John Winchell Tucker and Carrie Mabelle Woodbury, and sister of my maternal grandmother, Mary (Tucker) McGaw. Aunt Margery was the Blaine House chief cook for 25 years, hired by Mrs. Horace Hildreth, wife of Maine's 59th Governor, Horace Augustus Hildreth. Aunt Margery retired after 25 years at age 76, and we have many, very fond family memories of her and her sisters Julia, Dot, and Mildred at the Tucker homestead and the camp on Woodbury Pond. Margery contributed a version of this recipe to the *Maine Sunday Telegram* in the 1970s. It was a favorite dessert, reserved for special occasions at the Blaine House."

5 eggs, separated
½ cup sugar
Pinch of salt

½ teaspoon vanilla
2 tablespoons melted chocolate
Sweetened whipped cream, for filling

Tucker Reunion Cookbook
Litchfield, Maine
September 11, 1982

Beat egg yolks well. Add 2 tablespoons sugar, salt, vanilla, and melted chocolate. In a separate bowl, beat egg whites until foamy. Beat in remaining sugar, 1 tablespoon at a time and continue beating until very stiff. Fold in chocolate mixture.

Grease flat cookie sheet (that's right, no sides are needed) and cover with wax paper. (Margery lined pan with wax paper, then greased and floured paper.) Spread mixture and bake at 375 degrees about 15 minutes. If it needs more than 15 minutes, watch it closely. Remove from oven and turn out onto damp cloth. Remove paper and roll up jelly-roll fashion while still warm. Cool thoroughly; unroll, and fill with whipped cream—sweetened—and reroll. Serve with Chocolate Sauce.

Chocolate Sauce

2 squares (1-ounce each) semi-sweet
   chocolate
2 cups granulated sugar
Pinch of salt

2 teaspoons vanilla
2 tablespoons butter

Cut chocolate in 5 or 6 pieces. Melt over direct heat, stirring constantly. (Keep the temperature low so as not to burn chocolate.) Add 1 cup cold water and cook until thick. Add sugar and salt. Stir until dissolved. Boil 3 minutes. Add butter and vanilla.

7-Up Cake

Lyle Hall • Gardiner, Kennebec County

"In the years after World War II, my mom decided to try her hand at running a business. For many years, in the '50s and '60s, Muriel's Dress Shop operated profitably in Milbridge. Mom was both a successful business woman and a fantastic cook. The following recipe for 7-Up cake shares something in common with the fashions she brought to Downeast Maine: they both came 'from away.' In 1953, the 7-Up company included the recipe for this cake in a promotional recipe booklet. Exactly how my mom came by the recipe is not clear, but the cake became quite a hit and has now been a family favorite for three generations."

3 cups sugar
1½ cups butter
5 eggs
3 cups flour

2 tablespoons lemon extract
¾ cup 7-Up
Confectioners' sugar or simple glaze,
    for dusting

Preheat oven to 325 degrees.

Cream sugar and butter until light. Add eggs, beating well. Add flour and lemon extract and fold in 7-Up. Pour batter into well-greased and floured jumbo bundt pan. Bake 1¾ hours. Take care though this cake does *not* work with the toothpick test.

Let cool 10 to 15 minutes before turning from pan. Dust with confectioners' sugar or glaze, if desired. This cake has a splendid presentation and is delightfully rich, without being too sweet.

Arlene's World War II Spice Cupcakes

Erik Nielsen • Portland, Cumberland County

"During World War II, my mother, Arlene Nielsen, couldn't find eggs or butter, so she made do with this recipe. As a young mother, she wanted her kids to have something sweet. Growing up in Portland, these were our favorite dessert. She was mother to seven children and passed the recipe on to me, her youngest. My two boys grew up on these. Today both boys are grown and still want them for their birthday. My mom lives on in these, and we all smile and remember her when we have them."

1 cup sugar
1 cup raisins
1 teaspoon cinnamon
¼ teaspoon salt
½ cup shortening
1½ cups flour

1 teaspoon baking soda
¼ teaspoon baking powder
1 teaspoon vanilla

Vanilla frosting, for decorating
Maraschino cherries, for decorating

Heat sugar, raisins, 1 cup water, cinnamon, salt, and shortening in a large saucepan. Bring to boil. Lower heat. Cook 3 minutes.

Remove from heat and cool.

Preheat oven to 350 degrees. Add rest of your ingredients to the sugar and raisin mixture. Stir to make a batter. Pour into greased muffins tins.

Bake for 25 to 30 minutes. Allow to cool. Frost with vanilla frosting. Put a cherry on top.

Islesford White Gingerbread, aka Islesford Sugar Gingerbread

Islesford Historical Society • Islesford, Hancock County

"The origins of this recipe are lost in time, but it is a signature favorite at every Islesford event and most island homes. It was served at the Wood-lawn Hotel from the mid-1800s through the 1950s. It is always available at every bake sale and fair, and was sought by tourists at the Islesford Market. After the Market closed, it is back by popular request at the Islesford Post Office. It is quick and inexpensive to make and has a distinct, memorable flavor and texture. It is good to make to take when one goes to visit relatives who have moved away, and to serve to guests 'from away,' as well as your close-by island friends."

2 cups sugar
2 teaspoons nutmeg
1 teaspoon salt
1 teaspoon baking soda
1 cup oil

1⅓ cups buttermilk
  (or 1 cup milk mixed with ⅓ cup vinegar)
Splash of vanilla or lemon juice
4 cups flour

Grease a 9 x 13-inch baking pan, and preheat oven to 350 degrees.

Mix the sugar, nutmeg, salt, and baking soda together in large bowl. Mix the liquid ingredients in a smaller bowl. Pour the liquid into the sugar mix and stir. As it bubbles up, stir in the flour. Pour batter into the baking pan, and sprinkle top with a little more sugar and nutmeg. Bake for 30 to 40 minutes.

Fairy Cake

Brenda Maxfield • Norway, Oxford County

"My Uncle John, who lived in Bryant Pond, was the first one to bake this cake and it continues to be made down through three generations. He first made it for a birthday celebration and it continues to be a requested cake for many of our family members' birthdays, all the way from Maine to Kentucky!"

½ cup butter
1¾ cups sugar, divided
4 eggs, separated
1 teaspoon vanilla
6 tablespoons milk
1 cup flour

1 teaspoon baking powder
Dash of salt
½ cup chopped walnuts
½ pint whipping cream
Small can (8 ounces) crushed pineapple

Preheat oven to 325 degrees.

Cream butter and ½ cup sugar. Add egg yolks, vanilla, and milk.

Combine flour, baking powder and salt, and add to creamed mixture. Beat well. Pour into two well greased, 9-inch layer pans.

Beat egg whites, gradually adding 1 cup sugar and beating until stiff. Spread egg white mixture on top of both cakes. Sprinkle nuts over both meringues and bake for 40 minutes.

When cool, place one layer, nut side down, on cake plate. Whip cream, adding remaining sugar to your taste, and pineapple. Spread over cake, then place second layer on top of whipped cream filling, with nut side up. Chill before serving.

Blitz Kuchen

Pam Russell • Cumberland, Cumberland County

"My grandmother, Louise Fettinger, was born in Portland on April 22, 1900. She spent part of her life on a dairy farm in New York State but returned to Maine when she became a widow at age 42. Her parents lived in Saco and she always considered Maine her home. Widowed, Louise had to find employment to support her children. She had a college degree from Russell Sage College and went to work in the Saco school system. She went on to get a master's degree in Home Economics from the University of Maine at Orono and went to work for the Maine Department of Education in the department of Home Economics.

'Nanny' created this recipe and it became her signature dish. The people in our family with June and July birthdays are often blessed with this special dessert. Her strongest gesture of love, and her legacy, was her time spent preparing meals in the kitchen, where she was a gifted cook and creator. Farm to table was all she knew, and her meals were from fresh, local ingredients. She had her favorite butcher, vegetable farmer, fruit stand, and fish market. Her special ingredient was love, and we all felt so special when we gathered around her pine dining room table. From breakfast to dinner, everything was delicious. In 1982, we attempted to compile many of the favorite recipes in a cookbook for the family. Nanny wrote the forward and it reads, 'I can't give you wealth so I give you this as a loving memory of all the joyful times we've shared around the old table at Whispering Pines.' "

½ cup butter
1½ cups sugar, divided
4 egg yolks, beaten
2 teaspoons vanilla, divided
⅛ teaspoon salt
1 cup cake flour

1 teaspoon baking powder
4 egg whites
2 to 3 cups fresh strawberries, chopped into small pieces, with juices
1 cup heavy cream
1 tablespoon confectioners' sugar

Preheat oven to 300 degrees. Grease and flour two 9-inch round cake pans.

Cream together the butter and ½ cup sugar. Beat the egg yolks, then add 1 teaspoon vanilla, salt, flour, and baking powder. Add to butter/sugar mixture. Batter will be stiff. Divide batter evenly into two prepared cake pans.

In a separate bowl, beat the eggs whites until very stiff. Gently fold in the remaining cup of white sugar until mixed. Spoon evenly over the raw batter in each cake tin. Bake in a slow oven for 30 minutes.

While cake is baking, whip the cream with the confectioners' sugar and remaining teaspoon of vanilla.

Loosen edges from pan and cool slightly, then carefully remove to a cooling rack. Once completely cool, place one cake layer meringue-side down on a pretty plate. Cover well with crushed strawberries, then layer about ½ pint of whipped cream over the berries. Place second cake layer (meringue-side up) on top.

Pistachio Cake

Karen Ellis • South Paris, Oxford County

"My father called this 'Margaret's soggy green cake.' It's a family favorite for three generations."

1 Duncan Hines white cake mix
1 box instant pistachio pudding
4 eggs
1 cup canola oil
1 cup 7-Up or ginger ale

Mix all ingredients well with a hand mixer for 2 minutes. Pour into a greased bundt pan. Bake at 350 degrees for 45 minutes.

Fiddlehead Cake

Claudette Rossignol • Van Buren, Aroostook County

"I was born and raised across the St. John River in New Brunswick, but I have lived for many years in Van Buren. My husband, Percy, and I are descendants of the French settlers of the region. For many years, Percy annually collected fiddleheads at his favorite local spot and I cooked them in a variety of ways, including this unusual cake. Several years ago, Percy told me he heard of a new way of cleaning fiddleheads by placing them in the dryer before cooking them to separate the dirt. I promptly tried it, in an effort to lower the cleaning time to use them. When I opened the dryer, what I found was a ring of dried fiddlehead ferns lining the dryer, not cleaned fiddleheads! Percy has never lived down the new cleaning suggestion."

3 eggs, beaten
1½ cups sugar
1 cup vegetable oil
2 cups grated fiddleheads,
    cleaned, and blanched
½ cup raisins

½ cup walnuts
2 cups flour
½ teaspoon salt
1 teaspoon baking soda
½ teaspoon baking powder
1 tablespoon cinnamon

Preheat oven to 350 degrees. Prepare a 9 x 13-inch pan.

Beat eggs, sugar, oil, and blanched fiddleheads together and mix well. Add remaining ingredients, stirring well until completely mixed. Pour into pan and bake for 55 minutes. Cool and serve with whipped cream or ice cream or frost with cream cheese frosting.

Great-Gram's Blueberry Cake

Briana Alman • Owl's Head, Knox County

"My father is a lobsterman in a long line and many generations of fisherman, and much of our family has been in Maine since the 1730s. Our family hails from Portland, Baldwin, Sebago, Bangor, and Bath, to name a few; perhaps most important, though, is the lobster boat out of Owls Head! Growing up, our lobster bakes over the summer always included the day's catch, fresh corn on the cob, and Great-Gram's blueberry cake. Looking back, this simple meal holds so many memories of the family gathered together, whether on the farm on Bald Mountain or down by the river where the *Rising Sun* is moored."

3 tablespoons butter
1¼ cups sugar
1 egg
¾ cup milk (scant)
1¾ cups sifted flour

1 teaspoon baking powder
Pinch of salt
1½ cups wild Maine blueberries,
    fresh or Wyman's frozen
1 teaspoon cinnamon

Preheat oven to 350 degrees. Grease and flour a shallow baking pan.

Cream butter and 1 cup sugar, break egg into it, and add milk, beating to mix. Sift together flour, baking powder, and salt, then add dry ingredients to the batter in three parts, alternating with the milk. Mix well. Add blueberries and stir carefully. In a separate bowl, combine ¼ cup sugar with cinnamon.

Pour batter into prepared pan. Sprinkle the top with sugar/cinnamon mix. Bake for 25 to 30 minutes.

90th birthday party at the Weston home in Harpswell.

Holiday Yule Log

Melissa Bailey • Penobscot, Hancock County

"Over the years, my mom Barbara has become an amazing baker and developed quite a hobby out of bread making, desserts, and coffee cakes. She often will bake from her cabin kitchen in the woods and frequently ships her yummy treats all the way to family in Virginia! It's always a nice surprise to come home to a box of homemade sugar cookies, fudge, and more. Mom has made this Yule Log recipe at Christmas since I was a kid, carefully modifying the right balance of ingredients to yummy perfection. When I was old enough to start cooking, she taught me how to make it. I have distinct memories of licking the filling beaters after mixing and tasting the leftover cake from trimming off the ends of the 'log.' After all these years, she continues to share this dessert with her three grandchildren at every winter holiday. I make the Yule Log each year for my family, carrying on her tradition. My mom has always been my best teacher—in baking and in life!"

Cake:
7 egg whites, at room temperature
¾ cup granulated sugar
7 egg yolks
⅓ cup cocoa
¼ cup flour
1½ teaspoons vanilla
Dash salt
Confectioners' sugar

Filling:
2 cups heavy cream
⅔ cup confectioners' sugar
¼ cup cocoa
1 teaspoon instant coffee (crushed)
1½ teaspoons vanilla

Maraschino cherries, for decoration

Grease 15 x 10 x 1-inch jelly roll plan. Line with parchment paper, and lightly grease paper. Preheat oven to 375 degrees.

To make the cake: At high speed of mixer, beat egg whites until soft peaks form. Add ¼ cup of the granulated sugar slowly until mixture makes stiff peaks. Put aside.

Using a new bowl, but with the same beaters, beat egg yolks at high speed, slowly adding remaining ½ cup of granulated sugar. Beat until thick, about 4 minutes. At low speed, add cocoa, flour, vanilla, and salt until the mixture is smooth.

With a hand whisk, fold cocoa mixture gently into beaten egg whites mixture just until blended (do NOT over-whisk!). Evenly spread batter into the jelly roll pan.

Bake 15 minutes, or until the top of the cake "springs" back. Sift confectioners' sugar onto a flour sack towel and turn out cake onto towel. Peel off parchment paper. Gently roll up cake with the towel and cool.

To make the filling: Mix together all the filling ingredients on medium to high speed until whipped. Unroll the cooled cake carefully to avoid cracking, and evenly spread filling onto cake. Re-roll, and decorate with confectioners' sugar and cherries as you like!

Vegan Lemon Raspberry Poppyseed Layered Cake

Betsy Harding • South Portland, Cumberland County

"This delicious vegan cake has been used in my family for sometime now for summer outings, birthdays, and up to camp."

Cake:
3 cups unbleached all-purpose flour
4 teaspoons baking powder
½ teaspoon baking soda
1½ cups organic sugar
½ cup poppy seeds or ¼ cup chia seeds
½ teaspoon salt
2 cups plain unsweetened coconut yogurt
½ cup vegan butter, melted
Zest and juice of 2 lemons

Frosting:
½ cup vegan butter
2 cups powdered sugar
Zest of ½ lemon
⅓ cup lemon juice
8-ounce jar organic raspberry jam

Preheat oven to 350 degrees. Lightly spray two 9-inch round cake pans.

Sift flour, baking powder, and baking soda into a large bowl, and stir to combine. Add sugar, poppy or chia seeds, and salt, and stir until well combined.

Put the yogurt, butter, zest, and lemon juice in a small bowl and stir until well combined. Add the wet ingredients to the dry, and whisk until combined. Using a rubber spatula, scrape batter into prepared pans.

Bake 40 minutes, or until a toothpick inserted in the center comes out clean. Let cool in the pans.

While cakes cool, beat together all frosting ingredients.

Transfer cooled cake to a cutting board. Using a bread knife, cut each cake horizontally. Frost between layers, and finish by frosting top and sides.

Luce's Maple Cheesecake

Elaine Luce • Anson, Somerset County

"Maple syrup has been a Luce family tradition since 1795. Our family has been making maple syrup on the same farm in Anson since 1884. I've been making this maple cheesecake for my family to enjoy for the past 40 years. I hope your family enjoys it as much as mine."

Two 8-ounce packages cream cheese
3 eggs
⅔ cup maple sugar
1 teaspoon vanilla
1 teaspoon lemon juice
2 tablespoons maple syrup

Topping:
1 cup sour cream
3 tablespoons maple sugar
1 teaspoon vanilla

Preheat oven to 350 degrees.

Beat softened cream cheese and eggs until smooth and yellow-colored. Add maple sugar, vanilla, lemon juice, and maple syrup, and pour into greased pie pan.

Bake for 25 minutes, then cool for 20 minutes. Combine topping ingredients and pour onto pie. Bake for an additional 10 minutes. Cool to room temperature, then refrigerate. Serve cold and enjoy!

Mom's Special Whoopie Pies

Cate Orser • Saco, York County

"Growing up in rural northern Maine, in the town of Fort Fairfield, we worked picking potatoes during harvest. My parents both worked full time—40-plus long, hard hours—trying to provide for six children. I'm not sure where my late mother, Margaret Stewart Orser, found the time to bake homemade desserts for our daily lunches, however one special sweet was her famous whoopie pies. Each day she packed our lunches in a shoe box, each one consisting of a mini thermos filled with hot chocolate, peanut butter sandwich, apple, and the best part, a waxed paper individually wrapped whoopie pie, or some other home-baked dessert. Sometimes our father would drive out to the potato field on his lunch break to deliver a forgotten shoe box lunch, where we looked forward to our home-baked surprise. The rest of the field workers tried to trade their store-bought desserts for our home-made, but there was no chance of us giving up mom's precious goods! It was less expensive for home-baked desserts, feeding six kids, and created more work, but they were filled with lots of love and care that we will cherish forever. Our family has precious memories of our mother's delicious home-made desserts. We have managed to continue her legacy to other generations by still baking her mouth-watering sweet treats during holidays and gatherings. Thanks Mom for all of your hard work, and loving, caring efforts. We cherish your old whoopie tin, wishing it was still filled with your loving touch. It will always be a heart-warming reminder of your famous home made treasures."

Mem's Holiday Cake

Claire Breton • Lewiston, Androscoggin County

"My mother-in-law, Dolly Breton, made this cake 50 or more years ago at Christmas and begged her family members to have a piece, but got no takers. I finally was brave enough to try a taste and was hooked, as well as everyone else! The trick is not to call it a 'Fruit Cake,' which has connotations of dry, candied chewy fruits held together by equally dry glue of some sort! This cake is very moist and tasty. I have been making it for my family for these past 50-plus years."

2 cups chopped dates
2 teaspoons baking soda
2 cups boiling water
2 cups white sugar, plus 1 tablespoon for
    sprinkling
4 tablespoons shortening
2 large eggs
2 teaspoons vanilla
1½ cups whole wheat flour

1½ cups regular unbleached flour
¼ teaspoon salt
2 cups maraschino cherries, well drained
    and patted dry
1 small can sliced pineapple, well drained
    and patted dry, cut into chunks
1 cup walnut halves
½ cup pecan halves

Grease well a 10-inch tube pan. Preheat oven to 350 degrees.

In a large bowl, beat together chopped dates, baking soda, and boiling water until mixture is thick. Set aside to cool.

In a separate large bowl, cream together sugar and shortening. Add eggs and vanilla. In a separate bowl, mix together flours and salt. Add flour mixture to sugar and shortening, alternating with cooled date mixture, beating well with each addition. Reserve 12 cherries and 12 chunks of pineapple for decorating, and fold in remaining cherries, pineapple, and walnuts.

Carefully pour batter into pan, and decorate top with reserved cherries and pineapple and pecan halves. Sprinkle top with about 1 tablespoon white sugar.

Bake at 350 for 15 minutes, then reduce heat to 300 and bake 1¼ hours, or until toothpick comes out clean. Let cool at least 2 hours in pan. Cut around edges of both outside and inner tube, invert over rack, and let cool completely. Serve with decorated side up.

Apple Walnut Cake

Julie Greene • Falmouth, Cumberland County

"This is from a dear friend of my grandmother, who was heartbroken when my sister and I moved from Missouri to Maine. It always made her happy to know that our family traditions were being carried on, even after we had moved far away. Growing up in Missouri, we picked Jonathan apples and shared 'funnel cakes' at the farm stand. Here in Maine, we pick Mackintosh apples and eat cider donuts as a treat. No matter where you pick your apples, we know you'll love this recipe! As a 'Missouri Compromise,' we added black walnuts from our home state, but the cake is just as tasty without nuts."

2½ cups all-purpose flour

1 teaspoon salt

1 teaspoon baking soda

2 teaspoons baking powder

1 teaspoon cinnamon

2 large eggs

2 cups sugar

1 teaspoon vanilla

1¼ cups canola oil

3 cups raw, peeled, chopped apples

½ cup Hammons black walnuts (optional)

Grease and flour a bundt pan. Preheat oven to 350 degrees.

Mix flour, salt, baking soda, baking powder, and cinnamon together in a large bowl and set aside. In a separate bowl, beat eggs and add sugar, vanilla, and oil. Add dry ingredients to the egg mixture (dough will be stiff).

Add apples, which will moisten the mixture, and optional black walnuts. Bake 45 to 60 minutes. Let cool in pan 10 minutes before inverting onto a serving plate.

Molasses Blueberry Cake

Sandy Oliver • Islesboro, Waldo County

"Molasses was an inexpensive sweetener very common in early New England. In Maine, change came a little less quickly than in other parts of New England, partly because it was less prosperous; many dishes continued to be made with molasses here long after other places switched to sugar. Hence, molasses doughnuts, a plethora of molasses cookies, prevalence of gingerbread, brown bread, and even cakes like this one for blueberry cake sweetened with molasses, originally found in *Maine Cookery Then and Now,* submitted by Mrs. Robert Sowton, Jr. of Camden, and published by the *Courier Gazette* in 1972."

½ cup sugar

½ cup butter or shortening

½ cup molasses

½ cup milk

1 egg

1 teaspoon vanilla

2 cups flour

2 ½ teaspoons baking powder

½ teaspoon salt

1 pint wild Maine blueberries, fresh or
    Wyman's frozen

Preheat oven to 350 degrees and grease a 9 x 9-inch baking pan.

Beat together the sugar and butter. Add and beat in molasses, milk, egg, and vanilla. Sift together the dry ingredients and add to the sugar and molasses mixture. Mix until flour mixture is incorporated. Fold in the blueberries. Pour into prepared pan. Bake for 30 to 40 minutes, or until a tester inserted comes out clean.

Nanny's High School Home Ec Class Gingerbread (1937)

Jodie Mosher-Towle • Smithfield, Somerset County

"This is my incredible grandmother, 'Nanny' Betty Marshall Mosher's recipe from her home ec class in 1937. Whenever I take out the tattered composition book where all her favorite handwritten recipes reside, I am taken into the old farmhouse kitchen where as a youngster I would gleefully help her. I can picture her in her bib apron pulling open the giant flour bin and reaching down to scoop a cupful into her mixing bowl. My five siblings and twelve first cousins still make recipes found in that book, like peanut brittle pudding, molasses popcorn balls, and

stuffed dates (Grampy's holiday favorites). Nanny made a habit of taking photos of her breads and yeast rolls because she thought they were always so beautiful! Her favorite way to bake was using her old kitchen wood cooking stove in the farmhouse. These recipes keep her spirit alive and well from the first ingredient to the last lick of the spoon!"

½ cup sugar

¼ cup melted shortening

1 egg

¼ cup molasses

1 ¼ cups flour

Speck of salt

1 teaspoon baking soda

¼ teaspoon each cinnamon, nutmeg,
    and cloves

½ cup boiling water

First put sugar into mixing bowl. Add melted shortening and cream well. Add egg and blend thoroughly. Add molasses. Then sift dry ingredients together and add to mixture. Add boiling water last, and mix. Bake in moderate oven (350 degrees) for about 20 minutes.

Sour Milk Chocolate Cake

Sue Sturtevant • Portland, Cumberland County

"My maternal grandmother, Lura Dell Barter Bell grew up on Barter's Island, but met her husband J. Vance Bell when she was working at a resort hotel in North Carolina with her older sister. After Lura and Vance married in 1916, she convinced my grandfather that she was homesick and they needed to move back to Maine. He opened Bell's Garage in Boothbay Harbor when he became convinced that automobiles were here to stay! Nana was the cook in our family—my mother said the talent skipped her generation—and was known especially for her baked beans, biscuits, apple turnovers, blueberry gingerbread with lemon sauce, roast lamb, doughnuts, and lemon sponge pie. She made this cake every year on my birthday, and even my mother learned to bake it for me! The copy I have of this recipe is one Lura contributed to the *Cookbook of Tested Recipes* compiled by members of Eucleias of the Methodist Episcopal Church, Boothbay Harbor, Maine, Second Edition, December 1, 1937."

One and a half cups sugar; one-half cup butter; two eggs; one rounding teaspoonful soda, dissolved in two-thirds cup sour milk; two squares chocolate melted in one-half cup boiling water; two scant cups flour; salt.

Cream butter and sugar. Add well-beaten eggs, milk, chocolate, flour, and salt. Bake in a moderate oven (350 degrees) for 30 minutes.

Tomato Soup Cake

Mary Jane LeCours • Gorham, Cumberland County

"This recipe has been in my family for many years. My grandmother, Irene Barstow, passed the recipe to my mother. My grandmother was a great cook but never measured anything; she didn't need to. She was also a messy cook; you could always tell when she was in the kitchen!"

½ cup shortening	½ teaspoon cinnamon
1½ cups sugar	½ teaspoon cloves
2 eggs	½ teaspoon nutmeg
2 cups cake flour	1 regular can condensed tomato soup
2 teaspoons baking powder	1 cup nuts
½ teaspoon baking soda	1 cup seedless raisins

Combine all ingredients until well mixed. Pour into greased 9 x 13-inch pan. Bake in 350-degree oven for 35 to 40 minutes.

Wowie Cake

Donna Dwyer • South Portland, Cumberland County

"My mother had a heart attack in 1974, and according to the American Heart Association, this very moist cake, sans frosting, was the treat to make. So we grew up with it. Once I had my own family, though, I added a cocoa peanut butter frosting. It was made on every birthday, and requested for cookouts. Now the infamous Wowie Cake is made once a month, five cakes at a time, for our monthly kids' birthday celebration at My Place Teen Center in Westbrook, an after-school program for at-risk youth. Last year we served 467 kids, ages 10 to 18, 9,100 meals, and 60 Wowie cakes!"

2 cups sugar
1¾ cups flour
¾ cup unsweetened cocoa powder
1½ teaspoons baking soda
1½ teaspoons baking powder
1 teaspoon salt
2 eggs
1 cup milk
½ cup vegetable oil
2 teaspoons vanilla extract

Frosting:
1½ sticks butter, softened
1 cup crunchy peanut butter
2 teaspoons vanilla
¼ cup unsweetened cocoa
3½ cups confectioners' sugar
Whole milk, to desired frosting consistency

Preheat oven to 350 degrees.

Beat all cake ingredients for 2 minutes. Add 1 cup boiling water, and beat on low until mixed. Batter will be very thin. Pour into greased bundt pan and bake for 35 to 40 minutes, or until cake tester comes out clean. Let cool, flip over on round plate, and then transfer cake.

To make the frosting: Cream butter and peanut butter. Add vanilla. Add cocoa. Cream again. Add confectioners' sugar and 2 to 3 table-spoons milk. Beat until mixed. Frosting may need more milk depending on your desired frosting consistency. Store in a cool place or refrigerate before use.

Maine Whoopie Pie

Amos Orcutt • Bangor, Penobscot County

"In 2009, I was President of the University of Maine Foundation and became concerned when I read an article in the *New York Times* that suggested the whoopie pie probably originated in Pennsylvania. So, I began to investigate the history. Many of our older University of Maine alumni said, 'Oh my grandmother made whoopie pies in the 1940's, this is a Maine tradition. Amos, you have to do something. We can't let Pennsylvania steal our heritage.' So, the Maine Whoopie Pie Association was formed. There was a ground-swell of supporters to have the whoopie pie designated as the State Dessert, which later became the State Treat. Ultimately, the bill LD 71 designated the blue-

berry pie the Official State Dessert and the whoopie pie as the State Treat. Pennsylvania fought back hard, declaring a Whoopie Pie War of 2011 with the State of Maine; however, Pennsylvania historians couldn't find any evidence of a whoopie pie recipe earlier than about 1960. Labadie Bakery in Lewiston, Maine, had been making whoopie pies since 1925, so Maine won the war."

Cookie:
½ cup shortening
1½ cups sugar
2 eggs
½ cup cocoa
½ cup sour milk
1 teaspoon vanilla
2⅔ cups flour
1 teaspoon baking soda

1 teaspoon baking powder
1 teaspoon salt

Filling:
3 tablespoons flour
¾ cup milk
¾ cup shortening
¾ cup sugar
1 teaspoon vanilla

To make the cookies: Preheat oven to 350 degrees. Cream shortening. Add sugar and eggs and mix well. Mix cocoa with ½ cup hot water and add to shortening mixture. Add milk and vanilla and mix well. Sift dry ingredients and add to mixture. Drop by teaspoons on a cookie sheet, flatten down slightly with bottom of glass dipped in water. Bake approximately 19 minutes, then cool on a wire rack.

To make the filling: Mix flour with milk, and cook over medium heat, stirring regularly, until thickened. Cool to lukewarm and add shortening, sugar, and vanilla. Beat with an electric mixer until creamy, about 5 minutes. Spread the filling between two cooled cookies.

State of Maine

Proclamation

WHEREAS, the whoopie pie is a distinctive Maine dessert; and

WHEREAS, whoopie pies in Maine date back to 1925, with the first whoopie pies having been reportedly sold at Labadie's Bakery in Lewiston; and

WHEREAS, many Maine bakers make whoopie pies to be sold in bakeries, convenience stores, grocery stores, local markets and even gas stations throughout the state; and

WHEREAS, the popularity of whoopie pies nationwide is growing, with bakeries around the country and national chains now serving up variations of the comfort food; and

WHEREAS, the Ashland Community High School Youth in Government has worked to ensure that the whoopie pie is recognized as a Maine creation; and

WHEREAS, the Whoopie Pie Festival is being held in Dover-Foxcroft on June 26, 2010,

NOW, THEREFORE, I, JOHN E. BALDACCI, Governor of the State of Maine, do hereby proclaim June 26, 2010 as

WHOOPIE PIE DAY

throughout the State of Maine, and urge all citizens to recognize this observance.

In testimony whereof, I have caused the Great Seal of the State to be hereunto affixed GIVEN under my hand at Augusta this twenty-first day of May in the Year of our Lord Two Thousand and Ten.

John E. Baldacci
Governor

Matthew Dunlap
Secretary of State
TRUE ATTESTED COPY

BICENTENNIAL BITES

Published in the Bicentennial year of our Independence by
Mrs. Rand's Reading classes, Grade 6, Central Middle School
Auburn, Maine

PUDDINGS & ICE CREAMS

Photo: Bicentennial Bites, compiled by Ms. Vesta Rand's 6th Grade Class, Central Middle School, Auburn, Maine, 1976. Dahlov Ipcar's Potato Almond Pudding from the cookbook is on page 231.

Worster House Baked Indian Pudding

Carla Gilley • Sidney, Kennebec County

"The Worster House in Hallowell was run by my paternal grand-parents, Thomas and Pauline Worster, from 1925 until 1960. It was famous for its fine dining and hospitality. Their slogan was 'Where Maine Goes to Dinner.' I have hundreds of their recipes and the original menus from 1925. I also have my grandmother's handwritten notes from the hotel, with the lists and amounts for large meals and celebrations."

1 quart milk, scalded and heated in a
   double boiler
¾ cup cornmeal
1 cup molasses (4 gulps)
1 cup brown sugar
2 cups raisins

½ cup real butter
2 teaspoons pure vanilla
1 teaspoon salt
1 teaspoon cinnamon
4 eggs
2 cans evaporated milk (12-oz size)

Sprinkle cornmeal into scalded milk, and whip.

Mix the remaining ingredients together in an 8 x 14-inch baking pan. Pour hot cornmeal mixture over all ingredients and mix well. Cook in slow oven (250 degrees) for 4 hours, making sure to stir every 15 to 20 minutes. Serve hot with your best vanilla ice cream.

Apple Cream

Rolande Lachapelle • Monmouth, Kennebec County

"My maternal grandmother, Marie Louise Gosselin Baril, made this recipe for her family in the 1930s. She lived in Little Canada in Lewiston, had eight children, and was a housewife and good cook. I grew up having it all my life, and my kids and grandchildren like it too."

3 apples
½ cup sugar
3 egg whites

Peel apples, then put into a saucepan with a little water. Cook until tender, remove from pan, let cool, then mash apple pulp from the core. Add the sugar, to taste, and egg whites, and beat with a mixer until foamy. Serve with either yellow or chocolate cake. Keep it in the fridge between servings, and you can rewhip until it is all gone.

Indian Pudding

Judith Ripley • Gray, Cumberland County

"Every Thanksgiving and Christmas, my grandmother, Marjorie Thomas Hammond, would bake the Indian pudding a day or two before the holiday, when the kitchen wasn't busy. The smell of molasses was unmistakable and would fill the house for days. My sister and I didn't appreciate it when we were young. When I met my husband, his family had Indian River Indian Pudding out of a can. Can you imagine that? To impress my new family, I offered to bring the Indian pudding for Thanksgiving and I have been cooking it every year since. My mother, Rosemond Hammond Morrill, interpreted my grandmother's recipe with the details that I needed, though I now realize that you can't go wrong. Really, 8 to 10 hours of cooking? That is very forgiving. I'm sure that my grandmother was cooking it in a wood cook stove and the cooking time would depend on how hot the fire was."

1 quart milk, plus more to top off
1 cup cornmeal
1 cup molasses
1 teaspoon salt

1 teaspoon cinnamon
Apples, peeled and quartered
   (enough to cover bottom of pot)

Heat a quart of milk in a double boiler. When it is boiling hot, slowly add cornmeal, stirring well, and molasses, salt, and cinnamon. Keep stirring until it thickens. Pour into a bean pot that is full of apples peeled and quartered. Fill the pot the rest of the way with cold milk, cover, and bake in a slow oven. (Start at 300 degrees and "slow it down" to 200.) Stir occasionally. Add more milk during cooking if needed. Bake 8 to 10 hours. Serve piping hot with vanilla ice cream.

Applesauce

John Bunker • Palermo, Waldo County

"Five or six days a week, from August to May, I make applesauce. It's easy, delicious and habit-forming. It's a great way to eat lots of apples. I never make vats of it; I never can it; I never freeze it. Not only that, I don't peel or core the apples. The skin and the cores are the best parts after all. Why throw away all that flavor and goodness? Not only will your sauce be more nutritious, less fiddling with the fruit means less prep time. A handful of apples cut into quarters or eighths, a little water, and a small saucepan is all you need.

Sugar and spices aren't necessary because the varieties speak for themselves. Use the right apples and you'll never again want to ruin them with additives of any kind. Just apples. That's all. After the cooked apples turn soft, I run them through a Foley hand-crank food mill. The Foley mill has only three pieces, doesn't need electricity, comes apart easily for cleaning, and requires nothing more than a rinse when you're done.

I eat most of the applesauce I make with my morning oatmeal. I also eat it with pancakes and waffles, and with most any meat. It's good on just about anything. The Maine orchardist Francis Fenton frequently declared that ice cream and hot applesauce for lunch everyday was the key to his health and longevity. (He lived to be ninety-nine.)

As you might expect, I've developed a selection of favorite sauce varieties. They all cook up in a few minutes, have interesting textures, inviting colors, and unique flavors. Sometimes I mix and match, but, more often, I prefer a 'single-variety' sauce. If you have access to an old Maine orchard, you're all set.

My favorite old summer sauce apples are Crimson Beauty and Cole's Quince; in fall, Duchess of Oldenburg and Kavanagh, and in winter, Roxbury Russet and Cherryfield. My favorite modern sauce apple is Redfield, a beautiful red-fleshed variety developed eighty years ago for the applesauce market. If you don't have access to any of these varieties, some Maine commercial orchards grow Paulared, Milton, Macoun, and St. Lawrence. All make decent sauce. And let's not forget McIntosh; it's worthless in a pie, but it makes quite acceptable sauce.

The most important thing is to experiment and keep it simple. Whenever I come across a new variety, I always cook up a small pan of sauce. You'll learn which ones you love. You might just find yourself making applesauce from late summer to late spring. Like I do."

Ada Foss Cobb's Grapenuts Pudding

Cindi Cobb Annis • Monson, Piscataquis County

"Ada Foss Cobb was one of five sisters, the Foss Girls of Harmony. They were raised by their dad as their mom died in 1933. When this happened the 'Girls' were 2 to 17 years of age. I refer to the five of them (Louise, Barbara, Myrtie, Ada, and Norma) as being like the fingers of a hand, forever attached at the base. They would speak to each other frankly and didn't mince their words, but if you messed with one of them then they unite together. As I was often told, 'Friends come and go, but Family is forever.' For several years, three of the widowed sisters, Myrtie, Louise, and Ada, lived all together in their childhood home in Harmony.

The Foss Girls were wonderful cooks. We have compiled three 'Foss Family Favorites Cookbooks.' My Uncle Paul designed each of three covers. In the family, we refer to them by their color: blue (1982), red (1988), and yellow (1995). The dedication in the 1988 red Foss Family Favorites reads: 'To the Five Foss Family Girls: It is from you that we have learned the true meaning of family. Your loyalty is unquestionable, your love is unbreakable, and your spirit of family is inspirational.'" —*Jayne Farrin*

4 eggs
½ cup sugar
1 teaspoon vanilla

¼ teaspoon nutmeg, plus more for sprinkling
3 cups milk
¼ cup Grapenuts cereal

Beat eggs, add sugar, vanilla, nutmeg, and milk. Add grapenuts. Stir all together. Pour into a buttered baking dish, sprinkle with nutmeg, and set baking dish into a pan of water. Bake at 375 degrees for about 5 minutes and turn back to 350 degrees and bake until knife comes out clean.

Bowdoin Logs

Millie Stewart • Brunswick, Cumberland County

"I edited the *Merrymeeting Merry Eating* cookbook, published in 1988. We sold about 11,000 copies of the book, which was published by the Mid Coast Hospital Auxiliary, celebrating the 250th anniversary of the incorporation of Brunswick in 1739. This recipe is an old-time dessert at Bowdoin College with a delicious chocolate sauce from the Wentworth Hall Dining Service."

Logs:
2 boxes Nabisco Famous Chocolate Wafers
1 cup sliced almonds
1 half-gallon block ice cream,
    flavor of choice

Chocolate sauce:
8 tablespoons butter or margarine
1 pound confectioners' sugar
12 ounces evaporated milk
8 ounces unsweetened chocolate
⅛ teaspoon salt
1 teaspoon vanilla extract

For logs, blend chocolate wafers in food processor or blender until fine and smooth. Toast almonds on cookie sheet in preheated 350 degree oven for 5 to 10 minutes. Remove and cool. Cut ice cream into 18 to 24 equal-size rectangular blocks. Place several scoops of wafer crumbs on flat surface and, working quickly, roll a block of ice cream back and forth on crumbs while pressing down lightly until it is shaped into log. Freeze immediately. Repeat with remaining blocks and crumbs.

For sauce, combine all ingredients in double boiler over medium or low heat. Cook until thick and smooth, ½ hour or longer. Set aside until needed. Reheat over warm water.

To serve, cut ends off each log. Put dab of chocolate sauce on dessert plate and place a log on sauce. Add another dab of sauce on center of log. Garnish with almonds. Makes 18 to 20 logs.

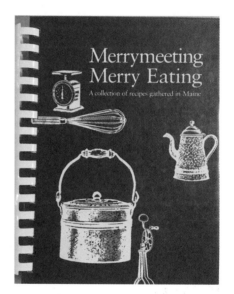

Mother's Holiday Fruit Salad

Rosanne Graef • Portland, Cumberland County

"The Mother in this recipe's name was Lillian Pitman Roakes (1901-1970) of Fryeburg, Auburn, and West Falmouth. Our family had this fruit salad at every holiday or birthday meal that she attended and many of us still do. She was active in the Grange and also the Farm Bureau and probably picked up this recipe over the course of her involvement with those organizations."

Fruit salad:
1 can pineapple chunks
1 can mandarin oranges
1 can dark sweet cherries
2 oranges, peeled and cut
2 or 3 bananas, peeled and sliced

Custard dressing:
2 eggs, separated
⅓ cup plus 2 tablespoons sugar
½ cup pineapple juice
¼ cup lemon juice
Pinch salt
¼ cup butter
1½ tablespoons flour

In a large serving bowl, combine fruit, except bananas.

Make the custard dressing: Beat egg yolks in a medium bowl, and add ⅓ cup sugar. Stir in pineapple and lemon juice. Add salt and mix well. Melt butter in saucepan. Stir flour into the melted butter. Add egg yolk mixture and cook over medium heat, stirring constantly until thick. Remove from heat and let cool.

In a separate bowl, beat egg whites, adding sugar 1 tablespoon at a time, until stiff. Fold egg whites into custard.

Combine custard dressing with fruit and mix thoroughly; add sliced bananas just before serving.

Banana Ice Cream

1908 • *Ninth Grade Cook Book*
Ninth Grade Pupils of Emerson Grammar School E.S.R. • Bar Harbor, Hancock County

The availability of tropical fruit has always been a treat in northern climes, and here a 9th grade class of students uses bananas to make ice cream. The instruction "freeze as usual" shows the popularity of the home ice cream making machine in early 19th century Maine. —*DL*

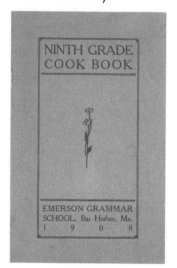

Peel six ripe bananas, split and remove the seeds and dark portion of the center. Rub the pulp through a puree strainer. Add it to the juice of one lemon, a little salt, and sugar to make it quite sweet. Add this pulp to a cream made of four eggs, one quart of milk and one-half cups sugar. It is much smoother if the yolks and whites of eggs are beaten separately. Freeze as usual.

Bread Pudding

Linda Labbe • Dayton, York County

"My Mom, Irene Paul, used to make a variation of this recipe she'd gotten from her mom, Florence Grant. I've reduced the sugar and added raisins."

6 to 8 slices bread
2 apples, peeled, cored, and sliced thin
¾ cup raisins
2 tablespoons butter or margarine, melted
4 beaten eggs

2 cups milk
½ cup sugar
1 teaspoon cinnamon
1 teaspoon vanilla extract

Preheat oven to 350 degrees. Slice bread and apples in triangles. Alternate slices in an 8 x 8-inch baking pan, sprinkle with raisins, and pour melted butter over top. In a medium bowl, combine eggs, milk, sugar, cinnamon, and vanilla, and beat until well mixed. Pour over bread, and press lightly until mix is absorbed. Bake until bread bounces back at touch, about 30 minutes. We love it hot, served with French vanilla ice cream.

Dahlov Ipcar's Potato Almond Pudding

Vesta Rand • Yarmouth, Cumberland County

This recipe was submitted by illustrator and author Dahlov Ipcar to *Bicentennial Bites*, compiled by Ms. Vesta Rand's 6th Grade Class, Central Middle School, Auburn, Maine, 1976. Ipcar clarified, in a note to the children, "This pudding makes its own sauce. The sauce forms at the bottom. This is not raw uncooked batter, but a combination of the sugar, egg yolks, and starch from the potatoes."

4 eggs, separated
½ cup sugar, separated
½ pound butter, softened
½ pound boiled potatoes, riced or put through a food mill

¼ cup almonds, blanched and chopped very fine
1 teaspoon vanilla
Pinch of salt

Beat egg whites until stiff and gradually add ¼ cup sugar and set aside. In a large mixing bowl beat butter and potatoes until well blended. Add egg yolks, almonds, ¼ cup sugar, vanilla, and salt. Beat until light. Fold in egg whites. Turn into buttered 2-quart casserole and bake at 350 degrees for 45 minutes. Set casserole on rack in pan of water while baking. Serve warm or cold.

Pop-Corn Pudding

1899 • *Cherryfield Cook Book*
Ladies of the First Congregational Parish • Cherryfield,
Washington County

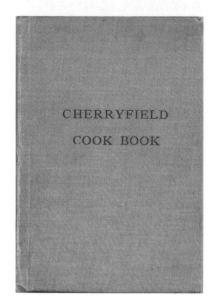

While Cherryfield considers itself the "Blueberry Capital of the World," surprisingly few blueberry recipes appear in this 1899 community cookbook. But Pop-Corn Pudding makes up for the lack in simplicity and novelty. —DL

Pop some corn nicely; then roll it as fine as you can. One pint corn, one quart sweet milk. Add small piece butter, one teaspoonful salt, two eggs, sugar to sweeten the milk. Mix all together and bake twenty minutes. —Contributed by Mrs. C. A. Ricker

Gram's Cracker Pudding

Phyllis Waldrip Pruett • Prospect Harbor, Hancock County

"My husband's family traces their history in Kittery and Kittery Point to before the Revolutionary War. His grandmother, Ruth Philbrick Pruett, passed this recipe to his mother, Lela Dame Pruett, and then to me and my stepson, Michael Pruett. It has been a Pruett family tradition to serve it with hard sauce at Thanksgiving and Christmas. Common crackers are hard to find now. My mother-in-law always used Saltines."

9 common crackers, crumbled
1 quart plus 1 pint milk
Butter the size of a walnut (2 tablespoons)
2 eggs

1 cup sugar (or to taste)
Salt, to taste
Vanilla, to taste

Soak crackers in 1 quart milk over low heat on the stove. When warm, add butter. Beat eggs and add sugar and dash of salt. Add egg mixture to milk. Put in oven and cook until brown on top. Then stir thoroughly and stir in the remaining pint of milk and vanilla, to taste. Cook until spoon comes out clean.

Frieda's Dessert

Jacalyn Mitchell • Naples, Cumberland County

"My grandmother, Velma Spencer, was born in 1899, and lived and raised her family in Maine. My parents both grew up here and graduated from the University of Maine, Dad as an engineer and Mom, now 96, as a teacher. We lived in Connecticut, but my maternal grandfather had built a camp on Beach Hill Pond, so every summer we stayed there and visited my grandparents. Whenever we visited Grammy Spencer, I begged her to make Frieda's Dessert and eventually convinced her to give me the recipe, which I have—and cherish—in her own handwriting."

12-ounce can evaporated milk
3-ounce package lime Jello
1¼ cups boiling water

½ cup sugar
Juice and rind of 1 lemon
Whipped cream, for serving

Chill evaporated milk overnight. Combine Jello with boiling water, sugar, and lemon juice and rind. Mix until dissolved. Put into refrigerator until just jelled. Then beat milk with electric beater and combine the two mixtures. Chill in the fridge, and serve with whipped cream.

Delicious Green Salad

Carol Tanner Proctor • Falmouth, Cumberland County

"We were served this Delicious Green Salad by the wife of the Air Force commander at the SAC refueling base in the Azores in 1960. Ever since we serve it every Thanksgiving and at special holiday gatherings."

1 cup heavy cream
1 cup hot water
3-ounce package lime Jell-O

8-ounce package cream cheese
1 medium can of crushed pineapple
½ cup chopped pecans

In a large bowl, whip cream. In a saucepan, bring water to a boil and add Jello, continually stirring to dissolve. Cool to room temperature. In a large bowl, beat together cream cheese and crushed pineapple. Pour Jello over mixture. Allow to gel in the refrigerator for 45 minutes. Then add to the bowl of whipped cream and beat until smooth. Add pecans. Pour into greased mold. Refrigerate until ready to serve. Just before serving, invert the mold.

Holiday Cranberry Pudding

Rachel Henderson • Portland, Cumberland County

"My mother, Paula Gendreau Cyr, made this at the holidays, and it was a recipe that she guarded closely—we never knew why, as she always shared her recipes with friends and relatives! It is simple and delicious, and one we continue to make in her memory for all the memories she made for us."

1 cup sugar
¼ teaspoon salt
2 teaspoons baking powder
2 cups flour
1 cup milk
3 teaspoons butter, melted
1½ cups fresh cranberries, cut in half

Sauce:
1 cup sugar
½ cup heavy cream
½ cup butter
1 teaspoon vanilla

Combine all the dry ingredients. Mix in the milk and butter using a fork. Add the cranberries. Place in an 8-inch square buttered pan and bake at 375 degrees for 30 to 40 minutes.

To make the sauce: Place all ingredients in a saucepan over low heat. Simmer—DO NOT BOIL—until sugar melts.

Serve each piece topped with a large scoop of the warm sauce.

Macaroon Ice Cream

circa 1935 • *Woodlawn Teas. Selected Recipes*
House Committee of the Colonel Black Mansion • Ellsworth, Hancock County

The teahouse became a popular place for women to gather, discuss the world, and snack on some light and often sweet foods. This simple ice cream made with yesterday's (perhaps) macaroons has a delicate flavor. —DL

2 quarts thin cream, 1 cup sugar, 2 or 3 macaroons (the macaroons can be dried in oven until you can roll them to crumbs with a rolling). Mix all together and freeze. —Contributed by Irma Eliason

Maple Cottage Pudding

Mary Anne Libby • Mount Vernon, Kennebec County

"My husband, Russell Libby, was the executive director of the Maine Organic Farmers and Gardeners Association from 1995 to 2012. A dish that he brought to a few of the many MOFGA potlucks was this Maple Cottage Pudding, a quintessential Maine dish from an old Maine Rebekahs cookbook from 1955. My daughter Rosa says that perhaps Russell's most iconic 'recipe' is: Amble through your orchard and pick a ripe apple from any tree. When you get home, cut it into slices, maybe add a slice of a locally made cheese, and share it with whoever happens to be there with you."

1 cup maple syrup brought to boiling. Cream 1 tablespoon butter, 3 tablespoons sugar. Add well beaten egg, ½ cup sweet milk, vanilla, 1 cup flour, 2 teaspoons baking powder, salt. Pour batter in hot syrup. Bake 25 minutes or until brown. Bake in an 8 x 8-inch pan for 25 minutes at 350 degrees or until brown.

Mrs. Gross's Apple Pudding
aka to family and friends "Mrs. Gross's"

Vickie Simpson • Bath, Sagadahoc County

"This is a recipe that my mother Jane Earl made, I believe starting in the late 1930s when she married my father, Ted Earl, who worked for Bath Iron Works during World War II. My parents were early skiers at Sugarloaf, and I can imagine my mother making 'Mrs. Gross's' after a day of skiing—she had the recipe in those early years of their marriage. And my dad loved it! Throughout my childhood, this was our favorite dessert and we had it fairly often, probably partially because it was so delicious, and also because it was not expensive and could feed our family of seven. My mother always made it only with apples. As an adult, I began to add other Maine fruit such as blueberries, rhubarb, or strawberries. My children now sometimes call and tell me they have taken 'Mrs. Gross's' to a party and it continues to be a hit! The topping is what makes it

different from other apple desserts; it is cake-like and crisp at the same time. And no, we don't know who Mrs. Gross was—perhaps another shipbuilder's wife also with a hungry family, but her name continues!"

6 to 8 apples peeled and cut into chunks or slices
½ cup to 1 cup rhubarb or wild Maine blueberries, fresh or Wyman's frozen
1 cup sugar
1 cup flour

1 teaspoon baking powder
½ teaspoon salt
1 egg, beaten,
1 teaspoon cinnamon
⅓ cup butter, melted

Put fruit in a greased baking dish, the approximate size of a pie plate but deeper.

Mix dry ingredients, except cinnamon, in glass or metal bowl, and mix egg in with fork until all is crumbly, like coarse cornmeal. Cover fruit with crumbly mix. Sprinkle cinnamon lightly over the top. Pour melted butter over whole surface.

Bake at 350 for 35 to 40 minutes, until top is lightly brown.

Inn Girl's Hot Fudge Sauce

Byrd Wood • Cape Elizabeth, Cumberland County

"In 1904, my great-grandparents brought their five children up from Boston by boat, train, and buckboard to spend a summer on the shores of China Lake. The family fell in love with the lake and the surrounding area and found a welcoming community of summer residents that soon expanded to include their extended family and many friends. They returned each summer to spend time on the lake. More than a century later, the descen-

dants of these families still return to their old summer cottages. For many years the summer residents hired a cook to provide meals at a central dining place. 'The Inn,' as we called it, was a sturdy, New England cape with a large barn that had been converted to a dining room. When I was growing up, we sat by family, with children, parents, and grandparents all together at the same large table. Lunch, served at noon, was buffet style. Dinner was more formal, and while it seems odd to think of it now, we used to dress up for dinner. Men would wear jackets, women wore dresses and low-heeled shoes. My sister and I wore little smocked dresses. The 'Inn girls' or 'table girls,' local teenagers who were hired at the beginning of the summer, waited on the tables, wearing starched white aprons. Meals usually consisted of baked chicken, pot roast, or fish, along with a salad, vegetable, and rice or boiled potatoes. Sunday dinner, which began at 1:00, was more elaborate, beginning with fruit cocktail, rolls, a hearty roast, vegetables, and dessert. The desserts made sitting through dinner worthwhile for the kids. The Inn girls would come out and recite a tempting variety of options: raspberry, strawberry rhubarb, or blueberry pie (homemade, of course); bread pudding; and ice cream or sherbet with a choice of toppings. My grandmother and I were particularly fond of coffee ice cream topped with hot fudge sauce. Here is the recipe from my grandmother's collection of handwritten recipes titled 'Inn Girls' Chocolate Sauce.'"

3 squares (ounces) unsweetened chocolate
1½ cups sugar
Pinch salt

⅛ teaspoon cream of tartar
1 cup unsweetened evaporated milk
1 teaspoon vanilla

Melt chocolate in double boiler over low flame. Stir in sugar, salt, and cream of tartar. Gradually add evaporated milk, stirring constantly, and continue cooking and stirring for 5 minutes. Add vanilla. May be kept in refrigerator and heated in double boiler. Serve over ice cream, preferably coffee.

CANDY

Photo: Tom Wilbur making chocolate in Freeport, 1985.
The Wilbur family recipe for Grandma Dobbins' Penuchi is on page 243.

Needhams

Deborah Ladd • Rangeley, Franklin County

"This recipe was given to me by Eleanor Huff Stinchfield, originally from Farmington, who was my mother's dear friend, my Home Economics teacher, and my 'third grandmother.' While I was growing up, her grandchildren, who were about my age, lived in Hawaii and she didn't see them often. She asked if my sister and I would like to call her Mimi. She didn't hear this from her own grandchildren often, since phone calls were so expensive then. Today, I am Mimi to my three young grandchildren in honor of Eleanor."

¾ cup mashed potatoes
½ teaspoon salt
¼ pound butter
2 pounds confectioners' sugar
½ pound flaked coconut

2 teaspoons vanilla
12-ounce package semi-sweet
   chocolate bits
4 squares unsweetened chocolate
½ cake paraffin wax

Combine mashed potatoes with salt. Melt butter in double boiler. Add mashed potato, sugar, coconut, and vanilla. Mix until well blended. Turn into a 9 x 13-inch pan. Chill.

While cooling, heat chocolates and paraffin wax in a double boiler. When potato mixture has chilled, cut into 2-inch squares. Dip the squares in the melted mixture, using a toothpick. Set on wax paper and let cool.

Molasses Corn Balls

Carlene Hill Byron • Topsham, Sagadahoc County

"These cornballs have been part of Christmas for our entire life. When Auntie (mom's unmarried Aunt Mina Clay) was still living in Gorham, we'd carry some, along with the tree we cut for her, to her home each year. When we kids moved away from home, Mom would send sacks of cornballs home with us after the family Christmas celebration. I've been known to eat my way through a half dozen during a two-hour drive back to my own home. The part I remember best about making these cornballs is the way the hot syrup billows into golden molasses clouds the instant the soda is added."

½ cup butter
1½ cups brown sugar
½ teaspoon salt
1 tablespoon vinegar

¾ cup molasses
½ teaspoon baking soda
12 cups popped corn

Prepare the work table where you will form the corn balls by laying out waxed paper—this is where you will scoop the hot mixture and lay the formed corn balls.

Put butter, brown sugar, salt, vinegar, and molasses in a pot, heat, and cook to 270 degrees (hard crack stage). Remove from heat. Stir in soda—it will foam up dramatically! Quickly pour mixture over popped corn and stir to (mostly) cover.

Scoop out coated corn onto waxed paper—anywhere from about ½ to 1 cup at a time, depending on the size corn ball you want. With clean, buttered hands, quickly press the hot mix into balls. The process has to go quickly so the mix remains soft enough to form—it's good to have an extra pair of hands or two helping.

Stretched Molasses Candy

1920 • *Cook Book No. 2*
Ladies of the Chesterville Grange • Chesterville, Franklin County

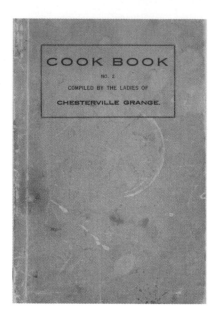

Candy recipes were a regular feature in community cookbooks, as home candy-making was a popular activity and because candy-making often required a degree of exactness that called for a written recipe. However, the recipes presume advance knowledge of candy-making, and often are written as simple formulas, without instructions. —DL

One cup molasses, 3 cups sugar, 1 cup boiling water, 3 teaspoons vinegar, ½ teaspoon cream tartar, ½ cup melted butter added just before it is done, ¼ teaspoon soda when taken from stove.
—Submitted by Mary J. Lowell

Microwavable Peanut Butter Fudge

State Prisoner Matthew • Warren, Knox County

This fudge uses ingredients found in the prison commissary, and was created by an inmate at the Maine State Prison.

> 1½ jars peanut butter
> ½ jar Fluff
> 1½ cups sugar (for less sweetness, use 1 cup)
> 1 bag M&Ms

In a bowl, empty out the peanut butter and Fluff. Place the bowl in the microwave and heat until it starts to rise. Take the bowl out of the microwave and stir. Let sit.

Pour a small amount of water in a separate bowl with the sugar. Mix. There should be a thick consistency to the sugar water. Place in the microwave and heat until the mixture begins to boil. Take out and stir for 10 seconds. Place back into the microwave and let the sugar boil until it turns a golden brown color. The sugar should be at the point of crystalizing.

Pour the M&Ms into the peanut butter/Fluff mixture. Then pour in the sugar mixture. Quickly stir, as the fudge will begin to harden fast. After mixing well, pour into a greased pan, or a box with a trash bag tucked around the corners. This is how we do it. Take a spoon and spread out evenly, with a gloved hand; press down on the top to compact the fudge. Let sit for 1½ to 2 hours and enjoy.

Grandma Dobbins' Penuchi

Andy Wilbur • Freeport, Cumberland County

"This is a family recipe that came from my maternal grandmother's friend, who the family called Mama Dobbins. She was a first-generation Irish immigrant living in Brighton, Massachusetts, where my mother grew up. My grandmother died when my mother was eight, and Mama Dobbins acted as a surrogate grandmother to my mother and her three brothers. This recipe uses the alternative spelling for Penuche, which we make at Wilbur's of Maine. Because of my mother's childhood memories, this was one of the first candies my father produced."

2 cups white sugar
2 cups brown sugar
1 cup milk
1 cup evaporated milk

1 cup walnuts, broken in medium-sized pieces
Butter the size of a walnut (2 tablespoons)
½ teaspoon vanilla extract

Combine sugars and milks and bring to a boil above 234 degrees (soft ball stage). Remove from heat and allow to cool to 100 degrees.

Add walnuts, butter, and vanilla extract, and beat until mixture is thick enough to pour. Pour into a greased baking pan. Cut as soon as mixture sets.

Flax Seed Candy

1882 • *Cuisine. A Collection of Family Receipts*
Ladies of Bangor • Bangor, Penobscot County

This recipe is not included in the printed text of this book, but is a handwritten recipe, laid-in to the book by an early owner. Cookbooks in the home became, and still become, depositories of new recipes, gathered from friends and family members or from published sources. Over decades they grow thick with new favorites. —DL

1 pound brown sugar
½ cup flax seed
2 or 3 ounces slippery elm

tThe flax seed and slippery elm are to be previously soaked, each in ½ cup cold water, then put all together and simmer. The seed and elm need to be soaked some hours.

Potato Fudge

Rosalie Colby • Hiram, Oxford County

"My grandmother Grace E. Locklin was well known in Kezar Falls for cooking her many specialties (baked beans, custard pie, and chocolate cake) at the Charter House Grange suppers. Potato Fudge was another of her specialties. The *Maine Sunday Telegram* did a feature about her in 1993 and called her 'A Lady of Maine.' She was a remarkable woman and truly a Lady of Maine."

1 small potato
½ teaspoon vanilla
1 pound powdered sugar (you may need more)
½ cup to 1 cup peanut butter

Peel and boil one small potato. Mash while still hot. Mix in vanilla and as much powdered sugar as you can to make a thick dough. Roll dough into a flat, thin rectangle. Spread with peanut butter and roll it up like a jelly roll. Cut into slices about ½-inch thick.

The Power of Sharing Food
By Micky Bondo

My first exposure to the changes when I moved to the United States was the food and the challenges that come with migration for immigrants. Migration can be a situation where the nutrition transition happens very quickly. It can be challenging to preserve our culture and adapt to the norms of a new society. But I was able to combine my traditional recipes and the mainstream spices found in an American supermarket to find a foundation of a better cooking style.

Many immigrants' stories go untold or are misrepresented. In Her Presence, the organization I began with Claudette Sara Ndayininahaze, was founded to recognize that each woman must maintain her own identity while creating new connections for herself and her family. As an organization, the best way we could help was to build a program, 'Connect to Your Community,' which serves as a platform to create a sense of belonging and appreciation.

Food is the essence that enables newcomers and mainstream communities to thrive and develop a common access to stories and culture, respect and inclusiveness. Sharing recipes, methods of preparation, and styles of presentation of traditional meals from their cultures allows women who have immigrated to Maine to contribute to their integration process, where fear will turn to self-confidence. It also helps with an increased mastery of the language, and intercultural connection and networking. The power of sharing food breaks barriers among people from different communities and builds strong human capital. Immigrant women are coming out of the shadows and onto the stage. They are building relationships between women from different cultures, bringing the value of their home food to the mainstream table, and forming a community in which hope and resilience take place.

Abusana "Micky" Bondo was born in Kinshasa, Democratic Republic of Congo, educated in Belgium, and has called Portland her home since 2009. In addition to running the non-profit In Her Presence, which she co-founded, Micky is a member of the Portland Board of Education and the mother of five children. She is an advocate for student-centered learning and is committed to empowering immigrant women.

Recipes in this cookbook from *In Her Presence* members:

Nahlah Alsafar's Kofta with Eggplant and Rice (page 150)

Angelique Bitshiluala's Makayabu (Salt Fish with Vegetables) (page 112)

Rachel Boyango Likabe's Wedding Ginger Juice (page 252)

THE WONDER BAR

PRESENTS

CROFT

CREAM ALE

SERVED AT ITS BEST

BY

KOOLER KEG SYSTEM

BEVERAGES

Photo: A vintage ad for cream ale from The Wonder Bar Steak House, owned by the four Droggitis Brothers of Biddeford. Their family recipe for Macoranadi can be found on page 144.

Hay-Time Switchel

Caryl McIntire Edwards • Harrison, Cumberland County

"Etta Pratt McIntire always served the 'men folk' this drink when they were haying at Sweet Hill Farm. A look at its history says that it originated in the West Indies and became popular as a summer drink in the American Colonies in the late 1600s. By the 1800s, it had become a tradition to serve it to thirsty farmers at the hay harvest time, thus it acquired the alternate name of 'Haymakers Punch.' There was always a lot of this on hand during haying season. It kept the workers hydrated and tasted very good."

> 1 cup light brown sugar
> 1 quart cold water
> 1 cup apple cider vinegar
> 1 tablespoon ground ginger
> ½ cup light molasses

Combine all ingredients and stir well.

Raspberry Shrub

1891 • *Choice Receipts from Many Homes*
Ladies of the Independent Society • Presque Isle, Aroostook County

Fruit shrubs and their non-fruity cousin, switchel, were used as both drinks and preserves throughout the 18th and 19th century. Recently, contemporary cocktail culture is bringing them both back as ingredients in specialty mixed drinks. Commonly, shrubs are described as easy to make, but this recipe gives us a good sense of the real labor and precision involved in cooking up a batch. —DL

To make this vinegar, as its now called, put the raspberries into a stone vessel and mash them to a pulp. Add cider vinegar—no imitation will do but the genuine article—enough to cover it. Stand in the sun 12 hours, and all night in the cellar. Stir up well occasionally during that time. Strain, and put as many fresh berries in the jar as you took out; pour the strained vinegar over them, mash and set in the sun all day; then keep in a cool place over night. Strain a second time the next day. To each quart of juice thus obtained allow one pint of water and five pounds of sugar to every three pints of this liquid, juice and water together. Only the best fine granulated sugar should be used for this, as for the preserves and jellies. Place this mixture of liquid and sugar over a gentle fire, and stir until the sugar is dissolved. Heat slowly to boiling, skim well, taking off every particle that arises to the surface, and as soon as it fairly boils take it off and strain. Bottle while warm and seal the corks with sealing wax.

Blueberry Maple Smoothie
Cynthia Finnemore Olin • Newcastle, Lincoln County

"I have always loved wild blueberries, with a full-on heart throbbing crush, like seeing your sweetheart across a crowded room. Every August when the roadside stands set out their 'Blueberries for sale' signs, my heart does a little tap-dance. Wild Maine blueberries are the best in the world. Sweet and sour little amethyst gems perfect for pie, muffins, jam, pancakes… just to pop in your mouth. I freeze them in gallon plastic bags and whenever I want a burst of summer sunshine, the blender is filled with the ingredients below. Maple syrup is the ideal complement, naturally sweet and mellow. If you're trying to get a few more healthy greens into your belly, you can even add a cup or more of fresh kale or spinach to the blender and blend it an extra minute before adding the ice. It'll be supercharged and delicious!"

1 cup blueberry juice or orange juice
1 cup skim milk
1 cup plain or vanilla yogurt
2 cups wild Maine blueberries, fresh or
   Wyman's frozen

2 ripe bananas, peeled or 2 cups of
   fresh fruit in season: pitted cherries,
   raspberries, or strawberries
2 tablespoons fresh lime juice
3 tablespoons Maine maple syrup
2 cups ice
Sprigs of mint for garnish

Place all ingredients in a blender. Blend on high until all of the ice is completely crushed and the mixture is smooth and delicious. Garnish with a sprig of mint. Serves 4 to 6.

Espresso Martini

Andrew Volk • Portland, Cumberland County

Andrew and Briana Volk are the couple behind the acclaimed Portland Hunt + Alpine Club and the book *Northern Hospitality*, which celebrates Briana's Scandinavian roots. This recipe is one of their favorites.

> 2 ounces Sweetened Coffee Concentrate (recipe follows)
> 1 ounce white rum
> 1 ounce Allen's Coffee Flavored Brandy

Add the coffee concentrate, rum, and Allen's to a mixing tin. Add ice to the tin, cap, and shake hard for 30 to 45 seconds. Fine strain into a chilled cocktail glass. Enjoy immediately. Makes 1 drink.

Sweetened Coffee Concentrate

> 1 pound coffee beans, ideally a darker espresso roast, coarsely ground
> Simple syrup of ⅓ cup sugar dissolved in ⅓ cup water

Combine coffee and 64 ounces cold water in a large glass pitcher, cover, and allow to sit at room temperature for 12 hours. After steeping, filter twice, first using a fine-mesh filter to remove grounds, and then a paper filter to remove sediment.

Measure the amount of coffee concentrate you made and add ⅓ that amount of simple syrup. Stir until fully combined.

Bottle, date, and store the sweetened coffee concentrate in the refrigerator for up to 4 weeks. You can use this in the Espresso Martini or simply dilute it with water and ice whenever you need a quick pick me up!

Christmas Season Egg Nog

James Marshall • Portland, Cumberland County

"This recipe has been in the family since at least 1950. I do not know exactly where it came from but at one point it was referred to as 'Colonel Lynn's' Egg Nog. Growing up in Cape Elizabeth we made it every year, and as an adult, my wife and I have continued the tradition: We hold an egg nog making party in early December. A single recipe will make just over a gallon, but we usually make five recipes and fill a 6-gallon crock. We leave the crock outside on the porch and serve from there. The colder the weather, the better the egg nog. It is really great when there are little ice slivers in your cup. A word of caution, more than one 'first timer' has asked for a third mug. That almost always proves to be one too many."

6 eggs, separated
¾ cup granulated sugar
2¼ cups cognac

¾ cup rum
4 cups whole milk
4 cups heavy cream

Beat yolks until very light. Set egg whites aside. Add sugar slowly to the yolks and beat until well blended. Slowly add the cognac, continuing to beat. Be careful not to "cook" the yolks. Stir in rum, then milk.

In a separate bowl (a chilled stainless steel bowl works well), beat the cream until stiffly whipped. Fold whipped cream into mixture.

In a separate bowl, beat the egg whites until they are stiff but not "dry." Fold into mixture. Be sure to use a clean bowl or they won't stiffen.

The egg nog will separate as it sits so be sure to mix totally before each serving. Sprinkle a little nutmeg on top.

The Droggitis brothers at The Wonder Bar in Biddeford.

Spruce Beer

1920 • *State of Maine Cook Book*
Democratic Women of Maine • Wiscasset, Lincoln County

Published on the occasion of Maine's Centennial in 1920, the State of Maine Cookbook drew recipes from around the state, as this book does. Mary G. Tucker of Wiscasset contributed a number of recipes, all with an eye to the past practices of cooking in Maine. This recipe celebrates the rich variety of local foraged ingredients, uses molasses from the West Indies, and reminds us of the difficult labor involved in putting food and drink on the table. —*DL*

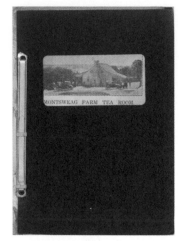

Put in a large kettle, spruce boughs, checkerberry leaves, yellow dock root, dandelion root, black cherry bark and spruce bark; cover with cold water and steep over a very slow fire for half a day. Drain and mix with two pails of cold water, add one and one-half pints of molasses to each pail of liquid and dissolve two yeast cakes in lukewarm water and add to mixture; strain through cheese-cloth, put in jugs in a warm place till it has worked off scum, then cork tightly. —Submitted by Mrs. Mary G. Tucker

Wedding Ginger Juice from Burkina Faso

Rachel Boyango Likabe • Bath, Sagadahoc County

Rachel and her twin sister came to Maine from West Africa and have lived in Bath for two years. As children, they loved following their mother around the kitchen, so starting at a young age, she taught them to cook. Here in Maine, they enjoy educating others about their culture through food. Rachel notes that ginger juice and hibiscus punch are two essential drinks at any wedding in Burkina Faso.

1 large ginger root
Sugar

Lemon slices
Fresh mint

Wash the ginger, then cut it into small pieces, leaving the skin on. Put the pieces into a blender and puree, adding water to make a thick juice. Add more water, sugar, sliced lemon, and fresh mint to taste. Serve cold.

80,000

Maine students rely on school meals
every single day.

SCHOOL MEALS FIRST

Maine's school nutrition programs are the first and best support for kids experiencing hunger. Full Plates Full Potential is working to increase participation in school meal programs. Our goal — every child in need has access to three nutritious meals a day at school and during the summer.

WE ARE ON A MISSION TO END CHILD HUNGER IN MAINE.

PLEASE SUPPORT FULL PLATES FULL POTENTIAL'S EFFORTS TO KEEP MAINE'S KIDS FED.

 Full Plates
Full Potential
fullplates.org

PHOTO ©BONNIE KITTLE

FOCUSED ON
FEEDING
OUR COMMUNITIES

Credit unions across the state collectively participate in Maine Credit Unions' Campaign for Ending Hunger. Through this initiative we are moving Maine forward and Maine families upward.

Since 1990, the Campaign has raised over **$9.4 million**—money that stays in Maine to provide healthy, nutritious meals to those in need.

Learn more at **mainecreditunions.org**

 CAMPAIGN FOR
**ENDING
HUNGER**
MAINE CREDIT UNIONS

 MAINE
CREDIT UNIONS

ACKNOWLEDGMENTS

A community cookbook is a labor of love. We have many people to thank by name, but there are countless others, whose identities are lost to the centuries, without whom this book would not have been possible. The tireless work of all those who put together previous community cookbooks, whose traditions and recipes are the foundation of this project, deserve our biggest thanks. Gathering and testing recipes, typesetting them, and working outside the traditional publishing channels to bring a book to fruition is hard work, and we applaud all those who took it on before us and offer them our deepest thanks.

The origins of the *Maine Bicentennial Community Cookbook* spring from an innocent question, posed on social media, and we are indebted to Marge Kilkelly for planting a seed in our fertile imaginations. Don Lindgren's thorough knowledge of the history and landscape of community cookbooks, and extensive library, gave shape to the project.

In the early days of the project, we were spurred on by the enthusiasm of Mary Herman and the encouragement of Governor Janet Mills. At the Blaine House (and so far beyond!), Leslie Oster's unflagging support truly made this project possible. We are grateful to Donna Loring for expanding our understanding of the Wabanaki Confederacy and helping us place the bicentennial of statehood in a larger context. We are grateful to the Jewish Farmer Network and Maryland's Pearlstone Center for their inspiration and example for the creation of our Land and Food Acknowledgment.

Early on, our excitement about this project was reinforced by the reception it received. Thank you to Dave Cheever of the Maine Bicentennial Commission; Sherri Stevens and Eric Blom at Hannaford; Susan Sharon, Jennifer Rooks, Cindy Han and Cory Morrissey at Maine Public; Micki Mullen at the Maine Office of Tourism; Charlene Williams; Kathy Gunst; Hannah Carter at the University of Maine Cooperative Extension; Amanda Beal, Commissioner of Agriculture, Conservation and Forestry; and Nancy McBrady, Bureau Director of Agriculture, Food and Rural Resources.

For providing a rich context to the food history and challenges of our state, thank you to those who contributed essays to the book: Darren J. Ranco, Nancy Harmon Jenkins, Sandy Oliver, Jim Hanna, and Abusana "Micky" Bondo. For helping us connect with new Mainers, thanks to In Her Presence, Amelia Garretson-Persans, Cultivating Community, and Diinkaa D. Lion.

As submissions came in and we got to the hard work of winnowing the recipes, we have been helped by Nancy Harmon Jenkins (again! always!), Jane Harmon Carr, Cynthia Finnemore Olin, Christine Burns Rudalevige, and Robert Bernheim. You helped us bring order to the chaos, see where we could tighten the copy, and fill in the "holes."

It's one thing to gather the recipes, but quite another to turn them into a physical book. Thanks goes to Melissa Kim, for making the introduction, and Dean Lunt and Islandport Press for including the book in its roster. The incomparable Ashley Halsey has designed a beautiful book, and done it with patience and heart. Thanks to our final readers and huge thanks to proofreader Amy Paradysz for her incredible attention to detail.

Thank you to Samantha Hoyt Lindgren for support and encouragement, Mark Germer for additional research and insight into the historical Maine books, and Anestes Fotiades and The Maine Menu Project for use of historical menus for research and image reproduction.

Thank you also to Vicki Akins, Heather Augustine, Nina Interlandi Bell, Ashley Benedict, Gillian Britt, Jim Britt, Glenn Chadbourne, Tom Easton, Emily Eckhardt, Julie Eugley, Jeff and Sonja Florman, Dawn Frankfurt, Meredith

Goad, Michael S. Graham, Rhiannon Hampson, Dan Jenkins, Craig Lapine, Sasha Leland, Taylor McCafferty, Susan Schatz Neudel, Amy Parker, James Pochurek, Cheryl Ramsay, Jamie Ribisi-Braley, Vanessa Santorelli, Ari Solotoff, Angie Stockwell, Carla Tracy, Ron Watson, Karen Watterson, Norma Jean Webber, Larry Westler, Alyssa Wood, and Nick Zeller.

None of this would have been possible without the ongoing support of Bruce & Nancy Schatz, Jeanine Hathaway, and Charlotte, Beatrice and Sadie Schatz.

Finally, thank you to everyone who cooks from this book, makes the recipes their own, and adds their family food story to the next 200 years of Maine cooking.

Great thanks to all the amazing Mainers who opened their homes, family cookbooks, recipe boxes, and family photo albums to us:

Abby Dunlap; Adam Hill; Ali Waks Adams; Alice Lynch; Allison Salisbury; Amanda Austin; Amber Lambke; Amos Orcutt; Amy Wight Chapman; Andrea Martin; Andrew Volk; Andy Wilbur; Angela Lundquist; Angelique Bitshiluala; Ann Sloatman; Anne Ashby Theriault; Anne D. Williams; Antonia Small; Arlene Goldstein; Attapol Sookma; Avery Kamila; Ben Diaz; Beto Guimaraes; Betsy Harding; Bill Nemitz; Billy Doukas; Brenda Athanus; Brenda Bourgoine; Brenda Broder; Brenda Kerr; Brenda Maxfield; Brett Johnson; Briana Alman; Byrd Wood; Caitlin Hunter; Carla Gilley; Carlene Hill Byron; Carlotta Keene; Carol Tanner Proctor; Carol Walsh; Carolyn Kelley; Caryl McIntire Edwards; Cate Orser; Cathleen Baylis Schwartz; Chad Conley; Cherie Scott; Chris Hart; Christine McDuffie; Christine Rudalevige; Christopher D'Amico; Cindi Cobb Annis; Cindy Colon; Claire Breton; Claudette Rossignol; Craig Sipe; Cynthia Dunbar; Cynthia Finnemore Simonds; Cynthia Palmer Sherman; Cynthia Scholar-Kellis; Cynthia Snow; Daphne Sanders; David and Maryli Tiemann; Dawnela Sheehan; Deborah Ladd; Debra Wallace; Dan Dostie; Diane Dostie; Diane Mann; Donna and Kate Mcaleer; Donna Dwyer; Donna Johnson; Donna Lambert; Doreen Duke; Elaine Baker; Elaine Luce; Elise Richer; Elizabeth DeWolfe; Elizabeth Stanton; Ellen Barnes; Ellen Densmore Booker; Ellen Farnsworth; Ellen Wood; Eric Houts and Susan Flynn; Eric Kangas; Erik Nielsen; Faye Luppi; Frances Harlow Clukey; Gail Ward; Gamana Yarow; Ginger Patterson; Heather Paquette; Heidi Symonds; Helena Strang; Henny Van Der Scheer; Hester Gilpatric; Islesford Historical Society; Jacalyn Mitchell; Jake Austin; Jake Metzler; James Marshall; James White; Jamie Gordon; Jane C. Legard; Jane Cleaves McKenna; Janelle Rhodeback; Jason and Lori Candelora; Jay Tall; Jayne Farrin; Jeanann Pollard; Jeff Holden;

Jennifer Scism; Jim Birkett; Jo Cameron; Jodie Mosher-Towle; John Bennett; John Bunker; John Kouronis; John Wilson; Jose Azel; Juanita Cuellar Nichols; Judith Ames Legendre; Judith Ripley; Julia Bailin; Julie Greene; Julie Terray; June LaCcombe; Karen Ellis; Karen Lancaster Morrill; Karen Soderberg Hinchliffe; Kate Fitzgerald; Kate Morin; Katherine Crosson; Katherine McGee Wilson; Kathy Gunst; Katie Murphy; Katina Stanwood; Kimberly Parsons; Kira Reed; Krista Kern Desjarlais; Krista Marvel; Larissa Crockett; Laura McCandlish; Lauren Webster; Laurie Taylor; Liana Hawes; Linda Labbe; Linda Morris; Linda Perry; Linda Russell; Lisa Millimet; Lois Blanchard Widmer; Lois Widmer; Lori Risner; Louis Fontaine; Louisa Edgerton; Lyle Hall; Lynne Holland; Margaret Harris; Margaret Stevens; Margie Kelly; Marilyn Meyerhans; Mark Messer; Marnie Reed Crowell; Martha Hadley; Martha McSweeney Brower; Martha Speed; Mary Anne Libby; Mary Drymon Derose; Mary Herman; Mary Jane LeCours; Matt Pelletier; Maureen Pease; Maya Flores; Melanie Wilson; Melissa Bailey; Michael Ball; Michael Pander; Michele Pfannenstiel; Millie Stewart; Mimi Gough; Nahlah Alsafar; Nancy Harmon Jenkins; Nancy McLaughlin; Nancy Wanderer; Nicole Castonguay; Nikki Gregory Erdman; Norma Dionne; Norma Salway; Norman Sullivan; Pam Russell; Patsy Messier; Patty Hymanson; Patty Pendergast; Paul Denckla; Paula Hopkins Dayboch; Paula Moore; Peggy O'Connor; Peter Berry; Phoebe Schilla; Phyllis Pruett; Phyllis Siebert; Poland Spring Resort; Rachel Boyango Likabe; Rachel Henderson; Rachel Tremblay; Randy Hatch; Representative Jared Golden; Representative Chellie Pingree; Rhea Cote; Rita Buckley; Rob Dumas; Robert Bernheim; Robert Kollmar; Robyn Norton; Rolande Lachapelle; Ronica Richardson; Ronnie Weston; Rosalie Colby; Rosanne Graef; Ruth Ristich;

Sally Foster; Sally Trice; Sally Walker; Sam Hayward; Sandy Oliver; Sara Jenkins; Sav Sengsavang; Senator Susan Collins; Sharon Bresler; Sheila Vaillancourt; Spiros Droggitis; State Prisoner Matthew; Stephen Dunham; Stephen King; Steve Peer; Steven Quattrucci; Sue Sturtevant; Susan Damm; Susan Goodwillie Stedman; Susan Koch; Susan Sanders; Susan Spector; Susan Vayda; Suzanne Trussell; Sylvia Pease; Sylvia Sim; Teresa Myers; The humble Farmer; Tyna Merdek; Ulla Meir; United Society of Shakers; Vanessa Seder; Vesta Rand; Vicki Doudera; Vicki Simpson; Victor Trodella; Wendy Thompson; Wes Judge; William Ginn.

Tremendous thanks to everyone who contributed to the Kickstarter campaign and made this book possible:

Abbe Levin; Alessandra Dreyer; Alexis Muskie; Alice Adams Melcher; Alisha Goldblatt & Zach Heiden; Amanda Beal; Amanda Roberson Austin; Amos E. Orcutt; Amy Austin; Amy B. Fagan; Amy E. Waterman; Amy L. Reams; Amy Wight Chapman; Andrew Molboski; Angela M. Morse; Ann Isobel Arnold; Anne Manning; Anonymous; Arthur Turcotte; Ashley Ferrer; Audrey & Q. Seddon; Avery Yale Kamila; B. Gunvaldsen; Barbara Bell Sturtevant; Barbara Hamilton; Beth Compton Interlandi; Beth Lubetkin; Betsy & Bob Gans; Betty Henriques; Blake Perkins; Bob Dodge; Bob Goodman; Bonnie M. Webber; Brenda Athanus; Brenda Kerr; Brenda Maxfield; Brenda Scott; Brian and Caity Hunt; Brian and Susan Starbird; Briana Alling Hogan Alman; Bridget Dickson; Brittany Cook; Bruce & Nancy Schatz; C. O'Connor; C.A.Prasch; Caleb & Jim Gerritsen; Carie Marie Wingert; Carla Suel; Carmen Harris; Carolyn Hardman; Caryn Crasnick-Maloney; Celestial Goldsmith; Chad Conley; Charlene Williams; Chip and Lisa Leighton; Chris Albee; Christine Burns Rudalevige; Christine O'Donnell; Claudette Rossignol; Claudia Hawkes; CSpaulding; Cynthia Finnemore Olin; Cynthia Graubart; Cynthia Mines & Toby Stucky; Cynthia P. Sherman; Dan & Kathy Camann; Dave & Hollye Seddon; Dave Hackman; David A. Sinclair; David and Dawn Homa; David Buchanan; David Ewick; David M. Grover; David Pearson; Dawn Frankfurt; Deb Harris; Deborah Bedard Ward; Debra K. Dean; Delbert Spine; Diana, Christopher, and Oswald Worcester Jr.; Diane A. Dostie; Diane Albano Vanpelt; Donna Currie; Donna L. Lambert; Donna Thomson; Donnell P. Carroll; Doris Harrison; Dorothy Adams; Dorothy T. Speed; Dragonfly Cove Farm; Duncan Ness; Dustin Rowles; E. Stanley; Elaine Bragdon; Elise, Archie, and Harry; Elizabeth & Robert Stoddard; Elizabeth Ansley; Elizabeth DeWolfe; Elizabeth Upham; Ellen Sylvia; Emery; Emily Beck; Enid Schatz & David Mitchell; Erik D. W. Greven; Erin Fitzimmons; Esther Martin-Ullrich; Ethan Welty; Evan J. Johnson; Fae & Jon Spath; Four Star Fresh; Gabrielle Lee Graham; Gail Gardner; Gibson Fay-LeBlanc; Glenn Baker; Gloria M. Boudreau; Hannah Maguire; Harvey Hatch; Heather Kiernan; In loving memory of Mary W. Sawyer; In memory of Edith Hill; Iva A Carroll; J + L Vine; J. Gunwaldsen; Jace Cooke; Jackie and Larry Vine; Jake Austin; Jake Metzler; James Greene, MD; Jamie L Gordon; Janelle Surace; Janice Gregg; Jasmine & Charlie Clayton; Jay and Kerri Buchholz; Jeanine Hathaway; Jeff Kirlin; Jennifer Pride Collins; Jennifer Wardwell; Jenny Stevens; Jessica Pantazelos; Jim Risner; Joan Levy; Joanne Anable; Jody Fein; Joel & Patty Robertson; Joel Miller; Jonathan LaBonte; Josef Kijewski; Josh, Samantha & Coby; Joy Ash; Joy Krinsky; Joyce Godsey; Julia Merriam; Juliette Denis Athanus; Kate Fitzgerald; Katherine; JB Simpson; Kathleen Benson; Kathleen Dunbar Later; Kathryn Langlois; Kim Hamilton; Kim Moore; Kimberly A. Hokanson; Kimberly Calderon; King Heiple; Kira, Kirk, Kennedy, and Anthony Reed; Kosta Psiakis; Krista Crommett; Kristi Gagne; Larissa Crockett; Lauren A. Carter; Lauren Cullity Sanford; Lauren Webster; Laurie Spooner; Leslie Oster; Leslie Thorndike; Liana Hawes; Lindsay Crooker-Mazariego; Lisa Botshon and Pete Milligan; Lisa Bradstreet Udelson; Lisa Gray Millimet; Lois Blanchard Widmer; Loraine Washburn; Lori Cheatle; Lori L. Norman; Lori Risner; Lori Schlenker; Lorna Mae Gordon; Luanne D Pachios; Lucky D'Ascanio; Luke Lorrimer; Lura Dell Barter Bell; Lynn Martin; Lynne Holland; Maria DiGiusto O'Neill; Marian Albee; Marianne Dodge; Marjorie Murray-Ure; Mark D. Grover; Martha L. Hadley; Martha A. Speed; Mary Merriam; Maryli and David Tiemann; Matt & Sara Gagnon; Matt Florell; Matt Hokanson; Matthew Pelletier & Family; Maureen A. Pease; Maybelle A. Blanchard; Melissa Bailey - In Honor of Her Mom, Barbara; Melissa A. Clark; Michael and Selena Conley; Michael Haselton; Michaela Paramo; Michele Metzler; Mildred Crocker; Molly Bogart; Mona Li; Morgan Bleimeyer; Muriel E.

Sayward; Nancy Markovsky; Nancy Wanderer & Susan Sanders; Natasha Baker; Neil K. Carroll; Nicole and Eric Sawyer; Nicole C. Castonguay; Nikki Erdman; Nikki G.; Nina Interlandi Bell; Noel Symons; Noni Strauss; Pajiba; Pam and Mike Sherrill; Pam, John & Chloe; Pamela Elder; Pat Woodard Havener; Patricia Eltman; Patricia L. Campbell family; Patricia L. Messier; Patt Murphy; Paul Greene; Paula Stewart; Pauline A Gudas; Peggy O'Connor; Percy Rossignol; Persis L. Thorndike; Peter Hertzmann; Phoebe Schilla; Rachel Harrington-Levey; Rachel Kahn-Troster; Rachel Lyn Rumson; Rachel Melcher Tremblay; Randy Hatch; Reade and Martha Brower; Red Stove Farm & Provisions; Renee Fay-LeBlanc; Rob Schatz; Robert Bernheim; Robert J.C. Buchanan III; Robyn Ferland Norton; Ron & Sheryl Adams; Ronnie Weston; Rosanne Graef; Ross; Ruby Rose Wright; Sam Hayward; Samantha Cote, Samson Graber; Sandy Nadeau Crockett; Sara Kahn-Troster and David Freidenreich; Sara Levensohn; Sarah Ferriss; Sarah Kaleko; Scarlet Peachey; Scott DeWolfe; Sean and Melodie Keating; Seth A. Reed; Shannon Sinkin; Sharon Freed; Sharyn Peabody; Sherrie Koocher Schatz and Stanley Schatz; Sofie Westra; Solwin Family; Sonia James; Sonja Ferris Florman; Sophia Inman; Spencer Droggitis; Spiros Droggitis; Steamboat Shire; Stella Stanley; Stephen Howe; Stephen Malarick; Steve Lewis; Steve London; Sue Sturtevant; Susan Bean; Susan Damm; Susan Greven "Vayda; Susan C. Koch; Susan N. Wagner; Susan Rottmann; Suzanne Trussell and Joseph A. Stupak, Jr.; Tara & Ashley Ingalls-Pratt; Tara L. Back; Taryn Kelley; Tatyana Herron; Taylor Jordan; Ted Kelleher; Teresa Close; Teri L. Willmore; The Allenby Family; The Cook Family; The Davis Family; The Green Hand Bookshop; The Mysterious Backer 'X'; the Okolita/Newbury family, The Phelan Family; Tin Pan Bakery; Town of Woodstock; V. Ness; Victoria Earl Simpson; Whitney Raymond; William Ginn; Winter Wren; Yasuko Hatano Collier; Yeto's; and all the unnamed cooks.

Huge thanks to all of our business sponsors — we could not have done this without your support:

Lobster Bake: Maine Office of Tourism; Maine Department of Agriculture, Conservation, and Forestry

Clam Bake: Hannaford; Miranda Restaurant Group; Stonewall Kitchen; Wyman's

Grange Hull Dinner: Maine Credit Unions; Maine Public; Sherman's Books

Bean Pot Supper: Austin Street Brewery; Bixby & Co.; The Cryer; Dirigo Food Safety; The Holy Donut; Home Remedies; Law Offices of Joe Bornstein; Luke's Lobster; Norway Savings Bank; Now You're Cooking; Oakhurst Dairy; The Press Hotel; University of Maine Cooperative Extension; Wilbur's of Maine

Seafood Platter: Bar Harbor Foods; Dean's Sweets; Maine Harvest Federal Credit Union; Maine Farm & Sea Cooperative; Maine Farmland Trust; Maine Grains; Maine Organic Farmers and Gardeners Association; Lee Auto Mall; Lorne Wine; LT's; Rose Foods; Sebago Lake Trading Company

Blueberry Pie: Maine Food for Thought Tours; Print: A Bookstore; SKORDO; York County Community College

Special thanks to: Sarah Alexander; Justin Alfond; Rachel Ambrose; Roxanne Ames; Jake Austin; Nate Bergeron; Dean Bingham; Ben Bornstein; Julia Bretz; Jeff Buchhalter; Scott Budde; Jennifer Burke; Patrick Carroll; Pam Chamberlain, Josh Christie; Jennifer Pride Collins; Chad Conley; Ben Conniff; Colleen Craig; Charles Crosby; Jeff Curtis; Emily Eckhardt; Jean English; Heather Fear; Lauran Franciose; Katy Green; Leigh Hallett; Sarah & Bryce Hatch; Lynne Holland; Carson James; Anne Karonis; Amber Lambke; Adam Lee; Ashley Martin; Krista Marvel; Sam May; Kate and Donna McAleer; Joshua Miranda; Michele Pfannenstiel; Matthew Robertson; Emily Russo; Ellen Sabina; Mike Sansing; Dave Seddon; Erin Sheehan; Deb Taylor; Bill Toomey; Andy Wilbur.

COPYRIGHTS & CREDITS

The recipes and stories included in this book belong to the many generous people who submitted them. We also acknowledge specific copyrighted material we were given permission to publish or republish within these pages:

A Recipe for Public Policy, copyright Governor Janet Mills; The Community Cookbook in Maine, copyright Don Lindgren; Wabanaki Foodways and the State of Maine, copyright Darren J. Ranco, PhD; Martha's Peaks Island Donuts, copyright Robert Bernheim; I Wish I Had a Hot Dog, copyright Ada Foss Cobb; Riley Water Pickles, copyright Sandy Oliver; Martha Ballard: A Woman's Place on the Eastern Frontier, copyright Nancy Harmon Jenkins; Pullen Sisters' Recipe Box, copyright Ruth Ristich; The Way It Was: Church Suppers, copyright Thomas W. Easton; Marge and Brownie in Our Kitchens, copyright Sandy Oliver; Bluefish and Empanadas, copyright Juanita Cuellar Nichols; Red Hot Mumbai Spicy Lamb Chili Dog, copyright Cherie Scott, Chicken Croquettes, copyright Phoebe Schilla; Ending Hunger in Maine by 2030, copyright Jim Hanna; Mom's Special Whoopie Pies, copyright Cate Orser; Applesauce, copyright John Bunker; The Power of Sharing Food, copyright Micky Bondo

All photographs inset within a recipe are courtesy of the submitter or submitter's family, unless otherwise noted below. All additional photographs are courtesy of, or credited as follows:

p. viii-ix: Cookbook collection of Don Lindgren by Karl Schatz; p. x-xi: collection of Don Lindgren; p. xii-xiii: collection of Don Lindgren; p. xiv collage (top left to bottom right): Alice Lynch, Amy E. Waterman, Four Star Fresh, Kira Reed, Maryli and David Tiemann, Photo by Gabe Souza/Portland Press Herald, Marge Kilkelly, Maureen Mehlhorn, Amanda Austin, Kate Morin, Martha Hadley, Jane Hartglass Baker, Susan Neudel, Lynne Holland; p. xviii: Gibson Hurst/Unsplash; p. 4: Karl Schatz; p. 7: collection of Don Lindgren; p. 13: Martha McSweeney Brower; p. 21: collection of Jeffrey Florman; p. 23: Suzanne Trussell; p. 30: Nikki Gregory; p. 38: Martha Hadley; p. 43: collection of Don Lindgren; p. 47: Ruth Ristich; p. 52: Brenda Kerr; p. 57: Pittsfield Historical Society; p. 64: Sav Sensavang; p. 68: Marilyn Meyerhans; p. 75: Ruth Ristich; p. 80: Abbe Levin; p. 83: NASA/Josh Valcarcel; p. 87: Katherine McGee Wilson; p. 90: Katherine McGee Wilson; p. 94: Norma Salway; p. 104: Antonia Small; p. 108: collection of Don Lindgren; p. 113: June LaCombe; p. 118 collage (top left to bottom right): Wendy Thompson, Maine Department of Marine Resources, John Atkinson, Nicole Castonguay, June LaCombe, Maine Department of Marine Resources, Karl Schatz, Ruth Ristich, Karl Schatz, Laura McCandlish; p. 123: Arthur Nichols; p. 127: Carol Walsh; p. 130: United Society of Shakers; p. 133: Jane C. Legard; p. 134: Stephen King by Shane Leonard; p. 146: inset by Karl Schatz, bottom courtesy Chad Conley; p. 147: Lauren Webster; p. 164: Jessie Perkins; p. 167: Office of Representative Jared Golden; p. 171: Karl Schatz; p. 174: Sylvia Pease; p. 176: Phyllis Siebert by Stephen Muskie; p. 177: Dempsey Center; p. 179: collection of Don Lindgren; p. 184: collection of Don Lindgren; p. 185: President George H.W. Bush (public domain); p. 186: Michael Pander; p 188: Jake Metzler; p. 194: collection of Don Lindgren; p. 202: Martha Hadley; p. 211: Ronnie Weston; p. 221: Amos Orcutt; p. 222: Vesta Rand; p. 226: Laura Sieger; p. 227: Jayne Farrin; p. 228: collection of Don Lindgren; p. 230: collection of Don Lindgren; p. 232: collection of Don Lindgren; p. 234: collection of Don Lindgren; p. 235: MOFGA; p. 238: Andy Wilbur; p. 241: Carlene Hill Byron; p. 242: collection of Don Lindgren; p. 243: collection of Don Lindgren; p. 244: Rosalie Colby; p. 246: Spiros Droggitis; p. 248: collection of Don Lindgren; p. 251: Spiros Droggitis; p. 252: collection of Don Lindgren; p. 269: Karl Schatz (top), Knack Factory (bottom).

INDEX

INDEX OF SPONSORS & ADVERTISERS

COUNTY INDEX

ABOUT THE AUTHORS

Margaret Hathaway and Karl Schatz are the husband-and-wife team behind six books on food and farming, including the memoir *The Year of the Goat*, the guide *Living With Goats*, and the two volumes of the *Portland, Maine Chef's Table*. Margaret is a writer who has worked in book publishing, corporate communications, and as manager of New York's Magnolia Bakery. Karl is a photographer who has worked as an editor at Time, Inc., and as Director of Aurora Photos. Since 2005, the couple has lived with their daughters on Ten

Apple Farm, their homestead and agritourism business in southern Maine, where they raise dairy goats, tend a large garden and small orchard, make cheese, teach workshops, lead goat hikes, and operate a guest house. Visit them at tenapplefarm.com.

Don Lindgren is an antiquarian bookseller specialized in printed and manuscript books about food and drink. His bookselling business, Rabelais Inc., acquires, researches, and sells rare books, manuscripts, ephemera, and other materials related to culinary history. He has served as a Governor of the Antiquarian Booksellers' Association of America and is a member of the International League of Antiquarian Booksellers. He has lectured or presented at the Oxford Symposium on Food & Cookery, the Colorado Anti-

quarian Book Seminar, and the Rare Book School's Boston Seminar. In 2019 he published the first part of a multi-volume exploration of the American community cookbook, titled *UnXld: American Cookbooks of Community & Place*. Visit him at rabelaisbooks.com.

For more recipes, stories, and photos visit maine200cookbook.com

THIS IS
REAL🌲MAINE
FLAVOR

REAL MAINE RECIPES BEGIN WITH REAL MAINE INGREDIENTS

For centuries Mainers have been drawing from the land and sea to create recipes with iconic flavors. Celebrate Maine's bicentennial and build your own traditions with Real Maine ingredients. Learn where to explore, experience, discover, and connect with Maine agriculture at **GetREALMAINE.com**.

maine **ME** DEPARTMENT OF Agricultur Conserva & Forestry